No Property *in* Man

THE NATHAN I. HUGGINS LECTURES

No Property *in* Man

SLAVERY AND ANTISLAVERY AT THE
NATION'S FOUNDING

Sean Wilentz

Harvard University Press

Cambridge, Massachusetts
London, England   2018

First printing

Library of Congress Cataloging-in-Publication Data
Names: Wilentz, Sean, author.
Title: No property in man : slavery and antislavery at the nation's
    founding / Sean Wilentz.
Other titles: Nathan I. Huggins lectures.
Description: Cambridge, Massachusetts : Harvard University Press, 2018. |
    Series: The Nathan I. Huggins lectures | Includes bibliographical references
    and index.
Identifiers: LCCN 2018006851 | ISBN 9780674972223 (alk. paper)
Subjects: LCSH: Slavery—Law and legislation—United States. | Antislavery
    movements—United States. | Constitutional history—United States.
Classification: LCC KF4545.S5 W59 2018 | DDC 342.7308/7—dc23
LC record available at https://lccn.loc.gov/2018006851

To David Brion Davis

CONTENTS

PREFACE

In 1987, Supreme Court associate justice Thurgood Marshall, in a widely publicized speech, disavowed the official celebrations marking the bicentennial of the U.S. Constitution. The flag-waving festivities and gauzy invocations of the framers, he protested, ignored the original Constitution's protection of racial slavery. The celebrations' distortion of history could not have been more offensive: northern delegates to the Federal Convention, Justice Marshall recounted, had plainly traded principle for commercial self-interest, striking compromises with slaveholders that tightened the shackles of human bondage. The Constitution reflected a wider assumption among white Americans that blacks were inferior creatures and articles of property, to be bought and sold like any other chattel. To ignore this brutal dishonor, Marshall contended, would only deepen the moral stain left at the nation's founding. The bicentennial, he said, should instead commemorate the succeeding generations of Americans who rewrote the Constitution by destroying slavery and fighting for racial justice—"those," he remarked, "who refused to acquiesce in outdated notions of 'liberty,' 'justice,' and 'equality,' and who strived to better them."

Few persons if any could speak to the subject with greater moral as well as intellectual authority than Thurgood Marshall. Today, when much of what he and his generation of civil rights champions achieved is under assault, his dissent is as urgent as ever. Yet there remains in Justice Marshall's remarks a deep historical conundrum concerning the Constitution and the freedom struggles that followed. Somehow, a nation with a Constitution that was strongly entwined with slavery also generated political and legal forces that eventually destroyed slavery. To be sure, those forces included Americans outside the political system, chiefly resistant slaves, free blacks, and abolitionist radicals who pushed the issue when most political leaders tried to suppress it; and it took a horrific civil war to achieve emancipation. But the war came only because of undaunted antislavery political activities, the most effective of them claiming the authority of the Constitution. These activities culminated in the rise of the Republican Party, an antislavery mass organization unprecedented in world history.

The Republicans' democratic triumph in 1860 on a platform dedicated to slavery's restriction—and geared toward its destruction—sparked the events that led to slavery's downfall, a revolution completed not by scrapping the Constitution but by radically amending it. Hence the puzzle: how could a proslavery Constitution become an instrument for antislavery politics? Did antislavery advocates distort the Constitution in order to legitimize their case, as proslavery and certain radical abolitionist critics charged? Or did the Constitution, with all of its concessions to slavery, also provide the means to hasten slavery's demise?

Resolving the puzzle requires returning to what Justice Marshall identified as the Constitution's originating sin. For millennia before America's founding, presumptions of the validity of property in man had been more a rule of human existence than an exception. When the American patriots declared their independence in 1776, every one of the new United States fully sanctioned slavery; and rebel slaveholders believed slavery was perfectly compatible with the patriot cause. Yet the American Revolution also encouraged and enlarged an extraordinary moral upheaval that challenged slavery's power and legitimacy. This, too, was part of the history of the nation's founding. When the Federal Convention met in Philadelphia in 1787, northerners had begun ridding themselves of the institution, charging, in the words of Rhode Island's emancipation law, that to hold humans "in a State of Slavery, *as private Property*," repudiated natural rights and subverted "the Happiness of Mankind." Southern slaveholders, aghast, were determined to ensure that the new national government could in no way interfere with slavery.

The Federal Convention finally settled on the compromises with slavery that Justice Marshall cited and that historians now regard as the proslavery heart of the original Constitution. Despite the rising strength of antislavery sentiment, the proslavery delegates gained significant concessions, aided by a general presumption inside the convention that any national constitution ought to pay due respect to private wealth. Yet the slaveholders failed to win the absolute protection for slavery they desired. Most important, the convention took care to ensure that while the Constitution would accept slavery where it already existed, it would not validate slavery in national law; that is, the Constitution would tolerate slavery without authorizing it. No mere technicality, the framers' exclusion of property in man was important enough in 1787 for delegates to insist upon it. In coming years it proved enormously consequential.

To be sure, nothing in the Constitution prevented the new Congress from approving slavery's further expansion over the decades before the Civil War, making the United States the mightiest slave power on earth. But the framers' exclusion of property in man also gave Congress the leverage to act otherwise. The exclusion in turn helped inspire three generations of antislavery advocates to press for halting slavery's expansion as a step toward its complete eradication, using thoroughly constitutional means. And here lies the solution to the historical puzzle inside Justice Marshall's dissent: by affirming that it would be wrong, as James Madison said at the Federal Convention, "to admit in the Constitution the idea that there could be property in men," the framers left room for political efforts aimed at slavery's restriction and, eventually, its destruction, even under a Constitution that safeguarded slavery. Those efforts, although sporadic through the early years of the nineteenth century, would eventually bring the advent of the Republican Party, the outbreak of the Civil War, and the completion of emancipation in 1865.

I originally offered this reevaluation of slavery, antislavery, and the Constitution in my Nathan I. Huggins Lectures at Harvard University in 2015 and in subsequent lectures and writings. This book presents the same basic arguments but improved with the benefit of valuable comments, queries, and objections from friends, colleagues, and critics. The debate so far has been lively and even sharp, befitting the importance of the subjects at hand, and I would like to thank all who have joined in pushing me to make my case as precisely as I can.

I owe my largest debt to Henry Louis Gates Jr., who paid me the honor of an invitation to deliver the Huggins Lectures as part of a rewarding four-day visit to Harvard's Hutchins Center for African and African American Research. Among his many other accomplishments, Professor Gates has made the Huggins Lectures series one of the premier occasions of their kind in the world of American scholarship and letters. Joining the list of distinguished Huggins lecturers remains a source of great personal pride, made even greater because of my memories of all-too-brief encounters with Nathan Huggins himself during my undergraduate days at Columbia in the early 1970s. Apart, meanwhile, from Skip Gates's intellectual support, his abiding friendship over many years has been a joy. I am also grateful to the staff of the Hutchins Center for their attention and care during my stay in Cambridge.

At the lectures, I was treated to the serious engagement, mindful skepticism, and welcoming spirit of numerous scholars I have long admired—some of them old friends, some new—including Sven Beckert, Jennifer Hochschild, James Kloppenberg, Kate Masur, Orlando Patterson, and John Stauffer. Above all, I wish to thank Evelyn Brooks Higginbotham, who not only attended the lectures but generously read an early draft and offered singularly helpful suggestions.

I completed a great deal of the initial research and wrote the first draft of the lectures while in residence as the Leah and Michael Weisberg Fellow at the New-York Historical Society in 2014–2015. My thanks go to the Weisbergs for their support as well as to the entire staff of the N-YHS for many favors, especially Louise Mirrer and Michael T. Ryan. As ever, I am deeply indebted to the faculty and staff of the Department of History at Princeton, as well as to the librarians and staff at Princeton's Firestone Library.

Before giving the Huggins Lectures, I was able to present some of my early thoughts to a stimulating conference, "The Antislavery Bulwark: The Antislavery Origins of the Civil War," held at the Graduate Center of the City University of New York in October 2014. Several months after the lectures, I had the privilege to deliver a condensed version as the Constitution Day Lecture sponsored by the American Studies Program at Princeton. Thereafter, I presented ever-evolving forms of the argument to several audiences, including a Works in Progress series seminar of the Shelby Cullom Davis Center for Historical Studies at Princeton, a lunchtime seminar of the James Madison

Program in American Ideals and Institutions, also at Princeton, and a lecture sponsored by the Department of History at Colgate University. My thanks go to all who attended for their questions, and to the organizers and commentators who made the events possible: James Oakes, John Stauffer, Joseph Murphy, Hendrik Hartog, Anne Cheng, Sarah Rivett, Philp Nord, Amy Dru Stanley, Robert George, George Kateb, and Graham Hodges. Thanks as well to George Kalegorakis and Clay Risen at the *New York Times* for their help in publishing a very brief and pointed op-ed version, which elicited some equally pointed and highly useful replies.

Several friends and colleagues generously read and commented on the lectures or the manuscript of this book or both, or in other ways lent me their expertise: Richard Aynes, Michael Les Benedict, Paul Berman, Sidney Blumenthal, Andrew Edwards, Christopher Florio, Eric Foner, Annette Gordon-Reed, John Craig Hammond, Hendrik Hartog, Matthew Karp, Stanley Katz, Bryan LePoint, Jonathan Levy, Earl Maltz, James McPherson, Michael Merrill, James Oakes, Jack Rakove, David Upham, and Gordon Wood. I owe special thanks to Farah Peterson, who, in addition to scrutinizing and questioning my interpretations, offered candid and valuable advice about how I might present them more persuasively. Her comments also affirmed my decision to address the book as far as possible to a general readership, with the hope that our scholarly colleagues would abide explanations of events and concepts that are familiar to them.

At Princeton, I have long had the privilege to try out ideas in the classroom and in office hours with exceptionally smart and engaged students, including undergraduates as well as graduate students. In connection with this book, I am grateful to the students in three of my courses, History 373 and 588 and American Studies 361, for listening, pushing back, and forcing me to make further revisions. I am especially grateful to Gabriel Fisher, Mahishan Gnanaseharan, Jack Jiranek, Sam Maeglin, Ben Perelmuter, and Maya von Ziegesar for their help with various chores involved in preparing the book for publication.

Among the pleasures of delivering and revising the Huggins Lectures has been the opportunity to reconnect with Harvard University Press and to work at last with my longtime friend, the much-beloved editor Joyce Seltzer. Joyce's enthusiasm, encouragement, and editorial wisdom greatly eased the job of turning tattered rough drafts into a final manuscript. I would also like to thank Louise Robbins of HUP and Brian Ostrander of Westchester Publishing Services for overseeing the transition to print, and Sue Warga for a superb job of copyediting.

More than forty years ago, David Brion Davis agreed to direct my dissertation at Yale and proceeded to give my stumbling early efforts exacting and sympathetic readings beyond anything I could have hoped for. Already an intellectual hero, he became a mentor, an unfailing friend, and an exemplar of humane imagination and scholarly fortitude. This book, in every way, is dedicated to him.

A NOTE ON TERMINOLOGY

SOME READERS may be confused by my use of the word "abolitionist," especially when used to describe advocates of gradual emancipation during the decades after the American Revolution. In recent years, historians have largely reserved the term for the immediatist abolitionists—those who advocated the immediate abolition of slavery—who were associated most closely after 1830 with William Lloyd Garrison. There is justification for this practice, as contemporaries of Garrison also used the term that way, sometimes to embrace and sometimes to distance themselves from his uncompromising radicalism. Finally, though, I believe the usage is misleading. Both before and after the emergence of the immediatists, a wide variety of antislavery advocates called themselves abolitionists, so long as they aspired to commence slavery's eventual eradication. Referring to these self-described abolitionists as anything other than what they called themselves demeans their dedication to eliminating slavery, while it elevates one strand of the evolving antislavery movement as the only one deserving of the name. There were also, to be sure, Americans who criticized slavery but who did not push in any serious way for its abolition, and I have refrained from applying the term to them. Likewise, many antislavery political leaders who sought slavery's ultimate extinction, notably Abraham Lincoln, eschewed the word lest they be associated with the Garrisonians, and I have not called them abolitionists either. But those who desired slavery's abolition and called themselves abolitionists receive that appellation in this book, whether or not they subscribed to the immediatists' views on how abolition could and ought to be achieved.

Introduction

Did the constitution of the United States enshrine racial slavery? During the last thirty years historians and constitutional experts have forcefully argued that it did—that in 1787, the framers of the Constitution, through ignoble compromises, created a proslavery constitution worthy of condemnation as a hellish compact with death.[1] These re-evaluations have forced a reckoning with the Constitution's concessions to slavery that scholars had evaded for generations. They have exposed both the importance of slavery to the framers' deliberations and the powerful sway that belligerent slaveholders exercised at the Federal Convention. The new interpretations have refuted renderings of the Constitution as neutral with regard to slavery, let alone as an antislavery document. Yet those interpretations are also flawed and in need of amendment.

Descriptions of the Constitution as proslavery have misconstrued critical debates inside the convention. They have slighted the antislavery impulses generated by the American Revolution, to which the delegates, for better or worse, paid heed. They have missed the crucial subtlety, which is this: although the framers agreed to compromises over slavery that blunted antislavery hopes and augmented the slaveholders' power, they also deliberately excluded any validation of property in man.

This exclusion, insisted upon by a majority of the delegates, was of profound and fateful importance. It rendered slavery solely a creation of state laws. It thereby opened the prospect of a United States free of slavery—a prospect some delegates deeply desired and many more believed was coming to pass. Above all, it left room for the new federal government to hinder slavery's expansion, something which, after the Constitution's ratification, slavery's opponents struggled to achieve. Through the early years of the nineteenth century, the antislavery efforts mostly failed. Over succeeding decades, however, mounting antislavery pressure caused proslavery southerners to assert that the Constitution actually did recognize property in man, which antislavery forces fiercely denied. These conflicts, in turn, became the crux of the political struggles that led to the Civil War and then to slavery's abolition in 1865. This book explains how and why all of this happened. Starting with the nation's founding, it tells a largely forgotten story that lies at the heart of American history.

The basics of the story are disarmingly simple. The delegates to the convention in Philadelphia presumed from the start that their new national government would be barred from interfering directly with slavery in states where it already existed. Proslavery delegates, though, long on the defensive in national affairs and troubled by the recent enactment of gradual abolition laws in the North, feared that the new government still might try to emancipate their slaves, so they demanded additional protection, as close to ironclad as possible. At best, they would keep slavery completely outside the national government's reach. At the very least, they would make it impossible for the government to enact anything concerning slavery without the slaveholding states' consent.

Led by the delegates from South Carolina, the slaveholders gained provisions that substantially reinforced the slaveholders' influence in national politics and safeguarded their property rights in slaves as inscribed in state laws. They could not, however, guarantee slavery's future under the Constitution—a failure about which some discontented slaveholders complained furiously during the struggle over the Constitution's ratification. Although they salvaged major concessions, the Lower South delegates could not prevent the convention from authorizing the national government to abolish the Atlantic slave trade, a provision they had attacked as a direct and intolerable threat to slavery itself. The slaveholders' power in national politics, enlarged by the notorious three-fifths compromise, seemed at the time almost certain to grow over the coming decades, but the compromise did not secure to the slaveholding states anything close to impregnable control over slavery. Above all, the convention drew a line against acknowledging slavery's legitimacy outside of state law and took pains to have the Constitution make that line perfectly clear. This last resolve by the convention—to exclude from the Constitution what James Madison called "the idea that there could be property in men"—demands closer examination.[2]

Acknowledging slaves as property would have had far-reaching ramifications. It would have negated the then deeply radical belief, increasingly powerful in the northern states, that debasing humans into property violated the egalitarian principles of the American Revolution. It would have affirmed as a national rule a long-standing assumption, only recently challenged, that served as slavery's chief line of defense: that the slaveholders had obtained their human property lawfully and that their rights to that property were therefore inviolable. It would have, in time, rendered the new national government powerless to interfere with the institution of slavery anywhere in the country, including areas under the government's jurisdiction—a matter that would become critically important after 1815, in ways unforeseeable by the framers. More immediately, it would have upset working assumptions among the convention majority about slavery's place in the new constitutional order.

Most of the delegates to the Federal Convention supposed that slavery would exist under the new Constitution strictly as a state (or, in common parlance, local) institution. Here, they thought, was an essential balance: slavery would have to be tolerated and even shielded as a creation of individual states, but nowhere in the Constitution would it be deemed legitimate. Elbridge Gerry, a delegate from Massachusetts, made the point directly, telling the convention that the Constitution should have "nothing to do with the conduct of the States as to Slaves, but ought to be careful not to give any sanction to it."[3] This was not a compromise hammered out inside the convention: antislavery delegates did not agree to tolerate slavery where it existed in exchange for excluding it from the Constitution. It was, rather, an insistence on limiting slavery's legitimacy—a limitation that a majority of the convention would affirm repeatedly.

At first glance, this distinction may seem strange and even bogus: wasn't allowing slavery to continue where it existed the same thing as giving sanction to it? Some critics of slavery asked precisely this question at the time, and later critics would do so for many years to come. Recent historians have demeaned the distinction as at best a mere technicality and at worst a despicable evasion, born of embarrassment and chicanery rather than principle. It did absolutely nothing, they reasonably observe, to prevent a consolidation of the southern slaveholders' power in national politics and government through to the Civil War. In fact, though, the distinction was not just real, it was essential. Beginning in the very first Congress, it informed occa-

sional efforts—largely futile but still underappreciated by historians—
to oppose the slaveholders in national debates. After 1815, as antislavery agitation became much more formidable, the distinction—and,
specifically, the framers' exclusion of property in man—became the
constitutional basis for the politics that in time led to slavery's
destruction.

Between 1780 and 1787, five northern states as well as the state-to-be
of Vermont, without always abolishing slavery immediately, either destroyed or severely undermined the legitimacy of property in man—
to that point the largest emancipation in modern history and the crucial
departure from which all later antislavery activity would follow. (Two
other northern states seriously debated gradual emancipation, which
they would enact over the succeeding twenty years.) These states hardly
would have agreed to a Constitution that empowered the national
government to interfere with their new property laws. They could
recall all too well how, while still colonies, several states had had to
bend to the central authority of the Crown and Parliament, which
prevented them from abolishing the slave trade and, by extension,
slavery. Likewise, though, these states were in no position to demand
that the slaveholding states empower a new government to interfere
with *their* long-established property laws. Under the right political circumstances, a national government powerful enough to abolish slavery
summarily could just as easily impose slavery.

Northern emancipation had divided the American house, making
it partly slave, partly free (in Massachusetts and, at least implicitly, New
Hampshire), and partly on the way to freedom (in Pennsylvania, Connecticut, and Rhode Island). Accordingly, the framers tried to design
a Constitution that would bridge the divisions and keep the house
from collapsing. Sanctioning slavery, though, in the modern sense of
condoning it—as opposed to tolerating it in the states where it was

legal—would have entailed formally pronouncing property in man the national standard and freedom the exception. This the convention firmly rejected—confirmation of how far antislavery sentiments had advanced since the first statewide emancipation victories less than a decade earlier. Instead, by refusing to credit the legitimacy of slavery, the convention left open the possibility of declaring freedom as the national standard and slavery the exception.

In their early debates concerning representation in the new national legislature, the delegates granted that slaves would be counted toward the allocation of representatives and direct tax obligations, thereby giving the slaveholding states a distinct and potentially powerful advantage in national politics. But the delegates carefully described the slaves not as property but as "persons." That wording, borrowed from a proposed taxation provision debated four years earlier by the Confederation Congress, neither proceeded from nor provoked debates in the convention about property in man, but it signaled the convention's intention to cede power to slavery without also naming and thereby legitimizing it in the Constitution. The issue then arose in various debates during the latter phases of the convention, as the delegates found themselves arguing over provisions that, wittingly or not, "acknowledg[ed] men to be property," as Roger Sherman of Connecticut observed.[4]

The surviving evidence about these debates belies their significance. Although the records of the convention's proceedings do not lack moments of high moral drama, they largely describe lawyerly disputes, sometimes over tiny details, which can disappoint modern readers looking for vivid rhetorical clashes. Such is the nature of constitution making. Because the Federal Convention deliberately worked in secret, in a kind of Olympian isolation, with no public record of its debates to clarify intentions, the delegates weighed every word in the text all the more carefully.[5] On that account, the discussions of property in man are easy to overlook, as they consist mainly of fine-tuning, striving to remove any equivocation or blurring. Coming late in the convention's proceedings, they were conducted with a dry exactness that evokes unimportance. In the moment, though, the exactness underscored the delegates' painstaking concern about property in man. Read in the context of the convention's larger, more impassioned disputes over slavery, their vital meaning becomes much clearer.

On the pivotal issue of authorizing federal regulation and abolition of the Atlantic slave trade, the convention corrected language that Sherman claimed could be read as describing persons as property. Later, according to James Madison's notes on the convention debates, a leading Lower South delegate "seemed to wish some provision should be included in favor of property in slaves," but the convention rejected the proposal by an overwhelming margin.[6] When confronted, during the final drafting process, with ambiguous wording in a clause guaranteeing the rendition of fugitive slaves—wording that might imply that property in slaves was legitimate in national as well as state law—a convention committee removed the offending ambiguities.

Historians today assimilate these seemingly minor refusals and revisions to what they describe as a hypocritical, even cynical bargain. At a moment during the Federal Convention when antislavery sentiments flared, the respected antislavery delegate (and former slaveholder) from Delaware, John Dickinson, wrote out notes for a speech he never delivered entitled "Acting before the World." After attacking the three-fifths clause and what Dickinson called the "new principle" of founding the right to govern freemen "on a power derived from Slaves," the notes expressed Dickinson's fear that in the eyes of all humanity, the omission of the word "slaves" in the Constitution would "be regarded as an Endeavour to conceal a principle of which we are ashamed."[7] This is precisely how recent historians have interpreted the framers' work. Drawing on stray comments during the convention and some later antislavery criticisms and proslavery defenses of the Constitution, scholars have ascribed the convention's exclusion of property in man not to an insistence on limiting slavery's legitimacy but to northern disgrace about the concessions the convention granted to slavery.

In order to spare antislavery sensibilities and minimize opposition to the Constitution in the North, as well as to disarm foreign critics of the American republic, the delegates supposedly agreed—indeed, conspired—to omit the offensive terms "slaves" and "slavery." In their place, the framers substituted labored euphemisms that avoided referring to slaves as property. The maneuver, one historian writes, amounted to calculated "damage control," cloaking the slaveholders' victory. Even when, at one juncture, the delegates specifically removed language they believed acknowledged property in man, the change was, supposedly, merely "semantic."[8] The convention "did not recognize the legality of slavery," another historian asserts, but only "in the most technical linguistic sense," by inserting circumlocutions "clearly designed to make the Constitution more palatable to the North."[9] With shifty word play—"a masterful stroke of linguistic subterfuge," so the argument goes—the delegates disingenuously approved a proslavery Constitution that did not once mention slavery or property in man.[10]

These claims, however, are based on meager evidence, suspect logic, and at times sheer supposition. Of course, some northern delegates expressed concern that their compromises over slavery would endanger support in their states for the Constitution. Bad consciences were no doubt at work behind the scenes, and may have had something to do with the delegates' choice of words. Historians have sometimes cited one delegate's remark, made during a debate over representation, that the wording of the three-fifths clause arose from men being "ashamed" to refer explicitly to slavery.[11] At one point, during a brief rhetorical detour in the debates over the Atlantic slave trade, Roger Sherman, supported by George Clymer of Pennsylvania, demurred from approving terms like "slave" that "were not pleasing to some people."[12] Shortly after the convention, the Maryland delegate Luther Martin, having turned fervently against the Constitution, claimed that when the convention framed the Atlantic slave trade clause, a process in which he had played a role, the delegates had deliberately avoided words "odious" to Americans, a charge that already had been making the rounds among Anti-Federalists.[13] A decade later, during the congressional debates over the repressive Alien and Sedition Acts, the Speaker of the House Jonathan Dayton of New Jersey, who had also been a convention delegate, stated that the "sole reason assigned" for avoiding the word "slaves" in connection with the Atlantic slave trade was "not to stain the Constitutional code with such a term."[14]

The convention majority certainly did not wish to stain the Constitution, but there is scarce reason to believe the delegates intended their wording to conceal the concessions to slavery and deflect criticism by antislavery advocates. The delegate who spoke of shame and the three-fifths clause, the antislavery New Jerseyan William Paterson, was imputing that motivation not to the Federal Convention of 1787 but to the Confederation Congress in 1783, of which he was not a member. (Indeed, as we shall see, by 1787 wording similar to the Constitution's provisions describing slaves as persons had already appeared elsewhere as a way to signify slavery without acknowledging property in man.) Sherman's and Clymer's passing objections to the unpleasant word "slaves" were virtually the only remarks in the convention debates to suggest as much, whereas the delegates struggled repeatedly to prevent the Constitution's references to slaves and slavery from condoning property in man. Martin's remarks must be taken for what they were, part of an impassioned polemic designed to make the Constitution look as proslavery as possible, in which Martin repeated what had become standard Anti-Federalist allegations and suspicions. Dayton's memory in 1798 was faulty: during debates over the Atlantic slave trade, quite apart from Sherman's and Clymer's momentary comments, delegates (Sherman above all) had insisted on inserting the word "persons" explicitly in order to avoid validating the legitimacy of property in man.[15] Nor is there persuasive evidence that the framers thought their wording would have the effect that historians claim they desired. John Dickinson's notes for his undelivered speech suggest just the opposite: warning the delegates about a candid world judging the Constitution's omission of the word "slavery" a foul evasion would appear to have been superfluous had the delegates intended all along to evade.

Had the framers, meanwhile, truly designed their phrasing in order to dupe the public, they would have proved themselves not canny connivers but artless blunderers. Antislavery advocates, far from deceived by the knotted passages, instantly seized upon and blasted them as outrageous double-talk. The framers' wording did not make the Constitution's provisions on slavery "more palatable"; it aroused angry charges that the Federal Convention had compounded a crime against humanity by trying to cover it up. Not surprisingly, northern Anti-Federalists, sincerely or not, fanned that anger and ascribed the basest of motives to what one leading abolitionist Anti-Federalist called the Constitution's "dark and ambiguous" words on slavery.[16] Historians, perhaps unawares, have engaged in similar accusation.[17]

In fact, the framers' choice of words was a substantive matter, not a cosmetic one. The convention's key arguments over how to describe slaves and slavery in the Constitution had little or nothing to do with the prudent suppression of distasteful language. They had to do with ensuring that the Constitution contained nothing that could be construed as acknowledging and thereby endorsing property in man. This was not wily subterfuge. It stemmed from the forthright insistence, as Elbridge Gerry explained, that the Constitution, while perforce tolerating slavery where it existed, would not sanction it. It aimed to exclude not just the word "slavery," but any validation of the thing itself. To stigmatize these efforts as ignoble damage control, let alone to charge that the framers actually *did* affirm the legitimacy of slavery, ignores both the vital principle at stake and the conviction that drove the convention majority. To dismiss the delegates' refusal to recognize the legitimacy of slavery as a linguistic technicality is to trivialize an important part of the convention's work.

The records of the Federal Convention, flawed though they are, plainly relate the convention's refusals concerning property in man.[18] Leading antislavery advocates in the mid-nineteenth century understood the importance of the refusal, albeit imperfectly, and made it central to antislavery politics. Abraham Lincoln stated the point as directly as anyone when he observed in his Cooper Institute address in 1860 that the framers referred to slaves as persons "on purpose to exclude from the Constitution the idea that there could be property in man."[19] Lincoln exaggerated the framers' collective antislavery intentions, but he accurately described the Constitution's purposeful exclusion. So did, in similar terms—and years before Lincoln—the escaped slave and abolitionist radical Frederick Douglass.

A century and a half of subsequent scholarship, though, especially over the last three decades, has misunderstood crucial aspects of the convention's debates and decisions over slavery and thereby made Lincoln's and Douglass's readings appear to have been commendable but wishful distortions. *No Property in Man* attempts to correct that misunderstanding and to describe and evaluate what actually happened in 1787. It tries to move beyond what has become a sterile debate among historians over whether the Constitution was antislavery or proslavery—or, in another formulation, "operationally proslavery"—and to frame the issue differently, as more of a paradox. It additionally tries to explain the vital implications of the framers' decisions for the subsequent history of antislavery politics as well as for the events that led to the Civil War and then to slavery's destruction.

Reconsidering the significance of slavery in the framing of the Constitution reminds us that the political struggle over American slavery was as old as the nation itself. Effective antislavery dissent did not begin with the rise of the radical, so-called immediatist abolitionist movement of the 1830s associated with William Lloyd Garrison. As historians have recently emphasized, the eradication of slavery involved a "long emancipation," which commenced in the northern states in the 1780s.[20] Yet even these more expansive accounts have continued to treat the framing and ratification of the Constitution as a thoroughgoing victory for the slaveholders, as if by tolerating human bondage the Constitution validated it. The story of antislavery politics may now appear to have begun much earlier than it did a generation ago, but historians still cling to Garrison's denunciation of the Constitution as "a covenant with death" and "an agreement with hell"—which was a minority opinion even in abolitionist circles. It would appear that, in the prevailing academic view, the only sound understanding of the Constitution was—and is—the Garrisonians', which ironically, as Frederick Douglass noted, was the same understanding propounded by slavery's hard-line defenders, including John C. Calhoun and Roger Brooke Taney.[21]

Comprehending fully the defects in this view requires an appreciation, first, of what the Federal Convention could and could not do regarding slavery; and second, of how suddenly and rapidly antislavery politics had arisen over the decade or so before the convention met.

While they were creating a new, more powerful national government, the framers were fully aware of the need to limit that government's authority. Even though they placed restrictions on states' power—barring states, for example, from coining money or imposing tariffs—the same respect for existing state property laws that compelled tolerance of slavery became the basis for counting slaves in allocating representation in Congress. A consensus inside the convention held that wealth and property ought to have weight in apportioning power. Accordingly, as slaves undoubtedly accounted for a large portion of their masters' wealth under their states' laws, so their numbers (as a measure of their value) would almost certainly be factored into apportionment, despite the misgivings and complaints of some northerners about conflating persons and property. Respect for slave state property laws, along with an expectation of state comity, also lay behind the clause requiring that slaves who had escaped to another state be returned to their masters.[22]

Yet despite the necessity of allowing for the slaveholders' wealth in slaves—indeed, because of that necessity—a majority of the Federal Convention was determined to prevent recognizing slavery as a normal institution in the new nation. The normality of American slavery had been self-evident before the Revolution, when slavery was legal in all thirteen colonies and antislavery political activity was virtually nonexistent. Apart from the breakaway republic of Vermont, slavery tacitly remained the American norm when the first national frame of government was drafted in 1777—the Articles of Confederation, which in saying nothing at all about slavery assumed its existence. "Prior to the great revolution," John Jay would observe to his British abolitionist counterparts, the great majority of Americans "had been so long accustomed to the practice and convenience of having slaves, that very few among them even doubted the propriety and rectitude of it."[23] By 1787, however, with astonishing swiftness, the political and intellectual foundations supporting slavery had come under concerted attack. Northern emancipation, including the gradual emancipation plans enacted in several states, contradicted claims that property rights precluded legislative or judicial emancipation and either overturned or severely undermined at the state level the legitimacy of property in man—the main legal and political pillar upholding human bondage. As never before, slavery was on the way to becoming a regional presence: "For the new American republic," one historian observes, "slavery would no longer be a continental institution."[24] In affirming that new reality, the Constitution carefully if for the most part silently limited slavery's legitimacy.

Why, though, given the push for emancipation in the North, did the northern delegates agree to a union with slaveholders without gaining some explicit guarantee that slavery would eventually be eliminated? The simple answer is that the slaveholding states, above all the Lower South, would have never ratified such a Constitution. But short of gaining a formal agreement about emancipation, why did the North then cut deals that bolstered the slaveholders' power? Why didn't they call out more forcefully the threats of disunion delivered most often by the delegates from South Carolina and Georgia? Above all, instead of choosing complicity with evil, why didn't the North simply form a nation of its own, free from the scourge of slavery? At the time there were certainly antislavery northerners who considered any connection with slavery morally unsupportable, anticipating Garrison and his allies by more than forty years: "If we cannot connect with the southern states without giving countenance to blood and carnage, and all kinds of fraud and injustice, I say let them go," one Massachusetts critic wrote.[25]

Like all counterfactual speculations, these raise a host of imponderables about how such changes would have played out, including possibilities that would have been deeply discouraging to the antislavery cause, let alone the enslaved. As we shall see, the northern delegates actually did confront the proslavery advocates over their disunionist harangues, occasionally replied in kind, and were not intimidated, although at key moments they were outmaneuvered. By the same token, one can imagine, for example, North Carolina and even Virginia abjuring the Union if South Carolina and Georgia refused to ratify, leading to a collapse of the Constitution before it was even established. Creating a separate northern nation, on the other hand, might have permitted antislavery northerners to verify their righteousness but it would have done nothing to help enslaved southerners, whose fates might well have been all the crueler in a formal, independent slaveholders' republic. What, meanwhile, would have become of New York and New Jersey under such a plan—two key northern states that had yet to commence emancipation? How would a free northern United States have found a way to include two slave states? Would New York and New Jersey slaveholders, who had fought emancipation tenaciously and successfully for years, have suddenly surrendered and put their states on the road to freedom? Alternatively, how might a northern republic have fared without New York and New Jersey?[26]

Speculation aside, though, the hard fact is that antislavery disunionist sentiment was far from common among free northerners. What there was turned up mainly among the antislavery minority in New England; elsewhere, even passionate antislavery Anti-Federalists objected chiefly to specific provisions they thought too proslavery, not to agreeing to a union with slaveholding states. At the same time, though, northern toleration of southern slavery hardly signaled indifference to human bondage. Having extirpated slavery in their own states, many antislavery northerners shared the view, still widespread outside the Lower South in the 1780s, that the glutted Atlantic market in tobacco spelled American slavery's doom, no matter the Constitution's immediate concessions to the slaveholders. Although complacent, even deluded in retrospect, that view was reasonable enough in 1787, before the cotton boom changed the course of American economic and political history.

Other northerners, meanwhile, saw no contradiction in supporting both the Constitution and the abolition of slavery. Quite the opposite: many antislavery advocates, including prominent abolitionists, considered the Atlantic slave trade clause the Constitution's truly important provision regarding slavery, and they saw it not as a setback but as a great triumph. By empowering Congress to abolish the trade even eventually, they thought, the Constitution took the first vital step toward eradicating American slavery completely. At least one group of free blacks in Providence, Rhode Island, mounted a celebration of the Constitution and its slave trade provision on July 4, 1788, and toasted the proposition, "May the Natives of Africa enjoy their Natural Privileges unmolested."[27] The idea that the North should repudiate the Constitution over the framers' concessions to the slaveholders would have struck them as preposterous.

On one important matter, the return of fugitive slaves to their masters, the framers certainly offered slaveholders at least a measure of direct protection not included in the Articles of Confederation in order to cover the exigencies of northern emancipation—that is, making a concession to slavery in an entirely new context of freedom.[28] Southern Federalists and northern Anti-Federalists alike would make much more of the provision than that, citing it as proof that the Constitution established a solid legal basis for slavery. Later, proslavery leaders as well as Garrisonians would repeat those assertions and enlarge them even further, to maintain—fancifully—that the clause had been a nonnegotiable concession to the slaveholders to ensure that the Constitution acknowledged property in man, without which the Lower South would have repudiated the Union. Through the early decades of the nineteenth century, northern as well as southern jurists, lacking any comprehensive record of the Federal Convention debates, read the clause pretty much the same way, as a broad protection for slaveholders' property rights.

Yet, as some commentators at the time and a few modern scholars have noticed, while the clause established a requirement of state comity—and while it made escape from slavery all the more difficult—it extended no legitimacy whatsoever to slavery. Indeed, the convention assiduously stripped the provision of any language that even suggested it legally sanctioned slavery or affirmed property in man.[29] Through the 1830s, antislavery advocates would deduce as much and more from their reading of the document itself, and then turn the point into the cornerstone of antislavery constitutionalism. Thereafter, those readings, now buttressed by Madison's notes on the convention debates, helped fortify critics of slavery who interpreted the Constitution very differently than the Garrisonian abolitionists.

In the early 1840s, just as the Garrisonians consigned the Constitution to perdition, other antislavery advocates, including sometime allies of Garrison, reformulated existing abolitionist arguments into a wholly constitutional program through which, they believed, the federal government would achieve slavery's demise chiefly by halting slavery's expansion. (A much smaller group of abolitionists claimed that the Constitution's Preamble and the Fifth Amendment had already abolished slavery.) The framers, they contended, had pointedly refused to recognize the legitimacy of property in man; therefore, they reasoned, the Constitution empowered the national government to prohibit slavery everywhere that fell under the government's jurisdiction, including the national territories. Contained by a cordon of freedom and incapable of augmenting their political power by adding new slave states, the slaveholders would recognize the hopelessness of their situation and abandon slavery.[30]

In the 1840s, the antislavery restriction strategy, based on the Constitution's exclusion of property in man, helped inspire political antislavery efforts by the schismatic Liberty and Free Soil Parties. Into the 1850s, numerous radical abolitionists, including Frederick Douglass, broke with Garrison and embraced that political movement, now persuaded that, even at its worst, the Constitution, as Douglass later put it, "still leans to freedom."[31] After 1854, the Republican Party made that refusal a cornerstone of its political program to put slavery, in Abraham Lincoln's phrase, "in [the] course of ultimate extinction."[32] Upon Lincoln's election to the White House in 1860, that program sparked southern secession and the war that led to slavery's eradication.

This history of the struggle over the Constitution and property in man does not, to be sure, cover the entire history of antislavery politics. Statewide debates over slavery's future, along with conflicts over civil liberties, gender, American empire, and more, were all part of the rise and eventual triumph of American antislavery, which will require a more comprehensive accounting than is possible here. Still, in national politics, the fights over property in man were of unsurpassed importance.

The Civil War, meanwhile, was not simply an argument over constitutional interpretation. Wars, including civil wars, have multiple causes. That the human property being argued over in the United States consisted entirely of black people, for example, meant that it was impossible to talk about slavery without also talking about race. Nevertheless, like other issues distinct from race, including the vindication of free labor, the argument over property and the Constitution had a powerful logic distinct from race and proved fundamental to the nation's mounting crisis over slavery. Conversely, other issues commonly named as causes of the Civil War, including state rights and slavery's expansion, were generated by older and deeper conflicts over the Constitution and property rights. Indeed, as it played out in national politics, the issue of whether the Constitution sanctioned slavery in national law, more than any other, made the mounting conflict between the North and South irreconcilable. When the secessionist conventions in 1860 and 1861 explained why they were dissolving their ties to the Union, the issue of property in man was paramount, just as it had been during the presidential campaign of 1860.[33]

The framers of 1787 could hardly have anticipated these events. They could not have imagined, in the first place, how slavery would experience an explosive rebirth with the rise of the cotton kingdom after 1793. They could not have predicted the ratification of the Bill of Rights in 1791, with the Fifth Amendment's due process clause making their exclusion of property in man all the more significant. None could have envisaged the aggressive antislavery mass movements of a later time, or foretold how the convention's decisions would play out in the sectional politics that led to secession and war. The events of 1787 proved vital to the antislavery politics of Douglass and Lincoln, but they hardly dictated those politics. The implications for the future of the framers' decision to limit slavery's legitimacy only became fully apparent in the future, and in an America very different from that of 1787.

That the delegates to the Federal Convention lacked clairvoyance, though, does not diminish the significance of their limitation of slavery's legitimacy. Neither does the fact that later Americans fought bitterly over the events of 1787 foreclose describing and evaluating those events and the intentions behind them—events and intentions that vindicate the antislavery judgments of Douglass and Lincoln much more than they do the judgments of Calhoun and Taney (and Garrison). Evaluating the meanings imparted by the framers' actions does not in itself imprison understanding of the Constitution as an immutable and transparent writ laid down by the Federal Convention. The politicization in recent decades of the concept of the Constitution's "original meaning" ought not to nullify inquiry into what the convention did and the intentions behind those actions, as if those clashing intentions are either unknowable on every issue or of no historical account. Only by evaluating the events of 1787 is it possible to understand the struggles over the Constitution's meanings that unfolded over succeeding decades, the very struggles that defined the Constitution as a living document. Only by studying those events anew is it possible to comprehend why the proslavery interpretation of the Constitution seemed plausible—indeed, became predominant— which made antislavery advocates' dogged if imperfect retrieval of the Constitution's exclusion of property in man all the more remarkable. The interpretation presented here, like those it contests, does hold that certain later understandings of the convention's work were more in line with what actually occurred in 1787 than others. Neither line of argument, though, is "originalist"; both are simply historical.

No Property in Man reexamines what happened in 1787 in order better to understand the Federal Convention's debates over slavery, especially the convention's resolute exclusion of the idea of human property, and the long-term consequences of that exclusion. The book also develops a number of subthemes on important related issues. Propositions about the inviolability of private property, for example, have long stood as a supposed foundation of American political history. Yet current research has shown that certain seventeenth-century ideas about property, above all those developed by John Locke, were not nearly as friendly to slavery as has been generally assumed.[34] This book contributes to a linked line of argument: that battles over what constituted legitimate private property were at least as important to subsequent phases of American history as the sanctity of property in the abstract.[35] In that connection, the book also explores the hardheaded, contradictory, and sometimes deceptive role of the man widely regarded as the father of the Constitution, James Madison, in excluding slavery from national law while also placating his fellow slaveholders.[36]

Above all, *No Property in Man* draws attention to the antislavery presence in national politics from the very commencement of those politics in the American Revolution. If, through the first half of the nineteenth century, the Constitution enabled the emergence of the United States as a republic dominated by slaveholders, it also kept the nation from becoming a proslavery leviathan—but it did so only because of determined constitutional agitation by antislavery partisans against long odds that the Constitution also helped establish. Slighting that antislavery presence, including the activities and pronouncements of forgotten figures such as George Thacher, James Sloan, Charles Rich, and William Slade, distorts the history of the antislavery cause. It thereby also obscures the history of the proslavery politics that arose in response to the antislavery challenge, in particular the proslavery constitutionalism that finally justified southern secession.

Most important, overlooking the early antislavery advocates contributes to a long-standing evasion that is well captured in the familiar shorthand assertion that slavery was the cause of the Civil War. The assertion is, to be sure, an improvement over the thoroughly discredited but persistent claims that the tariff or state rights or some issue other than slavery caused the conflict. Still, institutions by themselves don't cause civil wars; political struggles over institutions (and much else) cause them. In the United States, slavery's opponents initiated those struggles against an obdurate slaveholder elite and its allies. There is more truth in saying that antislavery, rather than slavery, caused the Civil War.

The book begins by examining the birth of antislavery politics before 1787 and how the concept of property in man became central both to slavery's defenders and to its assailants. Turning to the Federal Convention, it scrutinizes how the concept arose in debate and how the delegates handled it. Succeeding chapters seek to explain how battles over slavery, property, and the Constitution developed, from the ratification struggles of 1787–1788 through the 1850s. While it focuses on the emergence of a particular antislavery view of the Constitution, the book also describes the slaveholders' reactions, and the rise of a proslavery view claiming that the Constitution guaranteed slaveholders' property rights. The final chapter describes the crucial role these conflicts over property, slavery, and the Constitution played in the political struggles that brought the nation's crack-up in 1860–1861.

No Property in Man argues that the Federal Convention created a terrible paradox. From the start of their deliberations, the framers struck compromises that strengthened the slaveholders' hand in national politics and acknowledged their property rights in state law. But by remaining vigilant and steadfast on the issue of slaves as property in national law, the convention majority also bequeathed grounds upon which slavery's expansion would later be challenged, with the ultimate objective of destroying American slavery completely. The paradox— of a Constitution that strengthened and protected slavery yet refused to validate it—created what have been perceived as the Constitution's confounding ambiguities over slavery. It encouraged the spread of antislavery and proslavery understandings of the Constitution that, though helpful in gaining the Constitution's ratification, could not coexist forever.

In 1787, proslavery supporters of the Constitution contended that it provided the slaveholding states with sufficient power to prevent the new national government from interfering with slavery without their approval. That view prevailed in the southern debates on ratifying the Constitution, over and against the objections of a minority of slaveholders worried by the Constitution's failure to provide specific recognition of property in man. The outcome of national debates concerning slavery during the early years of the new republic bolstered the slaveholders' confidence. But thereafter, as antislavery political efforts mounted, slaveholders sustained their conviction that the Constitution was proslavery by shifting their ground and claiming that the framers unequivocally validated property in man, something the framers had deliberately refused to do. Antislavery northerners would not let those claims stand. Decades of conflict followed that finally could only be settled in blood.

The Constitution's ambiguities and the paradox behind them were part of the price paid to create the new American nation. Today, as then, it is arguable that the price was too high.[37] It is essential, though, to recognize the paradox for what it was, and especially that it proved unstable. Over the next seventy years, as the paradox fitfully fell apart, so did the nation. The story, though, began more than a decade before the Constitution was framed, at the outbreak of the American Revolution—a revolution that, in a related paradox, left American slavery in some respects stronger than ever, even as it helped to inspire the first successful antislavery political movements in history. The early antislavery victories in the North heightened the stakes connected to slavery in designing the Constitution. They also brought to the fore contests over the legitimacy of property in man that would cast a shadow over the framers' deliberations in 1787.

I

Slavery, Property, and Emancipation in Revolutionary America

ORGANIZED ANTISLAVERY POLITICS originated in America. In 1775, five days before the battles of Lexington and Concord, ten Philadelphians, seven of them Quakers, founded the first antislavery society in world history, the Society for the Relief of Free Negroes Unlawfully Held in Bondage. The group disbanded during the war, but in 1784, with the Revolution won, it reorganized as the Pennsylvania Society for Promoting the Abolition of Slavery (also called the Pennsylvania Abolition Society, PAS), and by the end of 1790, at least seven more statewide antislavery societies had appeared, from Rhode Island to as far south as Virginia. When the Federal Convention met in Philadelphia in 1787, five northern states as well as the republic of Vermont (which would become the fourteenth state four years later) had either effectively banned slavery outright or passed gradual emancipation laws, commencing the largest emancipation of its kind to that point in modern history. In the Upper South, a combination of Revolutionary idealism and practical self-interest had loosened some whites' attachment to slavery and, in

Virginia, brought a liberalization of laws governing manumission. Even in the Lower South, where organized antislavery was out of the question, some masters expressed discomfort about slavery, and especially the public sale and punishment of slaves; Low Country South Carolina masters manumitted more slaves in the 1780s than they had over the previous thirty years.[1]

Antislavery advances were by no means easy or clear-cut, let alone foreordained. In most northern states, emancipation was heavily compromised, on terms that minimized the slaveholders' financial losses and kept slaves and their children bound to their masters. In the Upper South, gradual emancipation proposals got nowhere; and in the Lower South, whatever the humanitarian stirrings, emancipation was anathema. But no matter how limited their victories, northern antislavery advocates initiated and in some places completed the destruction of human bondage—an essential break from the past and a momentous turn in the history of slavery and antislavery. The break required, first and foremost, undermining and finally overthrowing the legitimacy of holding human beings as property, a principle that northern slaveholders defended to the bitter end as a matter of natural rights.

Southern slaveholders fiercely shared that principle and they took heed. At the Federal Convention in 1787, the most resolute proslavery delegates from the Lower South, leery of the North's emancipationist impulses, fought hard to uphold their property rights in slaves and keep those rights immune from the authority of the new national government. Yet while the convention conceded to the proslavery delegates on various points, a majority was equally intent on barring any recognition by the new constitution of the legitimacy of property in man. This mindfulness about property and slavery marked a profound shift in moral perception, signaled by the commencement of emancipation in the northern states, which no degree of southern manipulation or proslavery resolve could undo.

Between 1660 and 1710, virtually every English colony in the New World enacted laws defining slaves as conveyable property. Despite variations between colonies, they all grappled, David Brion Davis writes, with "the impossibility of acting consistently on the premise that men were things."[2] Although special provisions came to govern debt and inheritance, the universal assumption remained that slaves, although possessed of personhood, were also the same as any other form of sentient property, like horses or cows, which could be moved or alienated at the owner's will.

Enslaved Africans did not submit passively, but among white colonists there was scarcely any resistance to slavery's spread. From the late seventeenth century on, a few voices, chiefly Quaker sectarians, challenged the institution as sinful, building on antislavery sentiments that had surfaced in Britain during the revolutionary upheavals of the 1640s and 1650s. Yet even inside the Society of Friends, the practice of what one antislavery Quaker called "making slaves of men" only gradually fell into disfavor. In 1696, the Philadelphia Yearly Meeting cautiously advised that "Friends be careful not to Encourage the bringing in of any more Negroes," but implied that slaveholders' claims to property rights in humans did not violate God's word. This would remain basic policy among the Quakers regarding slaveholding for more than fifty years.[3]

From the start, firm presumptions about the sanctity of property rights in slaves thwarted antislavery protests. In his brief but powerful pamphlet *The Selling of Joseph*, published in 1700, the Massachusetts judge Samuel Sewall charged that anyone who bought or inherited slaves enjoyed no more rights to own other humans than the original slave dealer did. "He that shall in this case plead *Alteration of Property*, seems to have forfeited a great part of his own claim to Humanity," Sewell wrote. "There is no proportion between Twenty Pieces of Silver and LIBERTY." But Sewell's colleague Judge John Saffin replied swiftly and confidently with his own pamphlet, asserting that even if some of Sewell's objections to slavery had merit, slaveholders had incurred no moral obligation to free their slaves "and so lose all the money they cost."[4]

Only with the imperial crises and egalitarian agitation that culminated in the American Revolution did it become possible even to envisage slavery's demise. As early as the 1760s, spokesmen for what would become the patriot cause, notably James Otis, began linking resistance to Britain to calls for, in the words of a Boston town meeting petition in 1766, "the total abolishing of slavery among us."[5] Criticism of slavery mounted elsewhere in the British Empire, some of it directed from the mother country at the slaveholding colonists. In 1772, the landmark ruling by Chief Justice Lord Mansfield at the Court of King's Bench in the case of *Somerset v. Stewart* upset the legality of slavery in England, and specifically the right to recapture slaves on English soil—and, while it upset American slaveholders as well, the decision more broadly forced a moment of truth regarding slavery and the empire's future, in what one historian has called a "Mansfieldian moment."[6] In 1774, Rhode Island and Connecticut forbade the importation of slaves into their colonies. That same year, the slaveholder Thomas Jefferson, in a body of instructions to Virginia's delegation to the Continental Congress, remarked that "the abolition of domestic slavery is the great object of desire in those colonies where it was unhappily introduced in their infant state."[7] Jefferson exaggerated, but the accelerating revolutionary current had begun to challenge the principle of property in man, if only to blame Britain for supposedly foisting slavery on the colonists.

The slaves themselves certainly seized every opportunity for freedom. Once the war began, thousands turned the patriots' egalitarian rhetoric against them by running to British lines after Lord Dunmore (in 1775) and General-in-Chief Henry Clinton (in 1779) offered freedom in exchange for service. A smaller but still substantial number of slaves gained their freedom by fighting for the Americans. Wherever enslaved men and women had access to the law, they initiated freedom suits in courts and petition campaigns to legislatures, which in turn undermined public toleration of slavery.[8] Yet without at all slighting their unremitting determination to be free, the slaves could not have secured their individual freedom at law, let alone eradicated slavery, without the help of capable and steadfast white allies, including, in time, members of the new abolition societies.

Before 1787, battles against slavery by necessity occurred at the state and not the national level. The original national charter, the Articles of Confederation, included not a single direct reference to slaves and slavery. In their version of what would later become known under the Constitution as the privileges and immunities clause, the Articles did contain a phrase that could be construed as describing slaves as property.[9] Otherwise, the Confederation government had no authority whatsoever over either slavery or the Atlantic slave trade. The individual states could act as they pleased in regulating property rights in humans, including the international as well as domestic traffic in slaves. The Confederation government, feeble in so many respects, could do nothing.

Slaveholders, insistent on their property rights in slaves, would have it no other way, as they made clear at the outbreak of the Revolution, when the definition of slaves as property seemed momentarily in doubt. In July 1776, three weeks after the signing of the Declaration of Independence, the Second Continental Congress debated whether slaves should be counted as persons for the purpose of allocating taxes to support the new American government, which obviously would add an extra burden on the southern states. Southern slaveholders recoiled, not simply over the extra assessment but over the presumption that their slaves could be considered anything but their property. (Slaveholders would take a very different view a decade later, when counting slaves as persons figured to increase their states' representation in the national legislature.) A South Carolina representative harangued the Congress with one of the earliest disunion threats issued on behalf of his famously fractious state: "If it is debated, whether their slaves are their property," Thomas Lynch Jr. declaimed, "there is an end of the confederation." As slaves were property, he said, there was no more reason to tax them than there was to tax northerners' land, cattle, or sheep. Lynch's bombast raised a barbed reply from Benjamin Franklin—"Sheep will never make any insurrections," Franklin said—but there the northern response ended.[10]

Nor were the nation's national officeholders and diplomats, working in their official capacities under the Articles of Confederation, in any position to forsake the principle of slaves as property. Franklin demonstrated as much during the negotiations with Britain that led to the Treaty of Paris in 1783, securing American independence. In November 1782, with the treaty largely agreed upon and ready for signing, one of the American negotiators, Henry Laurens, a wealthy South Carolina planter and slave trader, suggested a clause about slaves, which was then added to the treaty's seventh article: British forces would begin their evacuation of America speedily, without destruction, and "without carrying away any negroes or other property of the American inhabitants." Article VII would become a subject of intense wrangling in American diplomacy for many years to come, through the crisis over the Jay Treaty in 1795 and after. In American politics, the issue aroused pro- and antislavery sensibilities over what, if anything, the British owed American slaveholders who claimed their slaves had been stolen. Related questions connected to wartime emancipation and international law would persist until the Civil War. Still, in September 1783, John Jay and John Adams as well as Franklin unflinchingly signed the Treaty of Paris, complete with its recognition of Negro slaves as property.[11]

Emancipation in America would have to proceed state by state.[12] In 1777, the rebels of Vermont, declaring that "all men are born equally free and independent," approved the first written constitution in history to ban adult slavery.[13] Nearly identical language in a bill of rights added to the New Hampshire constitution of 1783 seemed to affirm that slavery, already crumbling in the state, was now prohibited. Several Massachusetts towns objected to the lack of a provision specifically renouncing slavery in a draft state constitution debated in 1778; although the constitution finally adopted in 1780 contained no such provision, it did declare that "all men are born free and equal." Based in part on that assertion, antislavery rulings over freedom suits involving a resolute slave woman named Mum Betts and a runaway named Quock Walker battered slavery's legal supports in Massachusetts, and the institution rapidly eroded. The first federal census in 1790 reported no slaves at all in the state. Men, women, and children who had once been enslaved walked free.[14]

Elsewhere, legislatures passed their gradual emancipation laws. In Pennsylvania, after a protracted struggle, antislavery forces led by the egalitarian radical George Bryant approved the first gradual abolition law in history in 1780. Tentative moves toward abolition in Connecticut and Rhode Island concluded with the passage of gradual emancipation laws in 1784. Slavery was much stronger economically and politically in New York and New Jersey, where gradual emancipation was not enacted until, respectively, 1799 and 1804. Yet well before the framing of the Federal Constitution, New Jerseyans hotly debated emancipation in the wake of gradual abolition in neighboring Pennsylvania; New York lawmakers, after debating a proposed immediate emancipation, came close to enacting a gradual abolition bill more liberal than Pennsylvania's in 1785.[15]

From one angle, this piecemeal, so-called first emancipation can seem subdued and grudging, even conservative. Slavery was nowhere near as deeply rooted in the North as it was in the South, and in important seaport centers such as Philadelphia and New York, slavery was quickly becoming less profitable than free labor. Yet in three of the six states that before 1787 acted to end slavery, emancipation would unfold gradually as it would later in New York and New Jersey. That is, the vast majority of northern slaves were covered by laws that freed no slaves at all, only children born to slave mothers after a specified date, who were then subject to a prolonged indentured servitude. Under Pennsylvania's law, for example, slaveholders retained ownership of all slaves born before the law went into effect, and children born to slave mothers were bound to serve their mother's master until they reached the age of twenty-eight. Connecticut and Rhode Island followed the same formula, although with somewhat lighter indenture provisions (lasting to age twenty-five in Connecticut and to age twenty-one for males and eighteen for females in Rhode Island).

So gradual was gradual emancipation that there were still slaves counted in the federal census of Pennsylvania in 1840, and a handful of slaves had yet to be freed in New Jersey as late as 1865. Even in Vermont, whose constitution of 1777 barred adult enslavement, there is evidence of slaveholding into the first decade of the nineteenth century. Gradual emancipation laws contained loopholes that permitted slaveholders to evade the proscriptions in various ways, such as selling slaves out of state. In New York and New Jersey, slaveholders responded to initial emancipation efforts by securing comprehensive slave codes that systemized and tightened the regulations upholding bondage. The writers of Connecticut's gradual abolition law sounded singularly unenthusiastic about their reform: after burying the emancipation provision at the very end of a highly restrictive new law entitled "An Act concerning Indian, Molatto, and Negro Servants and Slaves," the lawmakers included a tepid justification, observing that "Sound Policy requires that the Abolition of Slavery should be effected as soon as may be consistent with the Rights of Individuals, and the public Safety and Welfare."[16] In purely economic terms, meanwhile, under what was referred to as post-nati emancipation—that is, emancipation only of infants born after a certain date—slaveholders stood to recoup virtually the entire market value of their investment from the labor of those who remained slaves and from the bound labor of their children. The laws effectively placed the financial burden of emancipation on the slaves themselves and their offspring.[17]

Northern slaveholders forced these concessions and sometimes put the emancipationists—already facing hesitant and sometimes hostile public opinion—on the defensive. The prospect of ending slavery unsettled long-established social norms, and at every step, pro-emancipationists, without curbing their attack on the enormity of human property, strained to prove that their plan aimed to do justice to masters as well as non-slaveholding taxpayers. Gradual emancipation, they insisted, would not be nearly as injurious to the slaveholders as their critics claimed it would be. "The difference in value between a black child, hereafter to be born in servitude, and another to be his own master at the age of 28, is very inconsiderable," the Pennsylvania antislavery leader Bryant observed.[18]

The prolongation of emancipation, meanwhile, was not entirely a concession to the slaveholders, as the abolitionist mainstream, white and black, had its own apprehensions about pushing emancipation too far, too fast. Slavery had left the slaves destitute of property, education, and (some feared) virtue. A rapid abolition, emancipationists worried, might prove ruinous to former slaves and only worsen white racism, especially as taxpayers would be compelled to pay any extra costs incurred for policing and poor relief. "A *gradual* restoration to the blacks of their rights is all that is desired or can with safety be hazarded," the editor Noah Webster wrote in 1796, while counseling against "the danger of taking too deep hold of *principles.*"[19] People who had suffered the "evil consequences" of slavery, the black abolitionist Rev. Peter Williams Jr. would later remark, had to learn "the lessons of morality, industry and economy" in order to enjoy the full fruits of freedom. Once elevated, blacks would be able to encourage the "gradual discardment of the illiberal opinions entertained against part of the human family" by most whites.[20] These paternalist concerns were not always as callous as they might appear to modern eyes; indeed, in some places they led to the establishment of schooling and apprenticeship training for bound children of slaves as a form of restitution as well as elevation. But the concerns also reinforced an approach to emancipation geared toward placating slaveholders and calming a broader white public fearful of what freedom for blacks might bring.

Northern emancipation, meanwhile, whether immediate or gradual, hardly delivered either slaves, ex-slaves, or their children from oppressive conditions; indeed, one historian writes, even those blacks who attained their full freedom "often found themselves living in circumstances that looked suspiciously like the old bondage."[21] Poverty forced many ex-slaves to enter themselves or their children swiftly into long-term indentures with white householders. Otherwise, most free blacks found themselves either locked in landless rural penury or relegated to the meanest city occupations, despised by whites as social outcasts. Even where slave codes died, new laws sustained severe civil restrictions, including barring blacks from voting, sitting on juries, testifying in court, and serving in local militias. And while adult slaves remained enslaved under gradual emancipation, their children remained under the control of a master or mistress, in most states well into the prime of their working lives, with the rights to their labor or service still subject to sale like any other piece of property.

A few abolitionists protested what they saw as a hateful bigotry embedded in gradual abolition, and they attacked the laws angrily for doing "things by halves," as the Philadelphian "Phileleutheros" wrote— enacting an emancipation that still left slaves "groaning under the rod of a cruel unfeeling tyrant."[22] Gradual abolition, the New Jersey abolitionist John Cooper remarked, told the slaves that "we will not do justice unto you, but our posterity will do justice unto your posterity." Almost certainly, the mass of slaves greeted the new law with disappointment as well as gladness. One out of numerous freedom petitions, this one addressed to the Connecticut legislature by a group of New Haven slaves in 1788, four years after the enactment of the state's gradual emancipation law, bitterly described the slaves' continued suffering in what was supposed to be "a free contry," and asked the lawmakers to "grant us a Liberration wee are all Deturmand we Can to[il] As Long as thir is Labor."[23]

From another perspective, however—the perspective of past norms and the laws of property—northern emancipation with all its limitations was a decisive blow for freedom, with lasting repercussions for slavery everywhere. Accounts that portray gradual emancipation in particular chiefly as a blessing for the slaveholders miss this point, and thus fail to explain why the slaveholders fought even the slowest of emancipation plans so intensely. Grasping the point requires jettisoning the commonplace fallacy whereby gradual emancipation and its advocates get judged according to the standards set by the protests of later abolitionists and the general emancipation of 1865. The fallacy lies in evaluating one set of events and actors on the basis of what preceded them while evaluating the other on the basis of what followed them.

That some abolitionists in the post-Revolution decades, anticipating the later immediatists, objected that the process was morally compromised in no way vitiated what was so profound in gradual emancipation. Like any emancipation, gradual emancipation involved nothing less than, in one historian's words, the "use of government coercion to outlaw a specific form of previously lawful property"—that is, proscribing and then eradicating an entire class of property. Even though the process would be gradual, even though it kept slaves in slavery and subjected their children to extended servitude, it was by any standard a dramatic change in slavery's legal status.[24]

Prior to northern emancipation, private individual manumissions, sometimes requiring official approval, along with individual court cases (and, of course, slaves escaping or purchasing their freedom) had been the sole means by which slaves could be freed from bondage, or could free themselves. Now pushed by restive slaves, and with the encouragement of the local self-declared abolitionist societies, antislavery lawmakers and jurists won official measures, legislative and judicial, that secured systematic if in most cases painfully protracted emancipation. Victory, meanwhile, did not come easily, especially in the states with the largest slave populations, not because the emancipationists were fainthearted but because their opponents were so strong. "Slaveowners in states like New York and New Jersey fought long and hard to maintain their property rights in slaves," one historian writes, "so that the policy shift was the outcome of an intense political struggle."[25]

The slaveholders' resistance and that of many non-slaveholders reflected in part the significant place of slavery in northern life. To be sure, slavery was not the dominant form of labor in the northern states; nor was it the model of an ideal society and polity, as it was in much of the South. Still, quite apart from northern connections to slave economies elsewhere, northern slavery was hardly negligible. Divided between farm labor in rural areas and a variety of artisan, laboring, maritime, and servant tasks in the cities, slaves made up nearly 8 percent of the population of Rhode Island and nearly 7 percent in New Jersey in 1760, and 12 percent of the population of New York a decade later. The proportion of households holding slaves in Manhattan and its adjacent counties was greater than that in any southern state; as late as 1790, one in every five households in the city owned at least one slave. Even if slavery was only one form of labor among others in the North, the political influence wielded by well-connected slaveholders was considerable.[26]

Abolitionists also had to overcome objections to the ways they organized in politics. The very existence of political opposition to slavery was obnoxious to the master class, as undertaken by the groups in existence in 1787, the Pennsylvania Abolition Society and the New-York Manumission Society (the New York group having formed in 1785, a year after the PAS reorganized). Although composed solely of white men, including well-known members of local professional and mercantile elites, the societies worked with and on behalf of free blacks and slaves more closely than any other voluntary associations of whites in the early republic. Organized abolitionists doggedly defended in court blacks wrongfully claimed as slaves; they initiated benevolent efforts such as the celebrated African Free School established by the New-York Manumission Society in 1787; they tirelessly petitioned and lobbied state officials both before and after the enactment of emancipation laws. Political activities were central to the societies' mission. Absent any "private interest" or natural constituency to end slavery, one Rhode Island abolitionist later remarked, it was up to the societies to agitate and make "a much stronger impression upon the mind" of lawmakers.[27]

Such coordinated efforts offended northern slaveholders and their southern allies as intrusions on sound government. Rarely, it needs noting, did the masters' counterattacks charge that opposing slavery subverted republicanism itself, an argument that would only emerge coherently among southern slaveholders many years later.[28] Rather, the abolitionists ran afoul of what slavery's defenders—and not just slavery's defenders—considered the limits of legitimate dissent. Although antislavery advocates were entitled to publicize their personal opinions, their critics charged, they had no business forming societies to put pressure on elected officials. A decade later, similar organizations of self-styled Democratic Republicans would earn the opprobrium of President George Washington and his supporters as illicit "self-created societies." The abolition societies were just as problematic if not more so, denounced by one Georgian as "government meddlers." Washington, who embraced gradual abolition, was among the organized abolitionists' detractors, affronted specifically by the Pennsylvania Abolition Society's efforts on behalf of blacks claimed as slaves by southern slaveholders. "It should seem that this Society is not only acting repugnant to justice so far as its conduct concerns strangers," he complained, "but, in my opinion extremely impolitickly with respect to the State."[29]

Worst of all—and here the essential radicalism of gradual emancipation fully emerged—slaveholders asserted that the abolitionists were blatantly invading their property rights. Antislavery proponents never doubted that state governments possessed the authority to effect abolition; even the antislavery moderate William Pinkney of Maryland, no abolitionist, argued that the positive laws that established slavery, and not those that abolished it, violated "the principle of a democracy."[30] But proslavery advocates, North and South, saw property *in* slaves as a natural right, like property in any other commodity, which could not be abridged. Emancipation of any kind, no matter how gradual, the slaveholders maintained, involved government engaging in what one proslavery New Jersey writer called "a solemn act of publick ROBBERY, or FRAUD," with disturbing implications for the property rights of every citizen.[31]

The slaveholders certainly had a point about the legal implications of gradual emancipation. Under the post-nati emancipation laws, for example, children born to slave mothers were bound to sometimes arduous labor without clear contractual arrangements, and with their masters still empowered to sell rights to their service or labor. Yet if still subjugated, they were definitively not slaves or "servants for life," their persons owned by their masters, a major shift as far as the institution of slavery was concerned.

Since antiquity, slave law had dictated that children born of slave mothers were their masters' property; the rule was duly adopted in the British North American colonies, in custom if not always in law. A master, it was presumed, enjoyed the same natural right over his slaves' children as a farmer did over the offspring of his livestock, a claim northern slaveholders would assert repeatedly. Eighteenth-century abolitionists, however, drawing on authorities ranging from Blackstone to Montesquieu, denounced inherited bondage as absurd and odious.

With the coming of northern emancipation, this form of slave property would be henceforth, as the Pennsylvania law stated, "utterly taken away, extinguished and forever abolished."[32] In this regard, although freedom would be achingly delayed, there was nothing at all gradual about gradual emancipation: it delivered these children from slavery immediately.[33]

More to the point, even as slaveholders retained full ownership of the children's parents, they did so now in accordance with laws that declared property in humans as at the very least unsound, in some cases as unnatural and abhorrent, and in all cases as destined for eradication—laws enacted over and against the slaveholders' manifest disapproval. Freedom would come by degrees, but slavery—what the Pennsylvania law called plundering "the common blessings that [slaves] were by nature entitled to"—immediately lost its prior legitimacy.[34] The continued presence of slaves and slavery pointed to the past and reinforced whites' enduring domination over blacks, slave and free. The emancipation laws pointed to the future and stigmatized, sometimes forcefully, the slaveholders' property claims. Not surprisingly, no matter how considerable the concessions in gradual emancipation, resistant slaveholders considered gradual emancipation repugnant and oppressive.

Nor could anyone assume that enactment of gradual emancipation would not soon produce additional attacks on the slaveholders' once-presumed property rights, up to and including a general emancipation. The abolitionists certainly did not see gradual emancipation as the final blow against slavery, but merely considered it as (in the Pennsylvania law's words) "one more step to universal civilization."[35] For many years prior to the laws' enactment, abolitionists had tried to chip away at the slaveholders' authority by enacting reforms of state slave codes; after the emancipation laws' enactment, they worked hard to liberalize further state legislation governing slavery and indentured servitude, closing loopholes and winning reforms. In New York, these continuing efforts led to the approval in 1817 of a law abolishing slavery, completely and without compensation, to take effect a decade later—the first general emancipation law in the United States.[36]

The northern slaveholders' counterattack on the emancipationists frequently appealed to racism—not as obsessive as the racism that emerged after emancipation, but direct and nasty enough. Ridicule of blacks as innately inferior was commonplace, coupled with terrible predictions of what black freedom would bring. The idea of turning "a sheep hairy African Negro" into "a spirited noble, and generous American freeman" was perverse, one proslavery polemicist wrote. The sight of black men in the seats of power, with "General Quacco here, Col. Mingo there," wrote another, would incur shame "from mixture of complexion and their participation in government." Ending slavery would sooner or later shift the burden of disciplining and (in the case of the destitute) providing for the mass of deficient and desperate Africans to society at large, the slaveholders claimed—a shift they were more than happy to spare the public if permitted to retain their property rights in slaves.[37]

Slaveholders and their supporters also ferreted out quotations from the Bible that supposedly sanctified human bondage, in order to rebut antislavery appeals to religious and ethical principles. "Let us next see what support this doctrine of perpetual servitude has from the Scriptures," one typical discourse began, before concluding, with copious citations from the Old and New Testaments, that slavery "was allowed and not merely winked at, by the God of Heaven."[38]

Finally, though, as Arthur Zilversmit observed in the most thorough study to date of northern emancipation, "all pro-slavery arguments turned on the question of property rights."[39] Prospects of racial chaos were just that, prospects; biblical strictures on their own were not enforceable at law; and so slavery's defenders consistently focused on the property issue. In northern New England, where emancipation advanced most swiftly, and where general abolition was more or less immediate, slaveholders and their supporters complained loudly about annulment of their natural rights to property. In 1783, one disgruntled Massachusetts writer proclaimed not "a shadow of advantage" in emancipation, which "deprive[d] the lawful owners of their Negro property" and created a class of "ragged, miserable, wretched creatures, covered with vermin, and a nuisance to all near them."[40] Twelve years later, the chief justice of the Massachusetts Court of Common Pleas remarked dolefully on how, because of what he called an official misreading of the state's constitution, "a number of citizens have been deprived of property formerly acquired under the protection of law."[41]

Defense of property rights loomed even larger where resistance to freedom was stronger and emancipation was gradual. In these states, and particularly in New Jersey and New York, Zilversmit observed, the proslavery argument "shed its coating of biblical justification and historical precedent and stood revealed as the armor of property, defending its interests."[42]

Writing in New Jersey—where proslavery advocates mounted the longest and most intense campaign of all the northern states—the essayist "Impartial" forcefully made the case about slavery and property rights in 1781, in direct response to Pennsylvania's gradual emancipation law of the previous year. Although emancipation might one day come to New Jersey, he observed, slaves were undeniably a legitimate form of property under law, meaning that "we cannot constitutionally be divested of them by legislative authority." New Jersey's "most excellent constitution," he continued, guaranteed due process to every freeman for his property as well as his life and liberty; therefore, "the liberation of our slaves . . . without the concurrence of their possessors, we apprehend, is an object infinitely further distant from the legal attention of our Assembly than are the heavens above the earth."[43] Or, as another New Jersey slaveholder put it bluntly that same year, slaves "bought with money, or for trouble or expense for bringing up, are as much their owner's property as anything we possess . . . obtained under the sanction of the laws of their country."[44]

Gradual emancipation laws such as Pennsylvania's were no less offensive than proposals for immediate emancipation. "We are informed that you do not desire an 'immediate liberation of our Negroes,'" the writer "Truth et Justice" said in reply to a gradual abolition appeal. Mandating a long period of servitude for the children of slaves supposedly provided just compensation to the slaveholders. But to proslavery advocates, the post-nati compromise made no difference, as they believed the children of slaves were no less their masters' property than the slaves themselves. "To free them then, without satisfying the owners for their undoubtedly lawful property," "Truth et Justice" wrote, "would be [no] less constitutional at that period than now." Any legislators who interfered in any way with property rights in slaves without the slaveholders' consent and without full financial indemnification would "deviate from their line of duty or trespass on our rights."[45]

The property argument proved stubborn, even among northerners who acknowledged that slavery was oppressive. A New Jersey writer who styled himself "A Lover of True Justice" expressed sympathy with the slaves' desire for freedom and averred that he "could cordially wish the emancipation of this class of my fellow creatures" at some future period that was "favourable . . . to their and the community's advantage." Nevertheless, he insisted, nothing could be done about slavery that did not respect "*the preservation of property, so that no one has his slaves forced from him.*"[46] The French reformer Brissot de Warville, visiting Philadelphia in 1788, was informed that the slowness of emancipation was due to the fact that slaves were considered property, "and all property is sacred." The greatest impediment to emancipation, another French visitor, the Duc de la Rochefoucauld Liancourt, noted in 1796 about New York, was "the respect due to the *property* of the masters."[47]

The abolitionists attacked the slaveholders' property claims by turning the tables and proclaiming their view that slavery robbed the slaves of *their* natural rights to property in their own persons. Their arguments drew freely on British political and legal writings, dating back to the radical tracts of the seventeenth-century English Civil War, which proclaimed that the natural condition of human beings was freedom, and that all property derived from that primary natural right. "The property which every man has in his own labor," Adam Smith contended in *The Wealth of Nations,* "as it is the original foundation for all over property, so it is the most sacred and inviolable."[48] By these lights, property in slaves could only be abominable.

Slavery, the New Jersey writer "A Friend to Justice" wrote in 1780, "is utterly repugnant to the very nature and spirit of the common law"—and if the common law ever did authorize slavery, it would have to be excised as "repugnant to the laws of God and nature."[49] "Property in the persons and labors of other men, is a thing in itself absurd," Noah Webster's *American Minerva* declared in 1796, "it is a violation of the law of nature and society—of course every constitutional declaration and every law, authorizing such violation, is *ipso facto* void."[50] In fact, slavery involved stealing the slave's personhood and then selling it—a double crime. "It is said by some, that the masters of slaves have a property in them," the abolitionist and Pennsylvania Abolition Society member Charles Crawford observed, "and that to deprive a man of his property is unjust." But "no man can have a property in stolen goods," Crawford charged, regardless of whether the goods were inherited or bought from another. "The common maxim," he concluded, "that 'The receiver is as bad as the thief,' extends to this as well as every other species of theft."[51]

Above all, the abolitionists singled out the slaveholders' claims to property rights in humans as offensive to the egalitarian principles of the Revolution, which they identified with the primacy of freedom and self-ownership. Samuel Miller of New York proclaimed the argument just as the final push for emancipation in his state commenced. "Avarice may clamorously contend, that the *laws of property* justify slavery," he began, and his response to that contention was plain: "The right which every man has to his personal liberty is paramount to all the laws of property." Miller laid aside how emancipation might be achieved in New York, and even left open the possibility that slaveholders be directly indemnified for their financial loss. Yet Miller did not think compensation was mandatory: he hailed the immediate, uncompensated abolition of slavery as completed in Massachusetts. Like most emancipationists, meanwhile, he sharply distinguished between compensating slaveholders either directly or indirectly, which he thought was a political necessity, and acknowledging the legitimacy of slavery, which he would never do. His point was more basic: "All I contend for at present is, that no claims of property can ever justly interfere with, or be suffered to impede the operation of that noble and eternal principle, that 'all men are endowed by their Creator with certain unalienable rights—and that among these are life, liberty, and the pursuit of happiness.'"[52]

The compromise implied by gradual abolition—that, by ending slavery over time, basic justice would supposedly be done to masters and slaves alike—certainly helped to wear down resistance to emancipation, even among some slaveholders. "The freedom of those unhappy black people, induced in so gradual a manner as it is in Pennsylvania," one New Jersey master, previously opposed to emancipation, wrote in 1781, "must remove every reasonable apprehension of danger to the state, or private loss to individuals."[53] But the victorious pro-emancipationists also knew that inside their own states, whether or not emancipation came rapidly, they had established a principle slave-holders had fought bitterly: courts and legislatures could commence the process of extinguishing the slaveholders' peculiar form of human property.

No matter how long that process took, the abolitionists had success-fully challenged slavery's bedrock principle, the legitimacy of property in man. The Rhode Island gradual abolition law of 1784 most pointedly of all the emancipation laws announced that achievement to the world: "All Men are entitled to Life, Liberty and the Pursuit of Happi-ness," it began, and "holding Mankind in a State of Slavery, *as private Property*, which has gradually obtained by unrestrained Custom and the Permission of the Laws, is repugnant to this Principle, and subver-sive of the Happiness of Mankind."[54]

The words were galling to northern slaveholders. They were truly alarming further south.

Nothing remotely comparable to the northern emancipationist drive arose in the southern states. Yet southerners were aware of what was happening in the North, and in the Upper South, slavery's defenders had to contend with antislavery rumblings, including a short-lived emancipation campaign in Virginia in 1785. Aghast at even these ten-tative antislavery developments, southern slaveholders, like their northern counterparts, insisted above all on the inviolability of their property rights in slaves.

Organized antislavery politics, unheard of in the Lower South, made some very limited headway in the Upper South before 1800. In 1789, a group of ninety men in Baltimore formed the Maryland Society for the Promotion of the Abolition of Slavery, and the organization soon expanded to include as many as 250 members in four separate chapters, but it had faded away by 1798. In 1789, the governor of Virginia, Beverly Randolph, sent copies of his state's slave laws to the Pennsylvania Abolition Society, stating that "it will always give me pleasure to give any aid in my Power to forward the humane & benevolent Designs of the Philadelphia Society."[55] A year later, a group of Virginians including the Quaker tobacco planter Robert Pleasants (who had freed the slaves he inherited from his father) founded the Virginia Abolition Society, in which a later sitting governor, James Wood, would serve as vice president. But the society disbanded in 1798, after the Virginia legislature passed a law forbidding abolitionists from sitting on juries in freedom suit cases.[56]

Nevertheless, in a limited way, the Upper South shared in the broader antislavery feeling that accompanied the Revolution. As in the northern states, Upper South newspapers carried polemics, including some written by free blacks, on slavery as an abominable denial of natural rights. In 1783, "Vox Africanus," writing in the *Maryland Gazette,* cited the Declaration of Independence in a diatribe against "our abject state of slavery," and said it was "insulting to the understanding of America at this enlightened period" to have to explain the absurdity and inhumanity of human bondage.[57] Antislavery advocates beckoned to northern emancipation: "If the state of Pennsylvania is to be applauded for her conduct," a pseudonymous Maryland writer, "Othello," observed in 1788, "that of South Carolina can never be too strongly execrated." Alongside the struggling abolitionist societies, meanwhile, members of disciplined and capable religious minorities—Quakers, Methodists, and to some degree Baptists—pushed as hard as they could against slavery.[58]

Antislavery activity initially focused on liberalizing manumission laws. After unsuccessful attempts in 1778 and 1780, the Virginia legislature, under pressure from a well-organized body of Quakers, passed an "act to authorize the manumission of slaves," which lifted the requirement that masters receive formal legislative approval before freeing any slave. Designed in part to sanction manumissions that the Quakers were demanding of each other, the law also heeded (in the words of one Quaker pro-manumission petition in 1780) "the great principle, that freedom is the natural rights [sic] of all mankind." Any person would now be able to set free any of his or her slaves under the age of forty-five by private instrument, without requiring the manumitted slaves to leave the state. In addition to empowering masters to end their own slaveholding voluntarily, the law made it possible for slaves to purchase their freedom as never before. Quite apart from helping the Quakers, it opened the way for hundreds of slaves to buy themselves out of slavery and for thousands of Virginia slaveholders to free their slaves.[59]

The 1782 law did not in the least question slaveholders' property rights; indeed, it reinforced those rights, specifying that manumission did not negate the title to a slave that any person other than the manumitting master might own, including creditors and heirs. At the heart of the law lay the assumption that slaveholders could do with their property as they wished, including rendering it no longer property of any kind. Yet for many Virginians, that very assumption was ominous, producing what one legislative petition protesting the law described as nothing less than "a Partial emancipation of Slaves."[60]

Slaveholders' fears came to a head in 1785, when Virginia Methodists launched their own emancipationist petition campaign. Methodist ministers riding circuit had long preached against slavery and urged individuals to free their slaves. Delegates to the annual Methodist conference held in Baltimore in December 1784 condemned the institution and concluded that Methodists should manumit their slaves wherever it was legal to do so. The following spring, Methodist preachers fanned out across the state to obtain signatures for county petitions in support of the conference's resolutions. Almost certainly written by Bishop Thomas Coke, the petitions declared "that LIBERTY is the Birthright of Mankind," claiming that "the Glorious and ever Memorable Revolution can be Justifyed on no other Principles," and entreating the Assembly "to pursue the most prudential, but Effectual method, for the immediate or Gradual Extirpation of Slavery."[61]

The campaign quickly picked up steam. Several substantial slaveholders signed the petitions. In late May, Bishop Coke and Bishop Francis Asbury obtained an interview with George Washington, who was living in temporary retirement from public life at Mount Vernon. Washington declined to sign, yet he assured his visitors (Coke later recalled) that he shared their views about slavery and promised that "if the Assembly took [the petitions] under consideration, [he] would signify his sentiments by a letter."[62]

The Methodist petitions also sparked intensely hostile reactions. At the end of April, Bishop Asbury, while visiting Brunswick County, a proslavery stronghold, "found the minds of the people greatly agitated with our rules against slavery, and a proposed petition to the general assembly for the emancipation of the blacks."[63] Memorials from important slaveholding counties in central and southern Virginia, containing hundreds of signatures, arrived in Richmond, demanding repeal of the

1782 manumission law as well as a summary rejection of the Methodists' pleas.

The protesters were more certain than ever that the manumission law had been just a step on the way toward complete abolition of slavery. "Persons We may reasonably suppose disaffected to our State and Government," the petition from Brunswick County asserted, were not satisfied with the manumission law alone, and so they agitated for "a general Emancipation," under the pretense of being "moved by Religious Principles and taking for their motive universal Charity." Easing manumissions had been a disaster, the petitions charged, as it unleashed violent blacks to commit the basest crimes and outrages. This terrible experience made it imperative, the petitioners from Lunenburg County declared, for the legislature to "discountenance, and utterly reject every Motion and Proposal for emancipating our Slaves."[64]

In attacking the Methodist campaign, the Virginia anti-emancipation petitions included their own concise if rough-hewn defenses of slavery. Much like the northern anti-emancipationists' appeals, the Virginians' defenses disparaged blacks as brutes and claimed scriptural authority for slaveholding, but they emphasized above all the slaveholders' property rights.

"We understand a very subtle and daring Attempt is made to dispossess us of a very important Part of our Property," the petition from Amelia County complained, "TO WREST FROM US OUR SLAVES, by an Act of the Legislature for a general Emancipation of them." The nation, the petitioners pointed out, had only just won a revolution to affirm the principle that no legislature could usurp the power to dispose of anyone's property without that person's consent. "Our Rights of Liberty and Property are now as well secured to us, as they can be by any human Constitution and Form of Government," the Halifax County petition observed. On its face, any emancipation law would violate those fundamental rights.[65]

Legitimate property rights could never be subject to debate. "Tho' we admit it to be the indisputable right of the Citizen to apply to the Legislature by Petition on any or otherwise Subject within the Cognizance of their constitutional powers," the men of Lunenburg County remarked, it was intolerable to admit that "any Man has a right, to petition or otherwise press the Legislature to divest us of our known rights of Property, which are so clearly defined; so fully acknowledged; and so solemnly ratified and confirmd." The Brunswick County petition flatly concluded, "We have a right to retain such Slaves, as We have justly and legally in Possession." The legislature ought not simply to defeat any proposed emancipation, but refuse even to consider it.[66]

Virginia legislators hastily blocked the Methodists' emancipation drive, although they did not precisely follow the proslavery petitioners' wishes. Presented to the House of Delegates on November 8, 1785, the petitions were tabled. Two days later, meeting as a Committee of the Whole, the House considered both the petitions and the proslavery protests. A proslavery delegate moved that the Methodist petitions be thrown "under the table"—that is, rejected without consideration—but according to another delegate, James Madison, the motion "was treated with as much indignation on one side, as the [Methodist] petition itself was on the other." The House then proceeded to debate a measure that the proslavery petitioners had called wholly illegitimate. According to Madison, "sundry respectable members"—possibly including Madison himself—spoke up on behalf of emancipation, but the opponents treated the Methodists' proposals (Madison wrote) "with all the indignity" of a summary dismissal.[67]

Finally, not a single member voted in favor of authorizing the appropriate committee to draw up an emancipation law. Thereafter, the chances for legislative emancipation of Virginia's slaves quickly evaporated, and no one doubted why. "The laws have declared them property," the antislavery Baptist elder John Leland noted, and thus emancipation was impossible, as it would be unconstitutional "for government to take away the property of individuals." The cost of purchasing and liberating all of Virginia's slaves—which Leland calculated would run in excess of $8 million—was prohibitive, even if the slaveholders assented to such a plan. "It is a question," Leland wrote, sadly but realistically, "whether men had not better lose all their property, than deprive an individual of his birth right blessing, freedom."[68] Virginia Methodists, like antislavery northerners, had nudged their legislators to consider freedom as superior to property claims; Virginia lawmakers emphatically refused.

Slavery's vindication in Virginia was not quite as thoroughgoing, however, as its strongest defenders would have preferred. Even if the House of Delegates unanimously rejected emancipation, it had permitted debate on the subject, and it had allowed representatives, possibly including Madison, to express their emancipationist sympathies. It followed that, contrary to the slaveholders' absolutist property claims, the legislature was in fact empowered to debate and approve emancipation. George Washington himself had said as much privately in a letter to his antislavery friend the Marquis de Lafayette, observing that "by degrees" emancipation "certainly might, and assuredly ought to be effected; and that too by Legislative authority."[69] On the issue of manumission, meanwhile, proslavery forces, a month after they had killed further discussion of emancipation, mustered enough support to win, barely, the drafting of legislation to repeal the liberalized 1782 law—but the repeal bill failed twice. The House also rejected a bill that would have amended the manumission law to require all free blacks to depart the state within a specified time.[70]

The ambiguities in the Virginians' actions had important implications. Emancipationists, in Virginia as elsewhere, held that liberty, "the Birthright of Mankind," superseded claims to property rights. Proslavery advocates held that emancipation was theft and thus wholly illegitimate. But between these groups there were leading Virginians, including slaveholders, who, although not outright emancipationists, were sufficiently disturbed by slavery to entertain the idea of emancipation, permit lawmakers to debate it, and keep alive the possibility of slavery's eradication in future.[71]

Emancipationists, a minority in Virginia, were nearly nonexistent further south, where proslavery politics were impregnable. As antislavery northerners fitfully abolished slavery in their own states, a sectional divide opened that would soon enough threaten national unity. That division, though, and the political struggles over slavery to come, would be complicated by the influence of slaveholders who were wary of validating and fixing property in man as an eternal American institution. Among those slaveholders was James Madison, who would play a vital role (though ultimately conflicted and compromised) in the first important national debates over slavery beginning in 1787.

No northern legislature sent instructions regarding slavery to their state's delegation to the Federal Convention, but the two existing abolitionist societies had ideas of their own. The societies were becoming practiced in petitioning and lobbying state legislators, and the calling of a convention to reframe the national government presented an obvious opportunity. The abolitionists also had good reason to believe they would at least receive a hearing, given the makeup of the delegations from the North and especially those from the Middle States. To be sure, as the convention debates would amply prove, a critical number of northern delegates, especially from the New England states, were perfectly willing to make concessions to the slaveholders no matter their personal views about slavery. Still, several delegates, including at least half of the delegates from the Middle States, were avowed antislavery men; the Pennsylvanians, for example, included two active members of the Pennsylvania Abolition Society, the lawyer Jared Ingersoll and, most auspiciously, the group's president, Benjamin Franklin.[72]

In June 1787, one month into the convention's deliberations, the emerging writer on political economy Tench Coxe, a moderate member of the PAS, approached Franklin with a petition decrying the Atlantic slave trade as an affront to "the citizens of republics," and invoking the certainty of divine judgment if the new government did not abolish it.[73] The society's members, having produced what Coxe later called a "very strong paper," bade him obtain Franklin's signature for presentation to the convention. Coxe followed through, but he was worried about the petition's passionate tone, and he suggested to Franklin "that it would be a very improper season & place to hazard the Application," especially coming so soon after the delegates had assembled. Coxe was not privy to the convention's proceedings, but Franklin, who very much was, followed his advice. Although it was still early in the convention's deliberations, Franklin could have foreseen that introducing a forceful plea from an abolitionist organization to ban the Atlantic trade would have been morally righteous but politically reckless. In any event, he assured Coxe, the delegates would in due course take up the future of the slave trade.[74]

Two months later, the New-York Manumission Society appointed a three-man committee, which included one of its founders and first president, the eminent lawyer John Jay, to prepare a document bidding the convention to do all "as may in their opinion tend to promote the attainment of the objects of this Society." On August 17, the society was informed that the convention would probably not consider the question of slavery at all, and the membership resolved not to send a memorial on the subject of "the manumission of slaves."[75] Four days later, though, the convention commenced a debate over the slave trade that in time would turn acrimonious, raising the question of slavery's legitimacy and the issue of considering slaves as property. The organized abolitionists had not intervened directly and the convention would not entertain even considering manumission of slaves, yet many of the abolitionists' concerns inflamed the convention anyway.

No less inflammatory were the proslavery positions that had fitfully emerged during the 1780s—positions rehearsed in a set of legislative instructions prepared in Virginia in 1786, in favor of calling what would eventually become the Federal Convention. The instructions ridiculed the Articles of Confederation—which, "whilst it presents a *Comedy* to the rest of the world, will prove in the end a *Tragedy* to ourselves"—and demanded a national convention composed of "the best and ablest men in the Union" to design a new national government. That new government would require substantial powers denied to the pathetic Confederation Congress: "Government, without coercion, is a proposition at once so absurd and self-contradictory, that the idea creates a confusion of the understanding—it is *form* without *substance*—at best a *body* without a *soul*."

The instructions then attached to these concerns the signatories' abiding fears about slavery. The signatories pleaded with the Virginia House of Delegates to reconsider repealing the state's manumission law, which they said encouraged a kind of secret emancipation. Above all, the instructions assailed legislative emancipation in any form as an attack on property rights and Revolutionary principles. "When instead of defending, a part of the community attempt to wrest from another part, perhaps their whole property,—it is such a violation of the fundamental laws of society, that, of itself, it presupposes a dissolution of its bonds,—and the injured are driven to the last resource of the oppressed—*the resisting of force by force.*"[76] So long as the law enshrined slaves as property, no legislature could abridge those laws without destroying the entire compact.

The southern delegates to the Federal Convention did not come to Philadelphia primarily to argue over slavery: their overriding purpose, like that of their northern counterparts, was to achieve a stronger and thus more perfect Union that would fortify commerce and provide for the common defense. But in pursuing that goal, the delegates were bound to debate what powers over slavery, if any, the convention would grant to the new national government. During the decade since the Continental Congress had approved the Articles of Confederation in 1777, northern abolitionists and their political allies had defeated inside their own states powerful arguments that the slaveholders' property claims were just and inviolable. Not surprisingly, in preparing for the Federal Convention, southern slaveholder delegates, especially from the Lower South, were touchy on the subject, lest the northerners take it into their heads to use the occasion to emancipate all the nation's slaves. To block any such efforts, then and in the future, the proslavery delegates would have to succeed at the national level where northern slaveholders had fallen short in their states, by affirming and protecting the legitimacy of property in man.

Among the most gifted of the slaveholder delegates was the aristocratic Charles Cotesworth Pinckney of South Carolina. Educated at Oxford and the Middle Temple, a battle-hardened officer in the Continental Army during the Revolution, Pinckney would establish himself as an urbane but insistent voice inside the convention. Conspicuously, he would argue in vain for limiting democratic influence under the new Constitution, advocating, for example, a Senate designed to exclude all but men of independent wealth. Pinckney also fought shrewdly and strenuously in favor of safeguarding slavery, and in this he was much more successful. He did not achieve all his aims, however. At one point during the proceedings, as James Madison noted, Pinckney "seemed to wish some provision should be included in favor of property in slaves."[77] That price, as Madison stated it, the Federal Convention would not pay. Indeed, the convention majority would take great pains to ensure that the Constitution excluded the legitimacy of property in man.

2

The Federal Convention and the Curse of Heaven

On July 12, 1787, seven weeks into the Federal Convention's deliberations, Charles Cotesworth Pinckney declared "that property in slaves should not be exposed to danger under a Gvt. instituted for the protection of property." The other delegates agreed with Pinckney about protecting property, but they differed over how much to protect slavery. James Madison had sensed a gathering conflict, and two days later he concluded that the chief struggle inside the convention was not between large states and small states "but between the N. & Southn. States" over "the institution of slavery & its consequences."[1]

It is easy to understand why historians have contended that Pinckney and his allies prevailed in that struggle, because in several respects they did. On the issue of representation, the slaveholders secured the three-fifths clause, which linked slaveholding to political power in the House of Representatives and the Electoral College and would affect the outcome of major political developments for decades to come. They also won a prohibition of national duties on exports, to the obvious advantage of their rural export economy. The delegates from the Lower

South extracted a ban on national abolition of the trade for twenty years—a period, we now know, when South Carolina and Georgia imported more slaves from Africa than during any previous twenty-year period. (The Lower South also evidently hoped that the twenty-year delay would help prevent later abolition of the trade.) In the closing days of the convention, the slaveholders won a so-called fugitive slave clause that backed their claims to runaways who had escaped to states where slavery either had been abolished or was in the process of being abolished. And because the new national government tolerated slavery in the states where it existed, the numerous provisions with potential implications for slavery—notably the clause that obliged the national government to suppress domestic violence—reinforced the slaveholders' regime.[2]

In hindsight, the slaveholders' victories can look utterly one-sided and forbidding, just as northern critics and southern supporters of the Constitution at the time claimed they were. Judging from what we now know about what happened in Philadelphia, though, the Constitution's proslavery features appear substantial but incomplete. Above all, the convention took care to prevent the Constitution from recognizing what had become slavery's main legal and political bulwark during the northern struggles over emancipation, the legitimacy of property in man. While they had no choice in the moment but to tolerate and even protect slavery where it existed, they would prepare for a nation in which there was no slavery, which would mean refusing to validate slavery's legitimacy in the Constitution. And during the decades to come, that exclusion proved the Achilles' heel of proslavery politics.[3]

Fights over slavery and property would lie at the heart of the prolonged national political struggle over slavery that, seventy years later, brought southern secession, the Civil War, and emancipation. The fights originated in 1787, less than three weeks after the convention assembled, during the delegates' protracted debates over representation.

On June 11, 1787, Charles Cotesworth Pinckney's fellow South Carolinian Pierce Butler told the convention that "every state ought to have its weight in the national council" proportional to its wealth.[4] Butler, like Pinckney, was a preeminent Carolina planter, but he had a very different personality. The third son of an Irish baronet, he had arrived in America in 1767 as a commissioned officer in the British army and served in the 22nd Regiment at the Boston Massacre, then sold his commission in 1773 and married into a prominent Carolina plantation family. After serving as an adjutant general in the patriot army during the Revolution, he recovered a fortune that had been destroyed in the war and went on to become one of the new nation's largest slaveholders and wealthiest men. Personally popular but with an authoritarian streak and a fondness for vituperation, Butler would in time own 500 slaves who worked more than 1,000 acres of cotton and rice in South Carolina. (An absentee master, he established a summer home in Philadelphia, where he would end up spending most of his days, living in sumptuous comfort.) Although he harbored private doubts about slavery, and especially about the inhumanity of the Atlantic slave trade, Butler, like Pinckney, would be an unflagging champion of his class at the Federal Convention.[5]

Butler's remarks aimed to advance the slaveholders' interest, but they reflected the general view inside the convention that, as James Madison remarked, "the primary objects of civil society are the security of property and public safety."[6] Because the framers, as the historian John Hope Franklin observed, were "dedicated to the proposition that 'government should rest on the dominion of property,'" it followed for most delegates that they would have to give slavery, the South's peculiarly valuable form of property, some sort of consideration under the Constitution.[7] Some delegates if not most came to Philadelphia clearly understanding as much; Rufus King of Massachusetts, for one, said that he "had always expected that as the Southern States are the richest, they would not league themselves with the Northrn unless some respect were paid to their superior wealth," which meant in considerable part their wealth in slaves.[8] How much respect, though, would the delegates pay to property in humans, as created and regulated by state laws? How much would slavery affect what Butler called each state's "weight in the national council"? And how much sanction, if any, would the convention give to slavery in national law?

Divisive and convoluted debates over representation in the new national Congress consumed the convention from the end of May until the middle of July. On June 11, the delegates had advanced as far as rejecting the principle that each state ought to have the same number of representatives in the lower house, in favor of "some equitable ratio of representation."[9] Roger Sherman of Connecticut—implying that he saw nothing equitable about property in man—backed a formula based on "the respective numbers of free inhabitants."[10] Pierce Butler, joined by his fellow South Carolinian John Rutledge, countered with a proposal based directly on the states' relative wealth, or what Rutledge called "quotas of contribution," which implied counting the full value of slaves toward representation.[11] James Wilson of Pennsylvania intervened with a compromise that would apportion representation on the basis of the number of each state's "white & other free Citizens," including women, children, and indentured servants, and "three fifths of all other persons," excluding "Indians not paying taxes."[12]

Wilson explained that he had taken the three-fifths ratio from an agreement reached four years earlier in the Confederation Congress over an amendment to the Articles of Confederation about assessing national taxation. (The amendment, its ratio a compromise proposed by James Madison, had passed the Congress but failed to gain the unanimous agreement from the states required to take effect.) Indeed, Wilson had copied that earlier proposal word for word. But referring to slaves as persons was not at all unique to these two examples; notably, an important if unsuccessful land ordinance bill for the territory north of the Ohio River, advanced in the Congress in 1785 by Rufus King (now a convention delegate), referred to slaves as persons "from whom labor or service is lawfully claimed," thereby lumping them with indentured servants and avoiding acknowledging them as property.[13] And even before the convention formally opened, northern and southern delegates had discussed applying the three-fifths ratio to determine representation.[14]

Behind the proposal lay the assumption that the size of a state's population was a rough but reliable indication of its wealth and was far easier to measure; but it would provide a middle way between counting only free inhabitants and counting all slaves in apportioning representation. In response, Elbridge Gerry of Massachusetts asked forcefully how slaves, "who were property in the South," could be counted as persons any "more than the cattle & horses of the North."[15] The delegates, seemingly untroubled by the contradiction, approved Wilson's motion by a margin of nine states to two.[16] The decision was not at all a sectional one: the great majority of delegates from the North as well as the South approved the three-fifths proposal without complaint. But the matter would not rest there.

Over the next four weeks, under the pressure of continuing debates about representation and the mechanisms for determining apportionment, the Lower South delegates grew uneasy. On July 2, Charles Pinckney suddenly noted that there was "a real distinction [between] the Northern & Southn. interests," specifying that North Carolina, South Carolina, and Georgia had a special reliance on rice and indigo production that northern merchants might sacrifice. Pinckney's older cousin Charles Cotesworth Pinckney then moved that a select committee of one delegate from each state consider anew the issue of representation of both houses of the legislature. Out of that committee's report came the crucial agreement, known to historians as the Connecticut Compromise, that would base representation in the lower house on population while giving states an equal vote in the upper house. As the convention debated the report, though, Charles Pinckney rose to declare that "blacks ought to stand on an equality with whites" in allocating representation to the lower house, even though he would "agree to the [three-fifths] ratio settled by Congs." Evidently, the Lower South had become dissatisfied with the three-fifths rule and, though willing to go along, would consider it a major concession.[17]

Proposals by another select committee appointed to allocate seats in the First Congress then caused considerable disputation, as the committee's computations had taken into account "the number of blacks & whites with some regard to supposed wealth."[18] The antislavery William Paterson of New Jersey, whose state consistently opposed any representation plan based on population, objected specifically to representation based on slavery, averring that he could consider slaves "in no light but as property" and now charging that by including slaves as persons in deciding representation the convention would encourage the overseas slave trade.[19] Another committee proposed a different allocation for the First Congress, which led to further sectional scuffling. Rufus King, while acceding to the three-fifths rule "for the security of the Southern" states, contended that "no principle" could warrant giving them a majority in Congress; Charles Cotesworth Pinckney replied that the South did not seek a majority but only "something like an equality," lest the northern states approve commercial legislation that would harm the planters.[20] Hugh Williamson of North Carolina backed up Pinckney, alleging that the northern majority proposed by the latest allocation committee would strive to perpetuate itself and leave the southern interest "extremely endangered."[21] Finally, the convention approved the committee's allocation—which would give the states north of Delaware a majority in the House of 35 seats to 30—by a vote of nine states to two, with South Carolina and Georgia in opposition.[22] At this point in the debate, it should be noted, the southern delegates were describing their sectional "interest" chiefly in terms of warding off unfavorable maritime regulation and commercial policy regarding the planters' staple crops; the southern interest in slaves and slavery entered in only indirectly, as a means to gain the representation required to protect the planters' commercial standing. Southern fears of emancipation lay just beneath the surface. That would change very quickly.

The setback over allocations to the First Congress infuriated the Lower South, and the next day, Pierce Butler and Charles Cotesworth Pinckney proposed scrapping the three-fifths rule entirely and counting enslaved blacks *"equally* with the Whites."[23] Butler and Pinckney's plan certainly would have enlarged southern representation, if only slightly, over what the three-fifths ratio provided. In South Carolina, for example, enslaved persons, according to the 1790 census, accounted for 43 percent of the total population. By that figure, under the three-fifths formula, the state's representation was entitled to be 43.4 percent greater than it would have been had slaves not been counted at all. Under Butler and Pinckney's formula, it would have been 72.4 percent greater—enough for the state to expect at least another seat or two in the House.

But Butler and Pinckney's proposal went nowhere, winning the support only of Georgia and Delaware alongside South Carolina. The wrangling continued. Rufus King expressed fresh misgivings about the three-fifths clause; Roger Sherman urged conciliation. James Wilson, who had originally proposed the ratio, now worried about the inconsistencies in considering slaves as persons for the purposes of assessing their value as property, but he relented, citing "the necessity of compromise."[24] Gouverneur Morris of Pennsylvania starkly announced that he would not do injustice to human nature and "could never agree to give such encouragement to the slave trade" such as that provided by the three-fifths clause, or indeed any representation based on slaves.[25] The convention then defeated the clause, six states to four, but not especially out of antislavery conviction: South Carolina, evidently holding out for better terms, voted with the majority, as did Delaware and Maryland.[26]

The next day, six southern delegates drew the line, arguing emphatically, in the Virginian Edmund Randolph's words, "that express security ought to be provided for including slaves in the ratio of Representation," lest the South reject the Constitution.[27] William R. Davie of North Carolina proclaimed that if the convention did not approve at the very least the three-fifths ratio, "the business [of the convention] was at an end."[28] Gouverneur Morris tried to call Davie's bluff and charged that the people of Pennsylvania "will never agree to a representation of Negroes," but no other northern delegate joined him.[29] Raising the stakes, or perhaps just making a feint, Charles Pinckney reintroduced his cousin's and Butler's motion from the day before that whites and blacks be counted equally, calling it "nothing more than justice," but this time only Georgia and South Carolina assented.[30] Finally, the convention reapproved the three-fifths clause by a vote of six states to two, with two states divided. Once again, the sections were united, as at least one state from New England, the Middle States, the Upper South, and the Lower South voted with the majority.[31]

Although the issue was essentially resolved, continuing disagreement over the clause flared the next day, leading to a disturbing turn. First, the convention, after considerable debate, passed a motion by Elbridge Gerry to base state obligations for direct national taxation on the three-fifths rule, until a proper national census was completed. Then, seeking to bring the convention's documents into conformity with each other, Edmund Randolph moved that all references to wealth be replaced with the wording of the three-fifths clause.[32] Gouverneur Morris objected: if slaves were indeed property, as the slaveholders assumed, then "the word wealth was right, and striking it out would produce the very inconsistency which it was meant to get rid of." Morris said he had been pondering the matter deeply, then he fiercely attacked the inflation of southern representation, charging that the South would not be satisfied unless it gained "a majority in the public Councils," after which it would align with new states to the west, oppress eastern commerce, and instigate a war with Spain to seize control of the Mississippi River. Rather than "attempting to blend incompatible things," he declared, "let us at once take a friendly leave of each other."[33] For once, an antislavery northerner spoke of disunion.

The aristocratic Morris had a gift for getting under his adversaries' skin, but this time his needling and denunciations did more than that. Pierce Butler, aroused, sliced to the heart of the matter at last, rebutting Morris with an unequivocal clarification: "The security the Southn. States want is that their negroes may not be taken from them which some gentlemen within or without doors, have a very good mind to do."[34] There it was: however great the southerners' apprehensions about the price of rice and indigo, they were truly alarmed by the possibility of a government that could emancipate their slaves. Some people outside the convention, obviously, wanted as much: every delegate knew about the abolitionists, not least the Pennsylvania Abolition Society which held its meetings nearby. But everyone also knew that notables inside that very room, men entrusted with the fate of the nation, also desired slavery's destruction, not least the president of the PAS, Benjamin Franklin. After hearing Gouverneur Morris's declamation, Butler decided that it was time to call out the troublemakers; reading his speech, it is easy to imagine him speaking the words "within or without doors" while shifting his gaze from Morris to Elbridge Gerry to the judiciously silent Franklin. James Wilson immediately followed with a speech supporting Randolph and praising representation based on population rather than wealth, and the convention then overwhelmingly approved Randolph's motion. With the three-fifths issue apparently settled, the convention stood adjourned.[35]

The adoption of the three-fifths ratio was certainly a boon to the slaveholding South, but how much of a concession it amounted to at the time is not so clear. Apart from some isolated protests, chiefly from Gouverneur Morris, the delegates never seriously questioned whether slaveholding would be reflected in states' representation. (As we shall see, the delegates would later crush a proposal to revisit the three-fifths clause and base representation on free persons.) Still, the most forceful delegates on both sides thought they were conceding a great deal; hence, neither side offered a quid pro quo.[36] The convention, in converging on the three-fifths formula, did not truckle to the proslavery delegates any more than it did to northerners who demanded no representation of slaves. When the South Carolinians proposed counting slaves fully toward representation, the convention rebuffed them, just as it rebuffed Gouverneur Morris. In the end, the proslavery delegates, with all of their bullying, obtained nothing beyond what they could have expected from the outset of the convention, an arbitrary but widely acknowledged figure borrowed from an unrelated proposal over taxation narrowly rejected by the Confederation Congress four years earlier.

Perhaps the greatest boost the South gained from the three-fifths rule was a prospective one. "It has been said that N.C. S.C. and Georgia only will in a little time have a majority of the people of America," Gouverneur Morris observed with alarm during the speech that so provoked Pierce Butler. As he concluded his retort, Butler corrected him—those states' populations, he said, were only expected to grow more rapidly than the rest of the country in coming years—but he allowed proudly that, indeed, "the people & strength of America are evidently bearing Southwardly & S. westwdly."[37] Butler was correct to be measured: as of 1790, the three states Morris mentioned contained only about 18 percent of the nation's population and would not have "a majority of the people" anytime soon. Still, it was commonly assumed, in and out of the convention, that the center of settlement was shifting west toward areas hospitable to slavery, which portended well for the slaveholders' power in the long run, especially with the help of the three-fifths clause. "In fifty years," the South Carolina physician and historian David Ramsay would soon have occasion to observe, "it is probable that the Southern states will have a great ascendancy over the Eastern."[38]

Not everyone agreed. The Georgia planter Lachlan McIntosh, for one, believed that the southern states "will continue from their extent and other circumstances [to be] the minority in Congress." (McIntosh also observed that "it is known to have been the intention of the Eastern and Northern states to abolish slavery altogether when in their power," which he hoped could be delayed until "the proper time for it.")[39] But if that were the case, and should the demographic trends turn out to favor the North, then the three-fifths rule could prove even more valuable, providing the South with what Charles Cotesworth Pinckney had called "something like an equality" in representation, or at least enough to prevent the South from becoming a permanent, isolated minority. Indeed, if the slaveholders managed to unite—by no means a sure thing, even on issues connected with slavery—and if they could then win over a sufficient fraction of northerners, the three-fifths rule might give them a durable majority. (Under the Constitution's allocations, the South voting as a bloc would only need to win over three northerners to win a majority in the House, and the addition of new states to the west could soon enough give the slaveholding states a small advantage in the Senate.) Certainly without the three-fifths representation, it would be virtually impossible for the slaveholding states, at least in the foreseeable future, to stop national legislation concerning slavery or anything else.[40]

Whatever its advantages to the South, though, real and prospective, the three-fifths clause did not come close to securing slavery in national law. To be sure, the clause acknowledged that that there were persons in the United States who were not free (although any provision to count only free inhabitants would have had to do so as well). But this was acknowledging the obvious, as slavery plainly existed under state laws; it did not at all imply that the Constitution approved of or legitimized slavery. Having decided to base representation on population and not assessed wealth, and by then duly borrowing the phrase "all other Persons" without alluding to property, the convention deflected any validation of property in man.

Most tellingly, the South Carolina and Georgia delegates scarcely believed that the three-fifths clause offered slavery adequate protection; the vision of a Congress half a century hence dominated by slaveholding states, although encouraging, hardly sealed the matter. Indeed, the protracted debate over representation had only raised to the boiling point the Lower South delegates' suspicions about northerners' antislavery intentions. On the last day of the three-fifths debate, even before Morris's aggravated exchange with Butler, Madison drew his conclusion that the deepest division inside the convention was between the slaveholding and non-slaveholding states. The previous day, Charles Cotesworth Pinckney had told the convention that he was "alarmed" at the northern delegates' statements "concerning the Negroes."[41] Worse was yet to come.

On July 20, the delegates gave their initial approval to what might have been the most decisive triumph on behalf of slavery of the entire convention, made possible by James Madison, and with no direct bearing on the legitimacy of property in man—the creation of the Electoral College. In considering how the new government's executive ought to be selected, the convention divided between those more and those less impressed by the competence of popular rule, with the latter pressing for less than democratic procedures. But southerners in both groups had an additional reason to oppose popular election of the president, as the existence of slavery would put them as a distinct disadvantage. As slaves "will have no suffrage," the North Carolinian Hugh Williamson observed, southerners were unlikely ever to win the presidency under a democratic system. Madison, who emphatically wanted "the people at large" to select the president, understood the problem: the southern states, he said, "could have no influence in the election on the score of the Negroes."[42]

Madison's solution—an Electoral College apportioned according to the combined representation in the House and Senate—would reverse the slaveholding states' severe deficit, providing them with an allocation that, although insufficient to carry an election on its own, would in time help assure that four of the first six presidents of the United States were Virginia slaveholders. The delegates approved the idea, six states voting in favor (including two of the three northern states present), three opposed, and one divided. It would take until the convention's final weeks before the delegates finally worked out an electoral system to their satisfaction, but the three-fifths rule held. No debate in the convention would illustrate more powerfully the contradictions of a slaveholding republic, further strengthening the slaveholding states in order to empower "the people at large"—a "people" which excluded and oppressed the slaves.[43]

Three days later, the convention, on the verge of a much-needed ten-day recess, appointed a five-man Committee of Detail to write a first draft of the Constitution. Like any such draft, it was bound to have enormous influence on the remainder of the convention's proceedings—and with that in view, Charles Cotesworth Pinckney put the committee and the convention on notice. The debates had now broached the future of slavery, and the three-fifths clause was not nearly enough to calm the South's and especially the Lower South's disquiet. And so, Pinckney solemnly warned, should the committee fail "to insert some security to the Southern States agst. an emancipation of slaves, and taxes on exports," he would be "bound by his duty to his State" to oppose its report.[44] Pinckney would have been encouraged by the selection of a fellow South Carolinian as the drafting committee's chairman, but he would also leave no confusion about the seriousness of the stakes over slavery.

John Rutledge, the committee chairman, was in 1787 among the most distinguished public figures in South Carolina and, for that matter, the new republic. The eldest son of a Scots-Irish immigrant physician's family, he had taken early to the law and studied, as Pinckney would later, at London's Middle Temple. He then built an exceptional career in politics and government, serving as a delegate to the Stamp Act Congress in 1765, as a delegate to the First and Second Continental Congresses, and as president and then governor of South Carolina. The extraordinary powers that he exercised in the last of these posts earned him the nickname "Dictator John." An effective speaker, if sometimes overly rapid in his delivery, he proved a formidable presence at the Federal Convention.[45]

Although he owned as many as sixty slaves before the Revolution and was a very wealthy man, Rutledge claimed that he disliked slavery. (His wife, Elizabeth, manumitted her own slaves, while his nieces Angelina and Sarah Grimké would become among the most famous American abolitionists in the 1830s.) But in Philadelphia, Rutledge defended his and his fellow Carolina slaveholders' interests as aggressively as Pinckney and Pierce Butler did. The other members of the drafting committee proved, on balance, amenable on issues connected to slavery. On August 6, after eleven days of furious labor, the committee reported to the convention a document that one historian has described as a "monument to Southern craft and gall."[46]

With the matter of representation now decided—or so it seemed—other issues before the delegates tested slavery's place in the new Constitution. The most difficult of them were related to the new government's expansive powers over commerce, and southern delegates had special concerns. Because their economy was based on the export of staple crops, southerners wanted to prevent the new government from either laying duties on exports or placing onerous tariffs on imported goods. Some slaveholders, meanwhile, worried that antislavery northerners would attempt to give the new national government the power to restrict or even abolish the importation of slaves from Africa. By restricting imports, they feared, northerners could indirectly advance their emancipationist schemes, cutting off needed new supplies of enslaved Africans while also minimizing the political bonus that slaveholding states would receive under the three-fifths clause.

The South united around an outright ban on export taxes and around a requirement that legislation on maritime commerce, including tariffs, gain two-thirds majorities in both houses of the new national legislature. On the sensitive matter of the Atlantic slave trade, though, the South was divided. Most of the Virginians wanted either to abolish the trade immediately or to empower the new national government to do so. Moved in part by humanitarian idealism and in part by a desire to stabilize the institution, the Virginians were also bolstered by the emerging fact that that their own state already had more slaves than it needed, and that they would stand to profit from selling off their redundant slaves in what would amount to a protected market. The Lower South delegates, however, demanded that the trade be exempted completely from national interference, which would require a special constitutional provision. As far as they were concerned, the slave trade was but an extension of the institution of slavery; if the national government had the authority to curtail, let alone abolish, the trade, slavery itself would be severely endangered. With Virginia opposed to the trade, though, the prospect of its restriction or even its abolition by the national government seemed strong. The Lower South slaveholders would need to convince three states north of Virginia to keep the authority over the trade in the hands of the states.

The Committee of Detail's report on these matters handed a lopsided victory to the Lower South. The report did not, to be sure, explicitly describe slaves as property; instead, the committee prudently opted for wording similar to that of the three-fifths clause already approved by the convention. The draft did include, however, one provision that barred the new government from imposing export duties and another that required a two-thirds majority in both houses of the legislature on matters concerning maritime commerce. Most glaringly, the report forever barred the government from either prohibiting the Atlantic trade or laying taxes or duties on imported slaves (described obliquely as "such Persons as the several States shall think proper to admit").[47] On the Atlantic slave trade as well as on slavery in the existing states, the new government would have no more power than the existing Confederation government, which was to say none at all.

As the Committee of Detail did not keep an official record of its proceedings, its work must be reconstructed from a handful of surviving notes and drafts, some of them incomplete and all of them in the hand of one of only three committee members: Rutledge, Edmund Randolph of Virginia, and James Wilson of Pennsylvania. These scrappy materials make it clear that Rutledge and Randolph, not surprisingly, were chiefly responsible for the report's provisions related to slavery. Both were ardently committed to the provision requiring a supermajority on navigation laws. Rutledge was the more insistent of the two about banning federal interference with the slave trade (about which Randolph would later change his mind). But Randolph, chosen instead of the far more formidable Virginian James Madison, would prove pliable enough for Rutledge's purposes on the committee.

Given James Wilson's antislavery views, the two New England committeemen were crucial to the southerners' plans on slavery. Oliver Ellsworth of Connecticut, a strong proponent of strictly circumscribing federal power, eventually proved a staunch ally of the Lower South over the Atlantic slave trade. The matter is only conjectural, but it seems plausible and even likely that he and Rutledge reached some sort of agreement concerning the committee report's slavery provisions— which may, in turn, have marked the beginning of what would soon become a fateful alliance between New England and the Lower South.

The second New Englander, Nathaniel Gorham of Massachusetts, the only nonlawyer on the committee, would later speak out against the supermajority requirement for navigation laws, but he would play an essential role in extending a ban on national abolition of the Atlantic slave trade. Based on those later alignments, one constitutional scholar has reasonably suggested that Rutledge, alongside his ally Randolph, had an opening to create a three-to-two and possibly a four-to-one majority on matters concerned with slavery, leaving James Wilson to hold his tongue, go along with the committee's report, and oppose specific measures as they came before the convention.[48]

Far murkier is the degree to which Rutledge may have fashioned the committee report's provisions on slavery as part of a deeper strategy to forestall objections inside the convention. The report certainly advanced, to the fullest extent possible, the protections to slavery desired by the Lower South at this point in the convention. But with Randolph agreeing to a ban on regulating the Atlantic slave trade, did Rutledge think he might embarrass the Virginia delegation, which was hostile to the trade? More craftily, did Rutledge truly support the supermajority provision as fervently as Randolph did, or was he envisaging it as a bargaining chip to get some of the northern delegates to go along with the Lower South on the Atlantic trade? It is tempting to read the sources in this way, projecting backwards from subsequent outcomes and ascribing intentions accordingly, as if everything turned out precisely as Rutledge had planned. But that logic is obviously flawed. It seems safer to say that Rutledge—goaded by Pinckney, in conjunction with Randolph, and with vital help from the New Englanders—simply pressed the Lower South's interests as hard as he could, on all fronts, with the hope of eventually winning as close to everything as possible.

What soon became perfectly clear was that neither Pinckney's bombast nor the report's staunchly proslavery stance had overawed opposition either from northerners or, on the Atlantic slave trade, from the Virginians. Indeed, some irate northern delegates now believed that all bets were off regarding issues connected to slavery—and at their earliest convenience, when the convention took up the report's section on representation, two of them exploded. Rufus King of Massachusetts denounced the three-fifths clause which he had earlier supported—"a most grating circumstance to [my] mind," he said—and explained that he had gone along only because he thought it might lead to a readiness on the part of the South to strengthen the national government. The committee's report had ruined those hopes, not least its provision allowing an unlimited importation of slaves, which would further increase the slave states' political power and increase the likelihood of foreign invasion and domestic insurrection. While he doubted he could agree to the committee's slave trade provision under any circumstances, King concluded that unless exports were made taxable, the three-fifths provision would have to be discarded.[49]

Protesting King's remarks, Roger Sherman of Connecticut—who despite his antislavery opinions was now emerging as a steadfast New England ally of the Lower South—allowed that the slave trade was "iniquitous" but insisted that the issue of representation could not be reopened, having already occasioned "much difficulty & deliberation."[50] Several delegates, including James Madison, then tried to change the subject, but Gouverneur Morris would not let them, and he rose to deliver what would prove to be the most powerful antislavery speech of the entire convention. Morris moved that, in light of the committee's draft constitution, the three-fifths rule be stricken and that only free persons be counted toward apportioning representation. "Never," he proclaimed, would he "concur in upholding domestic slavery," that "nefarious institution" based on "the most cruel bondages"—"the curse of heaven on the States where it prevailed." Giving extra representation based on the number of slaves rewarded "the inhabitant of Georgia and S.C. who goes to the coast of Africa, and in defiance of the most sacred laws of humanity tears away his fellow creatures from their dearest connections." The Committee of Detail, by proposing unrestricted importation of slaves, was apparently trying to foster and not merely shield slavery, actively encouraging the Atlantic slave trade "by an assurance of having [the slaveholders'] votes increased in the National government."[51]

The northern dissenters were certainly impressive. Rufus King, at age thirty-two—handsome, well educated, and rich in voice—was one of the youngest delegates at the convention, but he was well embarked on a political career, having served in the Massachusetts state assembly for three terms and, with distinction, in the Confederation Congress from 1784 to 1787. In 1785, he returned to a proposal advanced by Thomas Jefferson the previous year, and only barely defeated, that would have banned slavery in all of the western territories in 1800; King's version called for slavery's immediate exclusion in the territories north of the Ohio River, but it too failed. King's speech to the convention, though, was in no way explicitly antislavery, offering instead a detached defense of broad sectional interests.

Gouverneur Morris, who had already done so much to anger the Lower South delegates, also had an established antislavery record. A blunt and brilliant man with a fearsome wit and a well-deserved reputation as a rake, Morris came from a New York family of great landed wealth and power. (He also walked on a wooden pegleg, the result, he claimed, of a carriage accident seven years earlier which quite likely was in fact an escape from an amorous adventure.) As a delegate to the New York constitutional convention in 1777, he had proposed, unsuccessfully, an article favoring abolition, by which he made clear he meant gradual abolition. At the Federal Convention, Morris was known for his intense distrust of popular democracy and support for a strong national government; his speech on the slave trade, for all of its antislavery outrage, contained no practical suggestion that even hinted at emancipation. But both King and Morris made clear that the proslavery portions of the Committee of Detail's draft had outraged at least some of the northerners; and Morris now confronted the slaveholders directly with the kind of moral repugnance that was driving the northern emancipationists.[52]

That outrage, though, quickly proved unavailing. Formidable as King and Morris were, the convention defeated Morris's motion by a margin of ten states to one, loudly reaffirming the three-fifths ratio.[53] John Rutledge and Edmund Randolph had new reason to be confident that their draft constitution's slavery provisions would stand. Yet the southern gall in the draft remained offensive to many of the Middle States northerners—and, with respect to the Atlantic slave trade provision, to some important Virginia slaveholders as well. More outbursts would follow, leading to a debate that became snagged on the issue of property in man.

On August 21, the convention debated and approved, over the objections of the Middle States (and with the assent of Massachusetts and Connecticut), the Committee of Detail's prohibition of taxes on exports—a major victory for the South and major hurdle cleared by the report.[54] But then the convention began its formal deliberation over the committee's provisions on the Atlantic slave trade.

Before the Revolution, the colonial Virginia legislature had tried to place high duties on the importation of slaves, only to be rebuffed by the Crown. After independence, and under the Articles of Confederation, the individual states assumed control of the trade. By 1787, every state save Georgia had either imposed high duties on the trade or prohibited it outright; but at the Federal Convention, Lower South delegates declared their determination to bar the new national government from interfering with the trade in any way.[55] Although the importing of Africans had become increasingly odious to southerners as well as northerners, the physical devastation wrought by the Revolution in the Lower South, including the loss of thousands of slaves who ran to British lines, made it obvious to the South Carolinians, in particular, that ensuring their economic recovery required reserving the right one day to reopen the trade unilaterally. Their insistence fit with a general expectation at the end of the eighteenth century that, to flourish and expand, American slavery would require additional importation of enslaved persons from Africa. Along with the Georgians, the South Carolinians affirmed that any coerced restriction of the slave trade by the new national government would be an attack on slavery itself, which the Constitution was bound to leave solely the concern of the states.

The maverick Luther Martin, a bibulous but daunting Maryland trial attorney with abolitionist sympathies, opened the slave trade debate with a cutting attack on the Committee of Detail's draft. Born in New Brunswick, New Jersey, and educated at Princeton, Martin had been an early advocate of American independence, serving on the patriot committee of Somerset County, Maryland, in 1774. Elevated to the office of Maryland's attorney general three years later, he would serve in the post for twenty-eight consecutive years. At the Federal Convention, Martin was among the most stalwart defenders of the interests of the smaller states, speaking vigorously and at exhausting length against a plan for proportional representation in both houses of Congress. Although himself the owner of six slaves, he was also among the minority of delegates who opposed including slaves in determining representation. He would be named an honorary counselor of the Maryland Abolition Society at the group's founding in 1789.[56]

Martin's reasoning recalled the arguments that Rufus King and Gouverneur Morris had delivered two weeks earlier: if the slave trade was left unregulated (he would have preferred to see it abolished outright), the three-fifths rule would encourage it, which in turn would increase the likelihood of slave insurrections. But Martin's closing remarks were barbed, more like Morris's than King's, attacking the trade much as the northern abolitionists attacked slavery, as "inconsistent with the principles of the revolution and dishonorable to the American character."[57]

Martin touched a nerve. John Rutledge claimed he saw nothing in his committee's provisions that would encourage the slave trade, and he blandly added that, as he saw no danger of slave uprisings, he would readily release other states from any obligation to subdue them. But it was Martin's remarks about the shamefulness of the slave trade that truly provoked the South Carolinian. "Religion & humanity had nothing to do with the question," Rutledge asserted. "Interest alone is the governing principle with Nations." Ethics, honor, and the principles of the Revolution were all well and good, but the bottom line was always about property and making money. For the Lower South, the matter was crystal clear: either the convention would leave the slave trade untouched or the Lower South states "shall not be parties to the Union." The threat could not have been plainer. But Rutledge then took another tack, describing the slave trade as a national benefit, not merely a sectional one, and bidding the convention to understand why. "If the Northern States consult their interest," Rutledge concluded, "they will not oppose the increase of Slaves which will increase the commodities of which they will become the carriers."[58]

Some of the delegates from the New England maritime states rushed to back Rutledge, describing their own interests precisely as he had described them. Oliver Ellsworth of Connecticut—one of the three New England members of the Committee of Detail—spoke on their behalf, insisting that "what enriches a part enriches the whole," and that "the morality or wisdom of slavery" was not a matter of national concern but encompassed "considerations belonging to the States themselves."[59] Ellsworth also implicitly equated national interference with the slave trade with national interference with slavery itself, in line with the Lower South position, and thereby edged the slave trade debate toward becoming a debate over slavery. Charles Pinckney then warned the convention that South Carolina would "never receive the plan if it prohibits the slave trade," suggesting that permitting a tax on the trade was tantamount to abolishing it, and implying that a sizable number of delegates intended to do just that. On that ominous note, the convention adjourned.[60]

The next day's debates affirmed that an alliance had formed between the maritime New England states and the Lower South, just as the debates pressed even harder on the subject of slavery as well as the slave trade. Ellsworth's fellow Connecticut delegate Roger Sherman asserted that the right to import slaves involved no vital matter of "the public good" and should be left entirely to the state governments, to help ensure there would be "as few objections as possible to the proposed scheme of Government." Sherman also beckoned to northern emancipation, noting that "the abolition of slavery seemed to be going on in the U.S." and "that the good sense of the several States would probably by degrees compleat it." Everything the Lower South delegates had said and would say in the convention about slavery contradicted that speculation. Sherman, though, who could see strong ambivalence about slavery in the Upper South (as expressed by antislavery slaveholders like Luther Martin) seems to have believed it—and the Lower South delegates saw no reason for the moment to rebut him.[61]

An eloquent and highly respected slaveholder delegate then ripped into Sherman's argument and into slavery as well. George Mason of Virginia, at sixty-two, was one of the older men at the convention. As the author of both the first draft of his state's Declaration of Rights in 1776 and then its constitution, he was also among the leading political minds of the Revolution. The squire of Gunston Hall plantation, Mason owned some 300 slaves, second only in Fairfax County to George Washington, and at the Federal Convention, he would favor offering protection to slavery. Unlike Washington (or, for that matter, even Thomas Jefferson at Monticello), Mason would never arrange for the emancipation of any of his slaves, even at his death. Yet Mason declared a sincere loathing of slavery, which he had described in 1773 as "that slow Poison" which made of every gentleman "a petty Tyrant[,] Practiced in Acts of Despotism & Cruelty," and rendered him "callous to the Dictates of Humanity, & all the finer feelings of the Soul." He could not imagine a summary emancipation without grave social and economic unrest, but he could foresee commencing the institution's demise by halting the barbaric Atlantic slave trade.[62]

Mason denied that the "infernal traf[f]ic" in slaves involved "the importing states alone"; questions surrounding the trade's future, he insisted, concerned "the whole Union," as they concerned slavery's future as well. Rehearsing arguments that he had helped develop over the years, he blamed the origins of the slave trade on the British but noted that, if allowed to continue, the trade would entrench slavery further by spreading it to the West. Mason then switched from the evils of the slave trade to the evils of slavery: "Every master of slaves is born a petty tyrant. They bring the judgment of heaven on a Country. As nations can not be rewarded or punished in the next world they must be in this." Halting the Atlantic slave trade would be a blow against slavery's expansion and thus against slavery itself—a blow he believed the new government ought to have the power to inflict.[63]

Young Charles Pinckney would not abide what he regarded as high-handed slander, no matter how esteemed the source. "If slavery be wrong," he replied sharply to Mason, "it is justified by the example of the whole world." The ancient civilizations of Greece and Rome had been founded on slavery, and modern states including France, England, and Holland had sanctioned it: "In all ages, one half of mankind have been slaves." Giving the national government any authority over the trade, Pinckney charged, "will produce serious objections to the Constitution which he wished to see adopted."[64] Charles Cotesworth Pinckney then made it perfectly clear that the entire future of the Lower South's economy depended on the Atlantic slave trade: "S. Carolina & Georgia cannot do without slaves." All of the delegates' "personal influence," Pinckney claimed, "would be of no avail towards obtaining the assent of their Constituents" if the convention rejected the Committee of Detail's provision.[65]

With the issues of slavery and the slave trade now thoroughly entwined, the convention hit a perilous impasse. The Connecticut delegates Roger Sherman and Oliver Ellsworth continued to support the Committee of Detail's draft, in part to quiet southern warnings of disunion, and in part because, in Ellsworth's words, "slavery in time will not be a speck in our Country."[66] The South Carolina Pinckneys along with Hugh Williamson of North Carolina and Abraham Baldwin of Georgia warned that their states would not tolerate the slightest interference with their right to import slaves however they saw fit, although Charles Cotesworth Pinckney, in the first whisper of a possible compromise, now allowed that he thought it was "reasonable that slaves should be dutied like other imports."[67]

The Virginia majority, above all George Mason, stood adamantly against the slave trade; Charles Cotesworth Pinckney, laying aside any possibility of humanitarian motives, noted how much the Virginians stood to gain from the trade's abolition as "her slaves will rise in value."[68] Rufus King of Massachusetts, in response to the southern threats to reject the Constitution, declared that the North and the Middle States would likewise reject a singular exemption of slaves from import duties.[69]

John Dickinson of Delaware rebutted Charles Pinckney's historical defense of slavery and insisted that, as the importation of slaves concerned "the national happiness," so the national government should have sole authority over it. Dickinson also scoffed at the Lower South delegates' claims that their constituents would reject the Constitution if it gave the national government authority to abolish the Atlantic trade "as the power was not likely to be immediately exercised by the Genl. Government." (Here, as throughout the debates, the Lower South delegates' disunionist threats cut little ice—although Dickinson's remarks might later have offered means for a compromise.) John Langdon of New Hampshire declared that he "cd. not with a good conscience" leave authority over the trade with the states. It fell to Elbridge Gerry to remind the delegates of a key distinction, that the convention had "nothing to do with the conduct of the States as to Slaves, but ought to be careful not to give any sanction to it."[70]

Most interesting were Roger Sherman's pro-Lower South remarks on exempting the slave trade from national import duties. A distinguished lawyer, Sherman would be the only man to sign all four of the nation's founding state papers: the Declaration of Independence, the Articles of Association, the Articles of Confederation, and the Federal Constitution. An active and influential delegate at the convention—

though described by a Georgia delegate as extremely awkward in his speech, to the point of appearing "grotesque and laughable"—Sherman was deeply suspicious of popular government. He is best remembered for formulating, along with Oliver Ellsworth, the compromise that created the bicameral Congress, consisting of the House of Representatives (based on proportional representation) and the Senate (with each state represented equally). Although he detested slavery and was wary of giving the slaveholding states too much power—recall his bid earlier in the convention to exclude counting slaves toward representation—Sherman also believed that because slavery's days in America were numbered, and as the Lower South would never agree to a Constitution that failed to offer slavery special protection, dwelling on the issue would unnecessarily threaten the Union.[71]

In a speech addressing the proposed prohibition of import duties on slaves, Sherman raised the issue of property in man explicitly for the first time at the convention. Gerry had just warned the delegates against legitimizing slavery; now Sherman objected that permitting assessment of import duties on slaves would do precisely that, "making the matter worse because it implied that [the slaves] were *property*." It was not an objection the Lower South delegates would have made, least of all Charles Cotesworth Pinckney, who now was willing to concede placing duties on slaves. The Lower South would only have welcomed a constitutional provision that implied slaves were property, although to this point in the convention no one had hinted at such a thing. As Sherman's remarks indicated, for the majority of the convention and presumably for a considerable majority of the northern delegates, any such implication was insupportable. Yet now Sherman, a New Englander conciliatory to the Lower South, was arguing that the delegates would have to exempt the Atlantic slave trade from taxation lest the Constitution endorse slavery.[72]

It was a clever rhetorical turn, perhaps too clever: the Committee of Detail's report denying Congress the power to tax the trade in fact raised the same issue about which Sherman was objecting. In any event, no delegate appears to have picked up on Sherman's concerns. Yet if— at least for the moment—Sherman's complaint went ignored, it revealed the underlying importance in the convention debates of the issue of property in man. The issue had nothing to do with alleviating northern embarrassment by using circuitous verbiage: the words "slave" and "slavery" appeared nowhere, either in the Committee of Detail's report or in any of what would be suggested revisions. Yet the problem remained: was it was possible to permit taxation of the Atlantic slave trade without inherently acknowledging slaves as property?

The convention faced a stark political dilemma. Even Edmund Randolph, who had helped write the Committee of Detail's proslavery provisions, could see the need for a fresh compromise: were the convention to agree to the committee's slave trade clause "it would revolt the Quakers, the Methodists, and many others in the States having no slaves," he said. "On the other hand, two States might be lost to the Union."[73] To break the logjam, Charles Cotesworth Pinckney moved that a special committee consider whether "slaves might be made liable to an equal tax with other imports"—a change that Pinckney said "he thought right & wch. would remove one difficulty that had been started."[74] John Rutledge seconded Pinckney's motion but also expounded once more on the imperative of preserving "untouched" the individual states' authority to import slaves, lest North Carolina as well as South Carolina and Georgia reject the Constitution.[75]

Gouverneur Morris looked at the bigger picture and suggested that the committee reconsider "the whole subject," including the Committee of Detail's ban on export duties and requirement of a congressional supermajority to pass navigation acts. Morris was hoping, he said, to strike a comprehensive "bargain among the Northern & Southern states"; previously unyielding in debate, he now kindled a compromise.[76] Pierce Butler rose to say that he would never agree to any reconsideration of the ban on taxing exports—that is, like Rutledge on the slave trade, he would not soften on a demand he still thought nonnegotiable. Sherman backed him up, saying that as the export duty ban had already been approved by the convention, it could not be undone. But the convention swiftly approved a reconsideration of all three items in the clause: the provisions on the Atlantic slave trade, duties on that trade, and duties on exports. Only New Hampshire, Pennsylvania, and Delaware opposed the motion.[77]

Immediately, Charles Pinckney and John Langdon of New Hampshire moved that the convention also reconsider (as Morris had suggested) the navigation clause—a clear signal that the New England and Lower South delegations, or at least individual members of those delegations, had their eyes on a grand bargain. Oliver Ellsworth, lagging behind his colleagues, objected that removing the two-thirds requirement would cause the Lower South to bolt, but the convention, including all of the southern delegations, approved the expanded motion to commit.[78] The delegates duly appointed a Committee of Eleven, later known as the Committee of Slave Trade.[79] Very quickly, the committee worked out what one historian has described as the convention's "dirty compromise"—but in doing so offered up language that revived concerns about property in man.[80]

The Committee of Slave Trade consisted of one delegate from each state then in attendance at the convention, and a majority of its members were unfriendly to the Atlantic slave trade—a sharp contrast with the Committee of Detail. The chairman, William Livingston of

New Jersey, was a firm opponent of slavery as well as the trade who, as his state's governor in 1785, had supported passage of a state emancipation law along with legislation banning the buying and selling of slaves.[81] The rest of the committee included George Clymer, who had served as the first president of the reorganized Pennsylvania Abolition Society; Luther Martin, whose antislavery remarks had riled John Rutledge; Gouverneur Morris's sometime ally Rufus King; and two delegates who had previously voiced strong opposition to the slave trade, John Langdon of New Hampshire and John Dickinson of Delaware. The committee also included three of the most determined proslavery delegates from the Lower South—Charles Cotesworth Pinckney, Hugh Williamson, and Abraham Baldwin—along with one of the Lower South's reliable allies from Connecticut, William Samuel Johnson. Finally, representing Virginia, the committee included James Madison. Placing Madison with the first group would mean that there was a seven-to-four majority hostile to the Atlantic slave trade. To secure any kind of deal involving the trade, Pinckney and his allies would need support from at least two members on the other side.

Very little evidence survives about the committee's closed deliberations, but what there is offers a basic outline of how it struck its bargain. On the first of the four items under consideration, placing a duty on the Atlantic slave trade, Charles Cotesworth Pinckney had already allowed that he would accept a duty so long as it did not exceed the average for all import duties—a limit that would prevent the government from taxing slavery to death. The committee reported out precisely that provision, suggesting there was little debate about it.[82] On the second item, the pro-southern ban on export taxes, the committee appears to have done nothing, perhaps because, as Roger Sherman had suggested in the convention debate, the convention's prior approval of it took the matter off the table. This left two provisions for the com-

mittee to discuss, the proposed supermajority requirement for navigation acts and the ban on abolition of the Atlantic slave trade.

Regarding the slave trade, Charles Cotesworth Pinckney, although
referring to the convention in general, later recounted that the New
England delegates—which would mean King and Langdon as well as
Johnson—offered "to restrain the religious and political prejudices of
our people on this subject" if the Lower South would "shew some period" when the trade might be stopped. Luther Martin, like Pinckney
a member of the slave trade committee, went further to say that the
New Englanders on the committee, "notwithstanding their aversion
to slavery," were willing to indulge the South with "at least a temporary liberty" to continue the slave trade provided that the South
relented over the requirements for enacting navigation acts. In 1792,
shortly before his death, George Mason would affirm Martin's account,
telling Thomas Jefferson that the bargain involved the three New
England states acceding to South Carolina and Georgia on extending
the slave trade in exchange for revising "the clause which required ⅔
of the legislature in any vote." A quarter century after that, James
Madison related the same basic story in a private letter. And so critics
and scholars have described the agreement as a squalid deal in which
the New Englanders agreed to extend the slave trade in order to
secure commercial advantage.[83]

Certainly, from the evidence, two things seem plain—and with
some reasonable conjecture, these things point to an interesting possibility that may help clarify the "dirty compromise." First, it appears
beyond doubt that a majority of the slave trade committee, and quite
probably of the convention, supported replacing the Committee of
Detail's provision with one that gave the national government full
authority over the Atlantic slave trade. But that still left open how quickly
the government might act to abolish the trade. Congress, of course,

if so empowered, could do as it pleased, and given the approved allo-cation of representatives, this portended a rapid abolition. But here, in accord with the evidence, opens the unprovable but interesting possi-bility. As we have seen, amid the stalemate in the convention, one of the members of the slave trade committee who was hostile to the trade, John Dickinson, remarked that the power to close the trade "was not likely to be immediately exercised by the Genl. Government." Might Dickinson have returned to that point inside the committee, now sug-gesting a formal temporary stay in order to soften the blow and help coax the Lower South delegates into a deal? Or, no less in line with the accounts by Pinckney, Martin, and Mason, might one of the Lower South delegates—maybe Pinckney himself—have picked up on Dick-inson's remark and suggested a delay, as preferable to a looming rapid abolition of the trade? If so (following Martin and Mason's accounts), might the New Englanders have agreed to the proposal in exchange for dropping the provision on navigation laws?

It is at least plausible, if not probable, that something along these lines occurred. If so, the New Englanders would have regarded granting the Lower South states the power to import slaves for a limited number of years—that is, giving the region's slaveholders enough time to finish their economic recovery and prepare for the slave trade's abolition—as a fair-minded concession. Indeed, within the larger scheme of au-thorizing the trade's abolition—something the Lower South had loudly declared unthinkable—it would have looked like a fairly minor conces-sion. And in view of the second plain fact established by the evidence—that the New Englanders, in exchange for the temporary stay, got the Lower South to drop the navigation law provision—the concession to the slaveholders would have seemed all the more acceptable. Although the New Englanders Langdon and King, who clearly went along with the deal, would leave themselves open to charges of cupidity, they would have seen these terms as, on balance, a victory for their anti–slave trade principles as well as for New England's economic interests. Without question, as would soon become clear, the Lower South delegates, although receptive to the stay, were not at all happy with the year the committee settled on for ending it, 1800. Evidently, though, the committee majority would go no further.[84]

But no matter how the backroom bargaining proceeded, the Committee of Slave Trade delivered a report that diverged sharply from the Committee of Detail's proslavery draft constitution. Of the four discrete provisions under consideration, only one, the ban on export duties, survived intact. The slaveholders had to abandon completely the Committee of Detail's requirement of a two-thirds majority in Congress to pass navigation laws. And on the two remaining issues, the Lower South also had to abandon something its delegates had long insisted unequivocally they would never give up, and which the Committee of Detail had provided—a complete and permanent ban on national duties on slave imports and on national abolition of the Atlantic slave trade. Thanks to Charles Cotesworth Pinckney's preemptive maneuvers, the committee restricted the potential duties on the trade to a level acceptable to the Lower South, and with the deal struck inside the committee, Pinckney and his Lower South allies rescued a twelve-year extension of the trade itself. But on the matter of denying the national government any more power over the Atlantic slave trade than it did over slavery in the existing states, the Committee of Slave Trade majority would not budge.

A question arises about how seriously the Lower South delegates ever expected to keep authority over the slave trade completely out of the national government's hands. Beginning with John Rutledge's maneuvering on the Committee of Detail, the proposed ban may simply have been a negotiating ploy. With George Mason, James Madison, and the Virginians opposing them, the odds for success were all that much longer. Yet the Lower South delegates fought fiercely to carry the point, even to the bitter end; and they had good reason to believe that they could prevail. Well before the Committee of Detail convened, Charles Cotesworth Pinckney, Pierce Butler, and other Lower South delegates had made clear their intention to keep the national government perfectly powerless over slavery, which by their lights would require keeping it perfectly powerless over the Atlantic slave trade. Once the Committee of Detail's proslavery draft constitution became the starting point for debate, the Lower South grabbed an advantage. Only when Rufus King and Gouverneur Morris rose in angry complaint did the Lower South have a fight on its hands, and in that fight the Lower South delegates could count on their allies inside the New England delegations to back them to the hilt. In the first engagement on the floor of the convention, over possibly revising the three-fifths clause, King and Morris suffered an overwhelming defeat.

It took considerable wrangling and ferocious resistance thereafter from the Middle States and Virginia before hints appeared from Charles Cotesworth Pinckney and others that the Lower South delegates would back off from their disunionist bluster and consider some sort of compromise. Even then, when Rutledge seconded Pinckney's motion to reconsider the slave trade clause, he demanded that the "right to import slaves be untouched," lest the Lower South reject the Constitution.[85] Rutledge was willing to compromise over the slave trade, as long the national government remained powerless to abolish the trade, but the majority on the slave trade committee would not let that happen.

Once the committee met, Charles Cotesworth Pinckney, having already expressed to the convention his willingness to accept a duty on slave imports, was well positioned to limit the amount of those duties. But he and his Lower South colleagues also had to face the fact that, no matter what clamor might arise inside their delegations, the slave trade committee majority would not tolerate leaving alone "the right to import slaves." Pinckney and the others would not walk out; but neither could they surrender, lest they doom the Constitution's chances of winning over their own states. They could have hoped that an extra twelve years would give the Lower South time enough to import all of the slaves that it needed. Just as important, they could have hoped that gaining a delay might be enough to persuade their constituents that the final bargain was good enough to secure slavery's future. Still, as the debate over the committee's report would show, twelve years may have suited the committee majority but it was sizably less than the Lower South delegates (or Pinckney, at any rate) wanted.

Pinckney and his colleagues did, seemingly, get the committee to grant a further consideration: instead of providing for an automatic cessation of the trade in 1800, the report stated that Congress could enact no prohibition before that year. It might have looked like a clever move in light of the perceived drift of the nation's population to the Southwest; and it certainly could have been presented to skeptical slaveholders back home that way, as a point won in defense of slavery (which is exactly what happened at some of the southern ratification conventions). But to the extent that discussions over the slave trade had involved whether to give Congress the authority to abolish it—not whether to abolish it by constitutional fiat—the report was simply in line with those discussions. Moreover, given the strong opposition to the trade in Virginia—to which the convention had apportioned more House seats than South Carolina and Georgia combined—the prospect of increasing proslavery representation sufficiently to block abolition of the slave trade by 1800 would have been, at best, far-fetched.[86] The Lower South needed all the time it could get just to import all of the slaves it needed.

Charles Cotesworth Pinckney, though, did not give up easily. Once outside the less-than-friendly confines of the slave trade committee, he aimed to alter its proposals—and as soon as the report came up for debate on the convention floor, he moved an amendment that would extend the ban on congressional abolition of the slave trade to 1808. Nathaniel Gorham of Massachusetts (late of the Committee of Detail) seconded the motion. James Madison, like Pinckney a member of the slave trade committee, may then have objected that an additional eight-year extension would "produce all the mischief" the committee had tried to prevent and would be "more dishonorable to the National character" than no ban at all. (The remarks appear in Madison's notes on the debate, but there is some doubt about whether he actually delivered them; even if he did not, though, it would appear that the slave committee majority thought that, with a delay to 1800, it had driven a bargain that was hard enough.)[87] But with Gorham standing beside Pinckney, the alliance inside the larger convention between New England and the Lower South held firm. Predictably, Massachusetts, New Hampshire, and Connecticut, all three of the New England states present, backed Pinckney's amendment, insuring its approval.

Whether or not James Madison actually envisaged as much, Pinckney's bait-and-switch, if that is was it was, would in time pay off richly for the Lower South slaveholders. And the convention was now on the brink of considering a provision that, wittingly or not, just might have validated property in man.

The convention divided the debate over the newly revised slave trade clause in two, devoting the first part to the subclause barring national abolition of the trade until 1808, and the second to the subclause assessing a tax or duty on the trade. Gouverneur Morris, trying to embarrass the convention into acknowledging precisely what it was doing, moved to specify that the entire measure was concerned only with regard to importing slaves to North Carolina, South Carolina, and Georgia, and nowhere else. George Mason, for all of his scorn of slavery as well as the slave trade, said he had no problem with including the term "slave," but did not want to offend the people of the Lower South by singling out their states. Roger Sherman, who three days earlier had risen to exclude property in man—the thing itself, and not merely the words—objected to "the terms proposed, which had been declined by the old Congs. and were not pleasing to some people"; and the anti-slavery George Clymer agreed. Here was the one moment during the convention debates when northern delegates expressed a desire to suppress unpleasant words in order to avoid popular displeasure—and the moment quickly passed. Morris, his point made—delegates were uneasy with either taking or assigning responsibility for extending the slave trade—withdrew his motion. With the New England–Lower South alliance holding steady, the convention approved the first half of the Atlantic slave trade clause, prohibiting any congressional abolition until 1808, by a vote of seven states to four.[88]

Suddenly, though, in the debate over the second part of the clause, the property question resurfaced, and once again because of Roger Sherman. In wording its proposed revision, the slave trade committee had not fully accounted for Sherman's earlier protest that assessing duties on the trade would recognize slaves as property. The first part of its proposal, which the convention had just approved, used the word "persons" to describe the slaves, but the second part did not. Sherman duly objected to that second part "as acknowledging men to be property, by taxing them as such under the character of slaves."[89]

John Langdon and Rufus King, who had been the key New Englanders on the committee, immediately rose to say that they considered the second part of the clause to have been the price for obtaining the first part.[90] A literal reading of their remarks, as recorded in

Madison's notes on the convention debates, is a bit perplexing and even unsettling. Were they saying that the imposition of duties on the slave trade was the price paid by the Lower South in order to secure a temporary ban on congressional abolition of the slave trade? This is the most likely construction and would support the view that the committee majority favored authorizing an immediate end to the trade until Langdon and King cut a deal with the proslavery side. But why would the imposition of duties, a concession Charles Cotesworth Pinckney had basically agreed to beforehand, have become the basis for the compromise? What about the removal of the supermajority requirement on navigation laws, which Luther Martin, George Mason, and James Madison made plain was the true price for gaining a temporary guarantee on the slave trade? Indeed, if the deal simply involved exchanging the government's power to tax the trade for a temporary ban on national abolition of the trade—with the navigation law requirement settled separately in the North's favor—then the compromise was not that "dirty" after all. And Madison's notes raise additional questions. How had the committee arrived at its wording on taxing the trade, which Sherman found objectionable? Was the phrasing simply careless, the most likely reason, or did the Lower South delegates sneak by the others a subclause that quietly recognized slaves as property? The evidence does not say.[91]

Whatever actually happened inside the committee, Pinckney quickly "admitted" that what Langdon and King said was true—a deal had been cut—but this still left Sherman's objection hanging.[92] Three days earlier, Sherman had raised his point about recognizing property in slaves in order to back the Lower South slaveholders' efforts to prevent imposing duties on the slave trade. By making the identical point now, though, he threatened to undo a compromise that the prominent Lower South members of the slave trade committee had helped to craft. However much he was willing to back the slaveholders, Sherman's concerns about excluding property in man were genuine.

The Lower South's Massachusetts ally Gorham pushed back, urging Sherman to consider the duty not as an implication that slaves were property but as a measure to discourage the slave trade. Sherman would have none of it: "The smallness of the duty," he said, "shewed revenue to be the object, not the discouragement of the importation."[93] Regardless of other considerations, he persisted. His complaint had nothing to do with the disagreeable word "slave," as had his objection to Morris's sly motion a little earlier in the debate; rather, as when he first raised the property issue, it was a substantive matter—inserting, not substituting, the word "person" so that there could be no improper inference that the Constitution authorized property in man.

James Madison intervened. It would be wrong, he said, "to admit in the Constitution the idea that there could be property in men. The reason of duties did not hold, as slaves are not like merchandise, consumed. &c."[94] For the slave trade compromise to stand, it could not carry with it any implied recognition of slaves as property. Whether accidental or the product of quiet design, the committee's wording— wording that, as a member of the committee, Madison had approved— could not survive. The convention then revised the subclause on taxing slave imports to include the word "person."[95] It was a clumsy solution, but it at least stated explicitly that in this portion of the Constitution, as in the rest, slaves were persons, not property. The delegates approved the revised slave trade clause without opposition, and, with very minor revisions, it would appear intact in the Constitution.

Madison's remark about excluding from the Constitution "the idea that there could be property in men" would resound in antislavery writings of the 1840s and 1850s as what today we would call an authoritative sound bite. Taken out of context, the quotation makes Madison appear as if he were more fervently opposed to slavery than he actually was. The son of a wealthy tobacco planter, Madison had inherited one of the largest plantations in the Virginia piedmont, Montpelier, and he owned hundreds of slaves over his lifetime. He would never advance or support any practical plan for slavery's abolition or limitation; indeed, four years after the Federal Convention, he would decline to support a gradual emancipation proposal in Virginia lest he give "a public wound . . . to an interest" in which his constituents "had so great a value."[96] Yet he fully recognized that slavery violated fundamental principles of republican government; his writings and speeches contain numerous moral and political condemnations of slavery; he had been willing, as a state legislator, at least to express in private sympathy for emancipationist petitioners in Virginia in 1785; and, like other enlightened Virginians, he opposed continuing the Atlantic slave trade.[97]

At the Federal Convention and during the ensuing debates over the ratification of the Constitution, Madison was mostly circumspect about the slave trade and slavery. Unlike his fellow Virginia planter George Mason, he delivered no diatribes against the "nefarious traffic" in humans; what little he said on these matters aimed to keep the sectional divisions that he noted from wrecking the convention's work. It was in that vein that he weighed in to conclude the slave trade debate.

In stating that the Constitution could not admit "property in men," Madison was not delivering a grand philosophical reflection about slavery's injustice. He was acknowledging a much smaller point: that Roger Sherman's objection about the slave trade clause was reasonable and that the convention needed to address it lest the compromise over the slave trade—a compromise that Madison himself had helped to create—come unstuck. There was nothing exceptionally idealistic, let alone daring, in Madison's little speech. Yet it did sustain a principle that most of the delegates honored: that property in man had no place in national law. It affirmed that the convention was intent not on deviously avoiding the word "slavery," but on excluding from the Constitution the very idea that there could be property in man. And in doing so, it brought to a close the most dramatic contest over slavery of the entire Federal Convention.

In an intense debate over commerce, export duties, and the slave trade, strung out over four days, the slaveholders, and especially the ardently proslavery delegates from the Lower South, had secured what historians have judged a stunning triumph, consisting of a ban on national taxation of exports and a twenty-year prohibition on a national abolition of the Atlantic slave trade. Yet important as it is to see what the slaveholders won in the slave trade compromise, it is also important to see what they did not.

It is vital, first, to remember that slaveholders were actually divided about the central issue in the compromise, granting the national government authority over the Atlantic slave trade. The Virginians, in particular, pushed for the trade's abolition every bit as hard as the Lower South delegates did for its perpetuation. (George Mason was deeply embittered by the "precipitate, and intemperate, not to say indecent Manner" in which the convention agreed to permit the trade to continue for twenty years—a major reason, as we shall see, why Mason finally repudiated the Constitution.)[98] Slaveholders as a class did not all fare the same on the Atlantic trade issue: when considering this aspect of the compromise, it is more illuminating to perceive it as a bargain between the Lower South delegates and the rest of the country than between slaveholding and non-slaveholding states.

Accordingly, in some important ways, the Committee of Slave Trade's bargain was actually a setback for the South Carolinians and Georgians compared to what the Committee of Detail had proposed, especially on authorizing the national government to abolish the

Atlantic slave trade. To be sure, things might have turned out much worse for the Lower South delegates. By heading off an authorization for immediate abolition of the trade and then extending the ban on such abolition until 1808, Charles Cotesworth Pickney and his allies turned their disappointment into what looked to many, including the dejected George Mason, like a smashing victory. With that success, Pinckney and the others could bring back to their constituents additional assurance that their property in slaves, and the institution of slavery itself, would be perfectly secure under the new Constitution. They would also buy South Carolina and Georgia ample time to import tens of thousands more enslaved Africans, at unprecedented levels. Yet they could not keep the convention from according the national government something they had declared intolerable—a clear if limited and highly compromised measure of what Mason had called "the power to prevent the increase in slavery."[99]

Far less dramatically—indeed, almost as a side issue—the slave trade debates had also affirmed the convention's refusal to validate property in man. As the arguments inside the convention mingled contentions over the slave trade with contentions over slavery, so the delegates touched on how much legitimacy the Constitution ought to extend to slavery. Elbridge Gerry came to voice what appears to have been the majority view, that the new government had to be scrupulous about leaving slavery entirely in the hands of the states where it existed but it equally had to be vigilant "not to give any sanction to it." In that spirit—though with contradictory goals—Roger Sherman had objected to implying that slaves were property. And in that spirit, James Madison agreed that there was no room in the Constitution even for the idea that there could be property in human beings.

The exclusion of property in man, though, would be tested again. At stake in the subsequent arguments would be the status of slaves who moved from one state to another, either accompanying their masters or as fugitives. Northern emancipation had created new concerns about these matters. In addressing them, the delegates returned to the conundrum of how to tolerate slavery without admitting it into national law.

Three days after the convention approved the Atlantic slave trade clause, the undaunted Charles Cotesworth Pinckney objected to the wording of what we know today as the Constitution's privileges and immunities clause. We don't have Pinckney's direct statement as to his concerns, but his intentions were clear.

The fifth article of the Articles of Confederation stated that the free inhabitants of individual states, except for paupers, vagabonds, and fugitives from justice, "shall be entitled to all privileges and immunities of free citizens in the several States." The provision underscored that the Confederation, although loose-knit, was nevertheless a nation, that no state would discriminate against the citizens of another state, and that, by implication, citizens could travel freely from state to state. The article went on to deal with existing commercial relations whereby states imposed import and export duties on each other: under the Articles of Confederation, these impositions on interstate commerce would stand, provided they did "not extend so far as to prevent the removal of property imported into any State, to any other State, of which the owner is an inhabitant." The provision also stipulated that "any person guilty of, or charged with, treason, felony, or other high misdemeanor in any State" who fled to another state would, upon demand of the governor or executive power of the state from which he fled, be returned to that state.[100]

The Committee of Detail's draft of the new constitution included the provisions on privileges and immunities and on the return of fugitives more or less as they appeared in the Articles of Confederation, although as two separate articles. But the convention was determined to end the existing impositions on interstate commerce—doing so was one of the chief reasons the convention had been called in the first place—and so the committee simply removed that clause completely. It thereby, despite the committee's pro-southern leanings, overlooked a southern fear that the drafters of the Articles could not have anticipated.

As George Mason noted privately, by removing the impositions on commerce, the committee's draft specifically excluded what Mason now construed as a necessary protection of the slaveholders' property rights in light of northern emancipation. (While he advocated abolishing the Atlantic slave trade, Mason was no less insistent that the property rights of existing slaveholders be respected.) If the phrase in the Articles that protected "the removal of property imported into any State" were carried over into the Constitution, Mason said, masters would be able to bring their slaves into states that had abolished or were in the process of abolishing slavery without concern that the slaves would claim their freedom. Absent that stipulation, Mason believed, the slaveholders might lose the freedom to travel anywhere in the nation with their slaves.[101]

Mason's fears were exaggerated, at least for the moment, but Charles Cotesworth Pinckney was just as worried as Mason was. When the Committee of Detail's pared-down version of the privileges and immunities clause came up for debate, Pinckney expressed his dissatisfaction and, according to Madison's notes, "seemed to wish some provision should be included in favor of property in slaves." Madison's rendering of Pinckney's remarks strongly suggest that Pinckney was now seeking, in defiance of the convention's previous presumptions, an explicit recognition of property in slaves in the Constitution. It is also possible that Pinckney proposed simply that the Constitution compel all states to honor state laws creating and protecting property in slaves, but that other delegates, including Madison, reasonably understood him to be speaking more broadly. No matter: by a vote of nine states to one (with only South Carolina in support and with Georgia divided), the delegates ignored Pinckney's complaint and approved what would become the opening clause of Article IV, Section 2 of the Constitution, with no implied consideration for the slaveholders and no provision in favor of property in slaves.[102]

The convention next debated the other provision that the Committee of Detail had taken from Article Five of the Articles of Confederation, regarding the return of fugitives from justice. The slaveholders had concerns about this clause as well, as, in the wake of northern emancipation, they now wanted it to cover fugitive slaves along with fugitive criminals. On this matter, however, they could draw on a very recent precedent.

On July 13—one day after the Federal Convention approved the three-fifths clause—the Confederation Congress, meeting in New York, approved, with little discussion or opposition, the Northwest Ordinance, organizing the nation's territory north of the Ohio River. At the very last minute, Congress included a provision banning slavery in the territory, a measure deriving from the grander proposal advanced by Thomas Jefferson that would have banned slavery in all of the western territories by 1800, and which Congress had only narrowly defeated three years earlier. As slavery already existed in parts of the territory, an explicit provision prohibiting it was necessary.[103]

The mysterious connections between the passage of the ordinance and the Federal Convention's deliberations have long been subject to debate, as has the ordinance's actual impact on the spread of slavery. Without question, though, by passing the ordinance, the Congress, working under the Articles of Confederation, exercised authority to legislate decisively on slavery's future in territories outside the existing states. Alongside the gradual emancipation acts passed by the northern states, the ordinance was the most ambitious legislative measure yet enacted in America to limit slavery. Nevertheless, it provoked no opposition from the representatives of the slave South. Evidently, the exercise of congressional power over slavery in the territories per se raised no alarms among the slaveholders at the time; neither they nor, for that matter, antislavery advocates could have foreseen the momentous conflicts to come over that power. If the ordinance was at all troubling, the slaveholders found no basis in the Articles of Confederation on which to challenge it. Presumably they also had reason to believe that if they acquiesced over the Northwest Territory, the territories south of the Ohio would be opened to slavery.

The ordinance, however, also raised the issue of what should be done with slaves who escaped into the territory. None of the three state gradual emancipation acts passed before 1787 extended freedom to fugitive slaves or their children, but the issue had become a sore point, notably in Massachusetts (where slavery had been abolished in the courts). In 1783, a ruling by Justice William Cushing freed eight South Carolina fugitive slaves being detained in a Boston jail. Cushing, along with growing numbers of other northerners, was committed to upholding property rights but reluctant to honor the legitimacy of property in human beings.[104] Two years later, when Rufus King moved his land ordinance proposal banning slavery north of the Ohio River, he included a provision stating that persons "from whom labor or service is lawfully claimed" who escaped from any of the thirteen states to the territory could be "lawfully reclaimed" and returned to their masters.[105] Congress now picked up King's proposal virtually word for word, declaring that any fugitive "from whom labor or service is lawfully claimed" in one of the original states "may be lawfully reclaimed and conveyed to the person claiming his or her labor or service."[106] The slave states' property laws would be respected without compelling the free territories to acknowledge the legitimacy of property in man.

The southern delegates in Philadelphia, like the rest of the convention, were well aware of the proceedings in New York—indeed, several of them, including Pierce Butler and Charles Pinckney, were members of Congress as well as of the Federal Convention—and they came to expect nothing less than the same guarantee in the new national constitution. Moments after the convention dispensed with Charles Cotesworth Pinckney's motion "in favor of property in slaves," Butler and the younger Pinckney entered the debate over the clause on fugitives from justice with a motion "to require fugitive slaves and servants to be delivered up like criminals." James Wilson of Pennsylvania complained that linking the return of fugitive slaves to that of fugitive criminals would oblige the executives of free states to deliver up slaves "at the public expence"—obligations and outlays that, by inference, the public (or at least the citizens of Pennsylvania) would refuse to shoulder. Roger Sherman, echoing earlier remarks over the three-fifths clause, observed there was no more propriety in "surrendering a slave or servant, than a horse." The loose wording of Pinckney and Butler's proposal, meanwhile, as reported in Madison's notes, would explicitly validate slavery under the Constitution. Having just rejected Charles Cotesworth Pinckney's motion on slavery and the privileges and immunities clause, the convention was not about to acknowledge property in man in connection with fugitive slaves. Butler withdrew the motion "in order that some particular provision might be made," separate from the provision on fugitives from justice.[107]

The next day, Butler arrived with elaborate alternative wording: "If any person bound to service or labor in any of the U——States shall escape into another State, he or she shall not be discharged from such service or labor, in consequence of any regulations subsisting in the State to which they escape, but shall be delivered up to the person justly claiming their service or labor."[108] Butler and Pinckney were clearly reacting to the effects of northern emancipation. The core of their amendment was to affirm that the northern states that had undertaken or completed emancipation would not be free soil for fugitive slaves. Otherwise, Butler apparently borrowed from the text of the Northwest Ordinance, rephrasing its line about "any person . . . from whom labor or service is lawfully claimed" as "any person bound to service or labor." Like the ordinance, the clause lumped slaves with fugitive indentured servants as persons whose service or labor was owed to another person—thereby avoiding describing fugitive slaves as property.

There were, however, two major differences between the proposed clause and the Northwest Ordinance. First, and obviously, the clause, unlike the ordinance, would in some degree impinge on the authority of existing states, namely, those northern states that would now be required to permit the reclamation of fugitive slaves. That requirement would cause little stir, if any, in much of the North—indeed, Pennsylvania's gradual emancipation law specifically outlawed harboring or enticing escaped slaves—but there might still be concern in Justice Cushing's Massachusetts and possibly elsewhere in New England. Second, reflecting the clause's origin as a supplement to the clause on criminal rendition, Butler's proposal stated that the persons apprehended would be "delivered up," not simply captured and conveyed to their masters, as specified in the ordinance. The difference was subtle, but it clearly suggested that the Constitution's provision involved something more than, or at least different from, restating the long-standing common-law right to recaption.[109]

Yet if it had a more definitive and even coercive ring, the proposed clause, like the ordinance, remained silent on who would enforce its provisions and how. There was no hint that the clause would require the new Congress to enact a law of enforcement; indeed, because the clause would appear, like the clause on criminal rendition, in a portion of the Constitution dealing with issues of state comity, the matter of national authority was presumably irrelevant. Otherwise, Butler's proposal retreated into the passive voice and established a requirement for the return of fugitive slaves without stating who at the state or local level, let alone the national level, was obliged to make the return—a relatively ineffectual addition to a document enumerating government powers.

Had the retrieval of fugitive slaves been directly tied to the retrieval of fugitives from justice, which appears to have been Butler and Pinckney's original intention, the executive of each state would have been responsible for the return of all escaped slaves, upon the demand of the executive of the state from which the slave had fled. But James Wilson's objection led Butler and Pinckney to separate the two, leaving the convention to contemplate a clause in which the Constitution required the return of fugitive slaves but did not assign any duties whatsoever to any public authority.[110] This price, evidently, was one the antislavery northerners were willing to pay. Without debate, the convention assented unanimously, and Butler's proposal, in slightly (but, as we shall see, significantly) modified form, became the third paragraph in Article IV, Section 2 of the Constitution.[111]

Alone of the provisions now regarded as slavery's key constitutional protections, the fugitive slave clause offered slaveholders at least a degree of direct safety for their property in slaves beyond what they had enjoyed under the Articles of Confederation. That provision, meanwhile, eventually received unanimous support, signaling sectional unanimity on the issue of returning fugitive slaves. But there were complications and important distinctions in the clause as well. The brief debate that occurred when Butler and Pinckney presented their original motion showed that at least one northerner, James Wilson, was unwilling to bind his state's executive to capture and return fugitive slaves at the public expense. At least one delegate, Roger Sherman, objected to the clause altogether. That unwillingness and that objection would reappear in the northern states in later decades. Above all, though, by approving wording about persons "bound to service or labor," the convention affirmed, yet again, that it would not permit the Constitution to recognize property in man. The distinction, of course, would have meant nothing to a fugitive slave, for whom the provision simply obstructed an avenue to freedom. But with regard to slavery's place in national law, the difference was profound—a difference later generations of slaveholders would try to erase.[112]

There is an additional point to be made about how the fugitive slave clause barred northern states from summarily declaring themselves free soil. American slaveholders were well aware of the so-called *Somerset* principle, as enunciated by Lord Mansfield in 1772, whereby any slave who set foot on British soil was automatically freed. Indeed, American slaveholders instantly connected their apprehensions about *Somerset* to their concerns about northern emancipation.[113] The fugitive slave clause thus apparently denied *Somerset*, fixing a fugitive slave's condition in the laws of the state from which he or she had escaped rather than those of the state where she or he was discovered.

In fact, the clause was a bit more ambiguous. *Somerset* voided masters' claims to property but not to labor or service. It was thus arguable—as later antislavery lawyers would endeavor to argue—that the clause, written as it was, conferred no rights to property and thus conformed to *Somerset*. In any case, considerations in America, where slave states bordered free states, were different than in the slaveless British Isles. There was already precedent in American antislavery legislation, from Pennsylvania's gradual emancipation law to the Northwest Ordinance, that offered recaption without declaring slaves property. And as a practical matter, outside of northern New England, there was little chance in 1787 that the northern states would declare themselves sanctuaries for escaped slaves.

Most important, the clause's treatment of fugitive slaves "functionally as property" was scarcely the same thing as enshrining property in man in the Constitution.[114] Even if free states were now obliged, if only vaguely, to ensure fugitive slaves' remittance, and even if that obligation impinged, if only vaguely, on state authority, it still left the condition of slavery entirely a creature of state laws, its wording careful to avoid any recognition of slaves as property. To be sure, in decades to come, slavery's defenders as well as ambivalent northern jurists would claim that such recognition of state property law was tantamount to validating slavery itself. These claims would acquire considerable political as well as legal force, to the point where they formed the linchpin of proslavery opposition to federal efforts to limit slavery's expansion. But the claims were at odds with what the framers actually did and what the fugitive slave clause actually said. Indeed, some of the delegates in 1787 would go to exacting lengths to ensure that the clause contained no validation of property in man.

It was now the end of August and the delegates, after an exhausting summer, were pressing to complete their work, but the Lower South delegates would not relent, and the antislavery delegates remained attentive. On September 10, as the convention debated the amendment power, the South Carolinian Rutledge stopped the proceedings cold, saying that he would brook no provision that permitted "the States not interested in [slavery], and prejudiced against it," to amend the approved provisions on slavery.[115] The convention was on the verge of approving provisions that would have made the amendment process very difficult, but Rutledge, on the defensive, was taking no chances. Too often, in the course of the convention, South Carolina and Georgia had found themselves isolated; there was no guarantee that the New England states would sustain their alliance of convenience with the Lower South. Even if North Carolina were included, the Lower South on its own would count for thirteen votes in the House and six in the Senate, nowhere near the one-third minimum the convention would eventually establish for blocking constitutional amendments. Rutledge may also have been looking ahead, and seeking extra leverage in the ratification struggle to come. The convention gave way with a proviso specifically protecting the export duty and slave trade clauses from amendment until 1808, sealing the slave trade committee agreement. At no point, though, did the proviso recognize slaves as property.

The end of the matter would not come for another five days. On September 12, the Committee of Style and Arrangement, charged with refining the document's wording, reported it had revised Butler's fugitive slave provision to read: "No person legally held to service or labour in one state, escaping into another," should be discharged from service but instead "shall be delivered up on claim of the party to whom such service or labour may be due."[116] This version introduced three subtle and important changes regarding the status of slaves and slavery, one of which would disturb some of the delegates.[117]

The five-member style committee included not a single delegate from south of Virginia and was weighted against slavery. The member who ended up having the most influence over its revisions was Gouverneur Morris; in addition to Rufus King, the committee included Alexander Hamilton of New York, who had been absent from most of the convention's proceedings and said nothing at all about slavery, but who had joined the New-York Manumission Society soon after its founding two years earlier. (The two other members were James Madison and William Samuel Johnson.) Those antislavery proclivities would be reflected in the committee's revisions of Pierce Butler's wording about the claimants of fugitives, as approved by the convention.

Read one way, there was no substantive difference between the two renderings. Why the committee changed Butler's wording about persons "bound to service or labor"—the same wording used in the three-fifths clause in connection with indentured servants—to persons "held to service or labour" remains obscure, as it introduced no obvious change in meaning, except perhaps to clarify that the clause referred to slaves as well as bound servants. Butler's version, meanwhile, meant that fugitives would be returned only to those who could substantiate a claim on their labor; the committee's version said the same thing while it eliminated the slack wording whereby a slaveholder would have to prove the justice as well as the legality of the claim. But words carried compound meanings. To describe a person's claim as just could also imply that the state laws establishing such a claim were just. To say that the person may or may not be due the fugitive's service or labor avoided that implication while it conveyed uncertainty about the justice of the state law or laws in question. The committee's revision, that is, removed the possible implication that there was justice in slavery.

Alert about two phrases, though, the style committee introduced a problem in another. Butler's version of the clause opened by referring to the fugitive as a "person bound to service or labor in any of the U——States"; the committee altered that to refer to a "person legally held to service or labour in one state."[118] The precise reason for the change is unknown. Perhaps the committee was attempting to have this portion of the clause conform more closely to the Northwest Ordinance, which referred to any person "from whom labor or service is lawfully claimed in any one of the original States." But whatever the reason, the change raised a warning flag.

Three days later, certain unnamed delegates objected to the phrase "legally held to service." According to Madison's notes, these delegates "thought the term <legal> equivocal, and favoring the idea that slavery was legal in a moral view." The convention then approved new wording, stating that "No Person held to Service or Labour in one State, under the Laws thereof" could be discharged and had to be returned—which is how the clause appeared in the Constitution.[119] Gone now from the fugitive slave provision were both of the legitimating adverbs describing persons "justly" or "legally" held. The wording inserted at the very last minute by the vigilant delegates sealed what the clause meant and did not mean. This made the change much more than, as one account calls it, "a minor victory for those who were squeamish about slavery" and something that had "no practical effect."[120] Rather, as another historian remarked, by adding the words "under the Laws thereof," the convention "made it impossible to infer from the passage that the Constitution itself legally sanctioned slavery."[121] Or so it would have seemed at the time.

The contests over slavery at the Federal Convention, concluding with the Committee of Style's revisions, had been bitterly fought, which indicated a momentous historical shift. Prior to the Revolution, American antislavery sentiment resided almost entirely outside of politics, chiefly—at least among whites—in the Society of Friends. Since the late seventeenth century, slavery had become standard in all thirteen colonies, as it remained in all of the rebel states in 1776. Then remarkably, beginning in 1780, northern emancipation commenced. Four years later, the Confederation Congress very nearly prohibited slavery in all the western territories as of 1800. By the time the Federal Convention assembled in Philadelphia, the broad principle that governments could abolish slavery, practically unheard of before 1770, was rapidly gaining ground, reaching as far south as Virginia.

The proslavery delegates in Philadelphia, alarmed by the antislavery upsurge, came away from the convention with provisions that enlarged the slaveholders' power in national politics, above all the three-fifths clause, and protected their peculiar property in state laws, above all the fugitive slave clause. With that power, presumably, slaveholders would thwart any national lawmaking regarding slavery that lacked their approval—or so they could have hoped. Yet although it recouped a twenty-year ban on congressional abolition of the Atlantic slave trade, the Lower South failed to prohibit the national government from exercising any authority whatsoever over the slave trade and by extension over slavery. Less dramatically but even more importantly, the convention, in taking every step possible to make certain that the Constitution excluded property in man, rendered slavery a wholly local institution, the creature entirely of state laws. The results were not always elegant, least of all in the revision of the Atlantic slave trade clause, but they were consistent and would in time prove crucial.

The convention's great paradox on slavery—framing a Constitution that strengthened and protected slavery without sanctioning it in national law—left it to later generations to interpret the Constitution in conflicting ways. In the moment, though, the great test of the convention's compromises was whether they could withstand the debates in the states over the ratification of the Constitution in 1787 and 1788. As it happened, slavery and the slave trade would prove relatively minor issues in the ratification struggle, raising the greatest concern not in any offended northern state but in Virginia, where Anti-Federalists railed against the convention's failure to do more to protect slavery. Yet if slavery was marginal to ratification, the debates still raised critical issues about slavery's place in the new nation's government and laws. The perceptions formed in these early fights—of the Constitution as basically friendly or hostile to slavery—wound up leading some antislavery and some proslavery advocates alike to support the new government plan. Less happily, those perceptions would color the turbulent politics of slavery and antislavery for decades to come.

3

Slavery, Antislavery, and the Struggle for Ratification

Misinformation traveled quickly at the end of the eighteenth century. Rumors about the framers' work had been flying for months before the Federal Convention finally concluded in September. In early July, a gentleman in Philadelphia informed a friend in Charleston that he had heard "from undoubted authority" about a proposal inside the convention that "no slave whatever be imported into any of the states for the term of twenty-five years."[1] (This wild report would be reprinted at least seventeen times in newspapers from South Carolina to New Hampshire before the convention adjourned.) Similar reports appeared and reappeared during the ensuing year-long battle over ratification, crowding weightier and more carefully crafted remarks, including, most famously, James Madison's and Alexander Hamilton's contributions to the series of New York newspaper articles known collectively as *The Federalist*.

Because the delegates conducted their business behind closed doors and under a vow of secrecy, the public's understanding of what they had done would henceforth be based largely on the *Federalist* essays, some less elevated observations by a few other delegates, and a great deal of supposition and hearsay, as well as the text of the Constitution itself. Not until the posthumous publication in 1840 of Madison's private notes on the convention debates would the world have anything approximating a reliable record of the nation's founding. This appears to have been precisely how the framers wanted it, to have the public judge their handiwork not on the basis of their deliberations but on the document itself—concealing the convention's conflicts and compromises so that they might present a united front in support of the new plan.[2] And so, as Americans struggled over ratification late in 1787 and 1788, a swirl of explications arose over what the Constitution actually said about numerous issues, including slavery.

Except in some rare instances, slavery and the slave trade were not leading issues in the state ratification debates. Other matters more pertinent to the original call for a new Constitution, above all the division of powers with the states, dominated these battles; so much so, one historian has persuasively argued, that the slavery issue was mainly an instrument used by supporters and critics of the Constitution alike to help them press their deeper concerns.[3] To the extent that the slavery provisions entered in, there were no clear-cut alignments: forceful southern slaveholders appeared on both sides of the ratification fight just as forceful antislavery northerners did. Always, though, the Constitution's supporters, quickly known as Federalists, suppressed their personal disappointments and geared their remarks about slavery to suit their audiences, in battles that followed a regional pattern very different from the one that arose inside the Federal Convention. Whereas leading New England delegates had been conciliatory toward the Lower South at the convention, during ratification a vocal minority of New Englanders renounced what they considered the Constitution's complicity with human bondage. Opposition to the Constitution's slavery provisions was milder in the rest of the North, in contrast with the Middle States delegates' stern antislavery objections at the convention. Among southern slaveholders, strong admonitions about the Constitution's potential threats to slavery came not from South Carolinians and Georgians but from Virginians.

The outcome left critics from New England and supporters from the Lower South in agreement that the Constitution provided ample security to slavery—the former expressing embittered disgust, the latter confident assent. In the Middle States, some outspoken antislavery advocates assailed the Constitution, but others, including prominent abolitionists, sincerely and emphatically endorsed it, sometimes suggesting that the Federal Convention had paved the way for gradual emancipation throughout the nation. In Virginia, harsh criticism of the Constitution's less than absolute protection of slavery led Federalists (and Madison in particular) to resort to misleading ambiguity and elliptical reasoning, at one point conveying a false impression that the framers actually had admitted property in man.

These clashing views were significant, even if slavery played only a relatively minor role in deciding the results. Because the Federal Convention tolerated slavery but did not sanction it, because the delegates conducted their business secretly, and because communications over long distances were unreliable, the Constitution's supporters could create contradictory impressions, winning over antislavery advocates in some places and self-protective slaveholders in others. After 1789, the new government faced the task of settling the Constitution's stance on slavery, which led to further strife, compromise, and ambiguity but no resolution. Decades later, reclaimed and reformulated, the gist of the conflicting impressions created during ratification would reappear, marking a widened sectional divide while also distinguishing different approaches to advancing the antislavery cause. At the core of all of these differences would lie increasingly heated arguments over the Constitution's stipulations about federal authority and property in man.[4]

Barely a month after the Federal Convention finished its work, the Quaker convert and outspoken antislavery advocate Moses Brown of Rhode Island wrote in distress to his fellow Quaker James Pemberton, vice president of the Pennsylvania Abolition Society. Brown was worried that too many Quakers were rallying in support of the new Constitution "without bearing Testimony against those parts which give Countenance to if not directly Incourage Slavery."[5] Over the coming weeks, Brown corresponded with several New England antislavery Quakers who shared his concerns about the Constitution's proslavery implications. "Whatever high encomiums are given to it (the Constitution)," William Rotch Sr., a prosperous Nantucket Quaker merchant charged, "it is evident to me that it is founded on *Slavery* and that is on *Blood*."[6]

Quakers were the most outspoken critics in New England of the Constitution's provisions on slavery, but their sense of moral outrage and personal responsibility pervaded the region's complaints. "How does it appear in the sight of Heaven, and of all good men," the hyper-Calvinist New Divinity minister Samuel Hopkins wrote to an associate in January 1788, "that *these States*, who have been fighting for liberty . . . cannot agree in any political constitution, unless it indulge and authorize them to inslave their fellow men?"[7] "When a man is called to establish a frame of government, it ought to be such an one as his conscience will justify, or he must give his voice against it," the antislavery Massachusetts writer "Phileleutheros" asserted.[8]

Like their fellow emancipationists across the North, antislavery New Englanders denounced the supposed legitimacy of human chattel as an evil absurdity.[9] New Englanders, however, more than others, regarded the slightest connection to slavery as intolerable, and overlooked entirely the Constitution's exclusion of property in man. "I must confess it will be very wonderful to me, if the Massachusettensians (above all people in the world) should hold up their hands to give efficacy to a constitution which admits of slavery," the writer "Adelos" observed.[10] "If we cannot connect with the southern states without giving countenance to blood and carnage, and all kinds of fraud and injustice," "Phileleutheros" declared, "I say let them go."[11] For these writers, drawing a distinction between permitting slavery in state law and enshrining it in national law was so much flummery. For them, there could be no moral difference between tolerating slavery as the framers did and endorsing it outright. Their righteousness brooked no mitigation of the slaveholders' unspeakable offenses to God. It also framed the attendant legal and political issues around their own moral purity.

Echoing Puritan as well as Quaker precepts, many antislavery New England critics based their dissent on the heavy burden of collective sin, in accordance with what one Massachusetts writer called the "doctrine of imputed guilt in civil society."[12] Addressing the New Hampshire ratification convention, the ex-Loyalist antislavery Anti-Federalist Joshua Atherton reduced the antislavery argument to a simple proposition: "If we ratify the constitution," then "we become *consenters to* and *partakers in* the sin and guilt."[13] The slave trade, in particular, had "become a national sin, and a sin of the first magnitude," Samuel Hopkins proclaimed, and collusion in that sin, if not universal, was already widespread: "All the individuals in private stations, who have any way aided in this business, consented to it, or have not opposed it to the utmost of their ability, have a share in this guilt." Everyone understood the awful implication: acquiescing in a Constitution that tolerated slavery and the slave trade would bring down God's wrath—for slavery, as Hopkins warned, was a sin "which righteous Heaven has never suffered to pass unpunished in this world."[14]

New England critics raised more specific complaints as well, although on some issues more than others. The three-fifths and fugitive slave clauses would elicit forceful objections from New Englanders in decades to come, but they turned up less frequently than might be expected during the ratification debates. The three-fifths clause, the Massachusetts Anti-Federalist Silas Lee complained to a friend, would increase the representation of the southern states "to undue proportion."[15] So long as there was little chance that the national government would assess direct taxes, the speaker of the Massachusetts House of Representatives James Warren observed, New England would "receive no kind of benefit" from the three-fifths ratio but instead be at "the mercy of the states having slaves."[16] The fugitive slave clause, Moses Brown wrote, appeared to have been "designd to Distroy the Present Assylum of the Massachusets from being as a City of Refuge for the poor Blacks."[17]

New Englanders were also among the first to charge that the framers had sneakily covered up their concessions to slavery with confounding euphemisms. Just weeks after the Federal Convention ended, an aging part-time doctor and mill owner in Connecticut, Benjamin Gale, spoke his mind at the town meeting that had elected him to his state's ratification convention. The Constitution, Gale declared, was "as *dark, intricate, artful, crafty, and unintelligible [a] composition that I ever read or see composed by man.*" The three-fifths clause—designed, he said, to help create an oppressive national aristocracy—offended with its reference to "persons": "Why could they not have spoke out in plain terms— *Negroes?*" The slave trade clause was just as bad, resorting, he said, to a "sly cunning and artful mode of expression" in order to spare those "who may have some tender feelings and a just sense of the rights of human nature."[18]

The most impassioned New England disavowals came over the Atlantic slave trade provision. On no other issue concerning slavery had New Englanders at the Federal Convention done more to appease the Lower South; and no issue did more to arouse their antislavery constituents' opposition. It was bad enough that what "Adelos" called "that most cursed of all trades" would be permitted to proceed for an additional twenty years, enslaving men, a New Hampshire writer lamented, "contrary to all the principles of reason, justice, benevolence and humanity, and all the kind and compassionate dictates of the Christian Religion."[19] Worse, a trio of western Massachusetts Anti-Federalists explained, "it is wholly optional with the Congress, whether they abolish it or not," and there were "good reasons" to conclude "that the *nefarious practice*' will be continued" after 1808.[20] At the Federal Convention, Rufus King, before agreeing to the slave trade compromise, had opposed a wholly unrestricted slave trade on the grounds that, thanks to the three-fifths rule, it would give the slaveholders a grossly disproportionate share of political power. Now he had to defend the Constitution against adversaries who claimed, with similar reasoning, that a twenty-year extension would ensure the Atlantic slave trade's indefinite survival.[21]

New England Federalists, for their part, dismissed the opposition's maledictions about imputed guilt. "The idea that by civil connections, we become partakers of each others sins, I believe is of late date," the Massachusetts Federalist "Philanthrop" contended.[22] The distinguished revolutionary general William Heath, addressing the Massachusetts convention, seized upon the federal nature of the Constitution and its insistent rendering of slavery as a local institution, not a national one. "Each State is sovereign and independent to a certain degree, and they have a right, and will regulate their own internal affairs," he remarked; hence, "we are not in this case the partakers of other men's sins, for in nothing do we voluntarily encourage the slavery of our fellow men."[23]

The Federalists also benefited from a division within antislavery opinion over the Atlantic slave trade clause, less pronounced than elsewhere in the North but evident nevertheless. For some antislavery advocates, the clause was a strong reason for supporting the Constitution, not rejecting it. "If, for no other consideration than that it opens a door for the abolition of the Slave Trade, in America, in a given number of years," one vehemently antislavery writer affirmed, "the new proposed Constitution of the United States is incomparably preferable to the old one . . . and must therefore meet the wishes and derive the support of every friend to humanity, and the common rights of mankind."[24] The eminent Baptist leader Rev. Isaac Backus, an antislavery stalwart, made the same point in a pro-ratification speech to the Massachusetts convention, rejoicing that "a door is now opened" to end the importation of Africans—the latest sign, he said, that "slavery grows more and more odious through the world."[25] In Providence, a group of free blacks gathered on the Fourth of July to celebrate "the Prospect of a Stop being put to the Trade to Africa in our Fellow-Creatures, by the Adoption of the Federal Constitution."[26]

A few New Englanders saw additional antislavery implications in the new Constitution. General Heath acknowledged that he doubted emancipation would come to the southern states anytime soon, but he noted correctly that the Atlantic slave trade clause pertained "to the States now *existing only*," implying that any new slave states could be barred from the trade. In the Northwest Ordinance, Heath added, the Confederation Congress had pronounced "that the new States shall be republican, and that there shall be no slavery in them."[27] Nothing in the new Constitution would bar the national government from doing the same regarding other new states in future; indeed, as Article IV,

Section 4 guaranteed to every state "a Republican form of government," it could be read as encouraging slavery's future exclusion.

Thomas Dawes Jr., an esteemed Boston lawyer, went further, telling the Massachusetts convention that with the slave trade clause, the framers had all but secured slavery's eventual downfall. As the South held fast to its prejudices, he said, and "it would not do to abolish slavery, by an act of Congress, in a moment, and so destroy what our Southern brethren consider as property." But by authorizing Congress to abolish the Atlantic slave trade in twenty years and impose a ten-dollar duty on every imported African, while also leaving it up to each state whether to permit slaves to enter its territory, the Federal Convention had, he believed, sealed slavery's doom. "We may say," Dawes concluded, "that although slavery is not smitten by an apoplexy, yet it has received a mortal wound and will die of a consumption."[28]

Dawes was more confident than most New England antislavery supporters of the Constitution, but he was not alone in what would prove to be his premature optimism. In New Haven, the rising Federalist lawyer Simeon Baldwin delivered a July 4 oration that, while lamenting the toleration of slavery, congratulated the southern states for consenting to the "liberal clause in our new constitution" on the slave trade, "evidently calculated to abolish slavery upon which they calculate their riches."[29] And so the desultory debate unfolded in New England, both sides castigating the slave trade, with one side sharply criticizing the Constitution for permitting it to continue, the other celebrating the Constitution for taking a historic step toward banning it, and some New Englanders such as Baldwin denouncing and celebrating all at once. Only in fractious Rhode Island (which had not sent delegates to the Federal Convention) did the antislavery opposition, led by Moses Brown, have much impact on the result, as one of several factors that delayed the state's decision to ratify until 1790. Connecticut approved the Constitution with little visible opposition. The Federalist victories in Massachusetts and New Hampshire required much more effort, and in both states, Federalists highlighted the Constitution's antislavery features. New Hampshire's Anti-Federalist leader Joshua Atherton delivered a scalding speech at the convention calling a union with slavery morally reprehensible, but the well-organized Federalist forces pushed it aside. Slavery and the slave trade were even less important in the Massachusetts debates compared with clashes over the process of electing members to Congress, among many others matters.

Once their states agreed to ratify, New England's antislavery critics did their best to adjust to their disappointment. Samuel Hopkins, whose fear of anarchy finally led him to support ratification despite his chagrin over slavery, remarked that nothing remained but to rely on the Supreme Ruler to one day "vindicate the oppressed, and break the arm of the oppressor in his own way and time."[30] But there also remained a conviction that whatever its merits, the Constitution had intolerably created a new nation partly in order to make that nation safe for slavery. Some critics flatly believed (as the Federalist Jeremy Belknap observed of his Quaker neighbors) "that the Constitution was *intended* to establish Slavery for twenty years at least."[31] Others held fast to William Rotch's opinion that framers founded the new nation, pure and simple, on slavery and blood. Such certitude allowed little room for finding antislavery meanings inside the Constitution, whether about property in man or anything else.

Divisions over slavery developed very differently in the Middle States, where, from the start, influential antislavery spokesmen supported the Constitution. Few prominent Americans, for example, were more closely identified with the fledgling antislavery movement than Benjamin Rush, the renowned Philadelphia physician and signer of the Declaration of Independence. A leading force within the Pennsylvania Abolition Society, Rush could barely contain his enthusiasm for the Constitution, in part because of (and not despite) its provisions on slavery. Less than two weeks after the Federal Convention concluded, he emphatically told a friend that the new Constitution stipulated an end of the African trade to America in 1808. (He later remarked, more accurately but still hopefully, that "the new government will probably" abolish the trade.) Possibly confusing Virginia with the entire South, Rush imagined that the slave trade provision showed that "a spirit of humanity has at last reached the southern states upon the subject of the *slavery* of the Negroes," which in turn foretold slavery's complete demise. Everywhere in America, he exulted, "sentiments favorable to African liberty" had taken hold. Most propitiously, he noted—and here his zeal brought him closer to the mark—the Constitution included "no mention . . . of *negroes* or *slaves*," because "it was thought the very words would contaminate the glorious fabric of American liberty and government." That is, by excluding the word "slavery," the framers had refused to validate the thing itself.[32]

Rush's excitement was in character—in 1774, he had predicted to the British abolitionist Granville Sharp that "there will be not a Negro slave in North America in 40 years"—but his support for the Constitution was hardly eccentric among antislavery advocates in the Middle States.[33] To be sure, some antislavery commentators totally rejected Rush's line of reasoning, including his assertion that the Constitution's reticence on slavery signified a triumph of antislavery principle. Many more in the region, though, expressed optimistic views of the Constitution and slavery—views generally less passionate than Rush's, but still insistent that the proposed Constitution favored freedom.

As in New England, concern in the Middle States over the Constitution's slavery provisions was strongest among Rush's fellow Quakers, who otherwise generally supported ratification. Moses Brown's Philadelphia friend, the vigorous antislavery campaigner James Pemberton, had hoped for better from the Federal Convention, especially in closing the Atlantic slave trade, but Pemberton quickly apprehended that "the influence of the Southern Govrnmts has diverted [the convention] from that very important Object."[34] The New York City Quaker merchant Edmund Prior lamented to Moses Brown "the Great oversight of the Convention in respect to securing universal Liberty & Impartial Justice."[35] Some of the region's toughest antislavery critics, though, were non-Quakers. "Strange indeed!" Benjamin Workman, an Irish émigré and mathematics tutor at the University of Pennsylvania, exclaimed in a passage aimed directly at the Quakers, "that the professed enemies of *negro* and every other species of *slavery,* should themselves join in the adoption of a constitution whose very basis is *despotism* and *slavery.*"[36]

The specific antislavery complaints in the Middle States were much the same as in New England. The New York Anti-Federalist spokesman Melancton Smith focused on the three-fifths clause, which he said would give the southern states "an unreasonable weight in the government."[37] More frequently, as in New England, critics railed against the Atlantic trade clause for permitting (as the Philadelphia writer "A Caution" put it) "this abominable traffic" to be continued "for TWENTY years by the people of America!"[38] The fugitive slave clause caused even less consternation than in New England, where escaped slaves might reasonably claim their freedom—although Edmund Prior did note privately that if the Constitution was adopted, "the State of Massachusetts will no Longer be an Assylum to the Negroes."[39] Benjamin Workman along with the New York Anti-Federalist (and former member of the Sons of Liberty) Hugh Hughes protested the Constitution's clause guaranteeing the suppression of domestic violence, which would include slave insurrections.[40]

Some of this criticism was technically plausible but overwrought. According to "Timothy Meanwell," the Atlantic slave trade provision would "in a great measure contravene" Pennsylvania's gradual emancipation law by permitting the state to reopen its connection to the trade until at least 1808; thereafter, he claimed, American slavery would be established permanently.[41] "Algernon Sidney" of Philadelphia likewise feared that the provision would lead to a perpetual opening of the slave trade not simply by the southern states but "by all the states of the union."[42] William Findley, the formidable Anti-Federalist from western Pennsylvania, believed that the Constitution rang the death knell for gradual emancipation and that "SLAVERY will probably resume its empire in Pennsylvania."[43] Another writer fancied that the Constitution's commerce clause empowered Congress to authorize the importation of slaves "even into those states where this iniquitous trade is, or may be prohibited by their laws or constitution."[44]

Middle States critics picked up and amplified Anti-Federalist suspicions about the wording of the three-fifths and Atlantic slave trade provisions. Samuel Bryan, an abolitionist who was also one of the leading Pennsylvania Anti-Federalists, claimed he detected purposeful evasion in the slave trade clause: "The words dark and ambiguous; such as no plain man of common sense would have used, are evidently chosen to conceal from Europe, that in this enlightened country, the practice of slavery has its advocates among men in the highest stations."[45] A few days later, in New York, Melancton Smith beheld the three-fifths clause in mock wonder: "What a strange and unnecessary accumulation of words are here used to conceal from the public eye, what might have been expressed [concisely]."[46] Also in New York, the young DeWitt

Clinton charged that "good religious people" would be "all against the new government" if they understood what the clauses actually meant.[47] In Pennsylvania, William Findley asked why the fugitive slave clause was so abstruse. "Candor certainly required a manner of expression suitable to the people's uptakings."[48]

Despite these outbursts and attributions, though, the tone of antislavery dissent in the Middle States overall was less vociferous and moralizing than in New England, even among the Quakers. "Charity leads me to conclude that [the convention delegates] have done the best they could under the circumstances attending their deliberations," James Pemberton told Moses Brown. Not that these critics conflated charity with acquiescence. "It can not be expected that a Government on such an unjust foundation can be durable; animosity, dissentions, and commotions will be most likely to attend it," Pemberton wrote to his brother John. And when these commotions came, he insisted to Moses Brown, it would be "requisite for the Advocates for the enslaved Africans" to continue objecting to the Constitution's "very exceptionable parts."[49] Nevertheless, the Middle States protests lacked the New Englanders' condemning emphasis on collective sin.

Just as strikingly, the Middle States produced a distinctive strain of what might be called antislavery Federalism, attuned to the passion for the Constitution expressed by Benjamin Rush. Although some antislavery New Englanders read antislavery implications in the Constitution, in the Middle States, especially in Pennsylvania, the Federalists gained vigorous and vital support from prominent abolitionists, including some of Rush's fellow members of the Pennsylvania Abolition Society. One antislavery critic of the Constitution described his "mortification" at seeing men who he thought "would never attempt to encourage or connive at slavery" actually sign the Constitution, most grievously Benjamin Franklin.[50] It became all the more galling when other antislavery men, including Franklin's friend Tench Coxe, secretary of the PAS, fought for the Constitution (albeit, in Coxe's case, pseudonymously) on antislavery grounds.

Writing as "An American Citizen," Coxe commenced the Federalist attack by highlighting the Atlantic slave trade clause. "The importation of slaves from any foreign country," he began, "is, by a clear implication, held up to the world as . . . inconsistent with the dispositions and the duties of the people of America." That inconsistency laid the foundation "for exploding the principles of negro slavery, in which many good men of all parties in Pennsylvania, and throughout the union, have already concurred." As "the *temporary* reservation of any particular matter must ever be deemed an admission that it should be done away with," so liberty, justice, religion and *"sound policy"* dictated the presumed eventual elimination of the slave trade, with regard "necessarily paid to the peculiar situation of our southern fellow-citizens." Like his friend Rush, Coxe depicted the southern slaveholders as increasingly antislavery, sensible "of *the delicate situation of our national character on this subject.*"[51] But Coxe's chief contribution was to help establish the argument that the Constitution's authorization to abolish the slave trade, even with the twenty-year extension, was a blow against slavery, not for it.

Other antislavery Federalist writers repeated the point, sometimes emphasizing what they described as the slave trade provision's momentous historical significance. "How honorable to America," an oft-reprinted essay in the *Pennsylvania Gazette* declared, "to have been the first Christian power that has borne a testimony against a practice, that is alike disgraceful to religion, and repugnant to the true interests and happiness of Society."[52] The writer, "Plain Truth," insisted that the authorization to prohibit the trade, and not the delay, was the truly important thing. It marked the great blessing "that in this new country, we should, in less than 150 years, possess a degree of liberality and humanity, which has been unknown during so many centuries, and which is yet unattained in so many parts of the globe."[53]

At the Pennsylvania ratification convention, state chief justice Thomas McKean, a more conservative Federalist and no abolitionist, argued that, after considering the doleful circumstances of the southern states, "every man of candor will find more reason to rejoice that the power [to abolish the trade] should be given at all, than to regret that its exercise should be postponed for twenty years."[54] Benjamin Rush, for his part, called the slave trade clause "a great point obtained from the Southern States."[55] Even the widely read Anti-Federalist writer "Federal Farmer," in a pamphlet published in New York, conceded that the slave trade clause, although "not so favourable as could be wished for," was "a point gained" against slavery.[56]

In Pennsylvania, antislavery Federalists also emphasized a matter that touched on the commonwealth's recently enacted gradual emancipation law: although the Constitution might not affect slavery where it existed, it upheld the rights of the states to abolish slavery as they saw fit, regardless of claims about the sanctity of private property. "As each state is still at liberty to enact such laws for ye abolition of slavery as they may think proper, ye Convention cannot be charg'd with holding out any encouragement to [slavery]," the Quaker merchant and PAS member Robert Waln wrote to his abolitionist brother, Richard.[57] The Constitution, Tench Coxe observed, left intact not only the individual states' authority to abolish their involvement in the Atlantic slave trade but also their authority over "the emancipation of the slaves already among us." Coxe drove the point home: the power of the state governments to abolish slavery within their borders, he repeated, "can *in no wise* be controuled or restrained by the fœderal legislature."[58] If the new government could not summarily abolish slavery, neither could it establish slavery or prevent its abolition.

According to some excited antislavery Federalists, the combination of the Atlantic slave trade provision and the Constitution's refusal to interfere with state emancipation laws amounted to a clear endorsement of emancipation—and not just in those states where emancipation had already taken hold. "What alteration does the new constitution make in the present system adopted by many of the states relative to slavery?" "Plain Truth" asked. "NONE contrary to that system, but in favor of it, has taken a power of checking this abominable importation by laying duties on it."[59] Leaving unchecked the states' powers to emancipate their slaves while placing a duty on imported slaves, the author deduced, could only mean that the Constitution favored freedom for oppressed Africans.

From here, some antislavery advocates leapt to the even headier conclusion that the Constitution actually bade the new nation sooner or later to abolish slavery everywhere. "Plain Truth" was among them. By affirming emancipation as it did, he enthused, the Federal Convention signaled approval to emancipating states like Pennsylvania. "The constitution says, by implication, to such states,—'well done ye good and faithful servants, continue your endeavors to compleat the glorious work—our assistance is not very far distant; for, ere the child now born, shall arrive to an age of manhood, the supreme power of the United States shall abolish slavery altogether, and in the mean time they will oppose it as much as they can.'"[60]

The vivid imagination of "Plain Truth" got the better of him, but more sober commentators also suggested that the Constitution was at least conducive to slavery's eventual extinction nationwide. The antislavery Federalist editor Noah Webster, asked by Philadelphia's Federalists to write a pro-ratification pamphlet, contended that the Constitution "wisely left each state to pursue its own measures" regarding the Atlantic slave trade for twenty years—a prudent step, he claimed, toward a general gradual emancipation.[61] Benjamin Rush, tempering his enthusiasm, described the slave trade clause similarly, in line with what he called a consensus "that the Abolition of slavery in our country must be gradual in order to be effectual."[62] The Federalist Thomas McKean went further, expounding that the slave trade clause put the abolition of slavery "within the reach of the federal government," presumably on the grounds that cutting off the supply of slaves from Africa would kill southern slavery.[63] The Irish-born, pro-Federalist Philadelphia editor Matthew Carey enlisted in the ratification struggle with an ode of prayerful anticipation: "May servitude abolis'd be, / as well as Negro-slavery, / To make *one* LAND OF LIBERTY."[64]

The same presumptions informed one of the most prominent and extravagant descriptions of the Constitution as an antislavery instrument, delivered at the Pennsylvania convention by the Federal Convention delegate James Wilson. Now the leader of Pennsylvania's Federalists and the dominant force inside the ratification convention, Wilson had played a major part in framing the Constitution, second only to James Madison in pushing for a strengthened central government that would also adhere to majoritarian principles. On numerous issues, Wilson's participation at the Federal Convention had been essential, not least in settling the representation conflicts with the three-fifths clause. He was also avowedly antislavery and had been at least since his early service in the Continental Congress, when he strongly supported taxing the southern states for their slave populations.[65]

In the middle of the ratification debates, William Findley complained about the foggy phrasing of the three-fifths and slave trade provisions, and Wilson rose to rebut and clarify. The three-fifths clause's wording, he explained, far from invidious, came directly from the Confederation Congress's proposed taxation measure of 1783. The slave trade clause's purport, meanwhile, was not to allow the federal government to order importation of slaves (as Findley charged), but to empower the Congress to abolish that importation instantly, completely, once and for all. Although the slaveholders put up a staunch and effective fight and won a delay, Wilson said he felt "high pleasure" at the provision the convention finally approved. Indeed, Wilson contended, that provision laid "the foundation for banishing slavery out of this country."[66]

Wilson conceded that the convention had extended the slave trade longer than he would have liked; similarly, the Constitution's ten-dollar limit on taxing imported slaves was, on his view, too low. Still, the impost, which Congress could assess immediately, would operate as "a partial prohibition," and there was "reason to hope" that in "a few years" the Atlantic trade would "be prohibited altogether." As Congress, moreover, had control "in this particular" in the territories and new states—he was alluding to the Northwest Ordinance—then "slaves will never be introduced among them." With the Atlantic trade closed and slavery's expansion halted, a general emancipation would soon follow, overseen by a federal government that Wilson presumed would be intent on ending slavery.[67]

Wilson's remarks were, of course, rhetorical, intended to persuade. His replies to Findley were perfectly correct: The Constitution's slave trade clause aimed to limit the trade, not expand it. But the remainder of his speech at times stretched the facts past the point of credulity. Presenting the ten-dollar duty on the slave trade as a "partial prohibition" was particularly disingenuous, given the support the duty had received at the Federal Convention from, among others, Charles Cotesworth Pinckney. Wilson's most exhilarating statements, like those of some his fellow antislavery Federalists, took no account of the fierceness with which the Lower South slaveholders defended their rights to property in men—fierceness that Wilson had faced directly. Although the Northwest Ordinance suggested Congress would have the power to ban slavery in the territories, there was no guarantee that Congress would actually do so. In all, Wilson's speech illustrated how northern antislavery Federalists were willing to exaggerate the Constitution's antislavery features to northern audiences, no less so (as we shall see) than southern proslavery Federalists were to exaggerate its proslavery features in front of southern audiences.[68]

Still, antislavery Federalism was a considered view and not a ploy; and it was not at all irrational for Wilson, Rush, "Plain Truth," and others to believe sincerely that the Constitution would advance national emancipation. In Wilson's case, for example, it was logical enough to project that, with northern majorities, the new Congress might well ban slavery in the territories, a policy which, in combination with the Atlantic trade's abolition in 1808, would ensure slavery's abolition. And such thinking was in line with what had long been antislavery assumptions about emancipation. Since the 1770s, discussions on emancipation had consistently stipulated an end to the importation of slaves as the necessary first step.[69] The debates in Philadelphia showed proponents of ending the trade, most eloquently George Mason—to say nothing of their proslavery adversaries—interpreting an end to the Atlantic slave trade in precisely that way. By all accounts, Americans in 1787 believed that slavery would still require additional importation of Africans to flourish; and it followed that permanently closing the trade would hasten slavery's doom. It was hardly surprising that antislavery advocates outside the convention, upon reading the text of the Constitution, immediately seized on the slave trade clause and proclaimed it a great thing.

By the same reasoning, the Constitution did a great deal to encourage emancipation above and beyond authorizing the slave trade's abolition. Certainly the Constitution, even with its concessions to the slaveholding states, betrayed no intention, let alone imperative, of perpetuating slavery. With the non-slaveholding states holding congressional majorities, despite the three-fifths clause, there was reason to think that the federal government would do all that it could to impede slavery's growth. Moreover, as David Brion Davis has observed, a view had emerged by the end of the eighteenth century—in Europe as well as the United States, and not just in antislavery circles—that slavery was "an historical anomaly" that could survive only in the plantation societies where it was dominant.[70] The American experience certainly fit that description, as slavery had crumbled in northern states where it had formerly been well-entrenched, and as antislavery had begun to make inroads in the Upper South. Precisely because the Federal Convention majority had blocked any recognition of slaves as property in the Constitution—the basis for what Robert Waln, Tench Coxe, and others called the Constitution's affirmation of northern emancipation—it remained conceivable, even likely that one form or another of gradual emancipation would take hold rapidly in Delaware and Maryland and soon enough (despite recent setbacks) in Virginia. Were slavery to fall in Virginia, its status in the remaining slave states would have been at best precarious.[71] By tacitly upholding northern emancipation, the Constitution enabled those future emancipations as well.

The exuberance of the antislavery Federalists, finally, reflected the extraordinary growth and success that the antislavery cause had enjoyed in so brief a time. Whereas public criticism of slavery had been rare and organized antislavery nonexistent less than a generation earlier, slavery was now subjected to continual, vehement denunciation. Inside of a decade, five states (plus Vermont) had either abolished it or commenced its abolition. American abolitionists had good reason to perceive their efforts in world-historic terms, and it was equally reasonable for antislavery Federalists to perceive the Constitution the same way—as the instrument by which United States became the first power in Christendom, as the *Pennsylvania Gazette* writer proclaimed, to authorize abolition of the abominable slave trade.[72]

But no matter how we judge the antislavery Federalists, including their more dubious statements, the outcome of the ratification battles in the Middle States complicated Americans' impressions of slavery's place in the Constitution. Of course, the disputes over slavery were no more consequential in determining ratification in the Middle States than they were in New England: Pennsylvania and New Jersey approved ratification early, and although New York's approval took longer and involved more of a contest, in none of these states did slavery arise as a major issue in the final debates. Nevertheless, the Federal Convention's handling of slavery had come under public scrutiny, especially in Pennsylvania, and a distinct antislavery pro-Federalist view of the Constitution had emerged, one that contradicted and dominated the alternately resigned and embittered opinions of antislavery Anti-Federalists. Although in some cases disappointed that the Constitution granted as many concessions as it did to the slaveholders, the antislavery Federalists were also positive that the Constitution left sufficient room to undermine and then overthrow the slaveholders. This sort of confidence would soon motivate organized abolitionists to press for antislavery legislation by sending antislavery petitions to the very first Congress. Once those petitions reached the House of Representatives, though, they would enrage proslavery southerners, who were absolutely certain that the Constitution was completely on their side—a conviction shaped by their own states' struggles over ratification.

Divided at the Federal Convention, Upper and Lower South Federalists joined forces during ratification by depicting the Constitution as essentially proslavery. Important differences persisted, chiefly over the

Atlantic slave trade, but with regard to protecting existing property in slaves, the southerners, with the notable exception of one Upper South defector, were remarkably united.

To the extent that slavery became an issue in the southern state conventions, the Constitution's supporters had to rebut charges that the Federal Convention ought never to have ceded authority to abolish the slave trade, and that the convention had failed to adequately secure the slaveholders' property rights. Always, the Federalist supporters returned to the accurate but misleading point that the Constitution provided unprecedented protection to slavery, and for the most part this was sufficient to blunt slaveholders' concerns. But the fact remained that the convention majority had forced the proslavery southerners, and particularly the delegates from the Lower South, to back off some of their strongest demands, while it refused to recognize rights to property in man. When pressed about these shortcomings, southern Federalists resorted to dodgy justifications, some of which, especially statements about the fugitive slave clause, would return in proslavery political assertions through to the Civil War. More immediately, the proslavery Federalist arguments, along with the general tenor of the southern ratification conventions, helped consolidate support for the Constitution on the grounds that it firmly entrenched the institution of slavery.

"Though there is *very little* opposition to the proposed fœderal constitution in South-Carolina," the *Pennsylvania Gazette* reported in March 1788, some slaveholders were complaining that the Constitution would finally grant Congress the authority "*to regulate or prevent* the importation of slaves."[73] In fact, there was considerable Anti-Federalist opposition in South Carolina, especially in the newly settled backcountry, predicated chiefly on concerns about centralizing national power and its possible encroachments on individual liberty. The state's aristocratic, commercially minded Low Country planters, however, were strongly pro-Federalist, eager to foster national commerce. Exercising disproportionate power, they smothered dissent, leaving "no expedient untried" to get their way, the Anti-Federalist jurist Aedanus Burke later recalled with chagrin.[74] Ratification succeeded easily in South Carolina, where apprehensions about the Constitution's slaveholding provisions might have been expected to run higher than anywhere. The prestige and power of men like Charles Cotesworth Pinckney, Pierce Butler, and John Rutledge among their planter peers occluded misgivings. Still, what little opposition arose within Low Country ruling circles had to do largely with the slave trade, just as the *Pennsylvania Gazette* asserted. The criticism was sufficiently irksome to compel the Federalists inside the state legislature—which in South Carolina debated ratification before the state convention assembled— to make the strongest case possible for the Constitution on proslavery grounds.[75]

Rawlins Lowndes, an aging former governor from the Charleston district, delivered the most biting Anti-Federalist remarks in the legislature. Lowndes would have known from the start that his chances of winning over his colleagues were slight. ("A Mr. Lowndes, is the only opponent I can hear of," one South Carolinian reported, "but his influence is as feeble as his party is insignificant.")[76] Yet what he lacked in support the crusty Lowndes made up for in bluntness, and his accusations over slavery demanded refutation. Lowndes thought the Constitution inferior to the Articles of Confederation on several counts, but he emphasized his belief that it would subject the slave South to northern domination, not least because of its provision on the Atlantic slave trade. "Why confine it to a limited period, or rather why lay any restriction?" he demanded. Lowndes considered the trade a blessing "on the principles of religion, humanity, and justice," as it brought "a set of human beings from a bad country to a better." Without an absolute right to supply itself with slaves as it wished, he continued, South Carolina would become "one of the most contemptible [states] in the Union."[77]

Charles Cotesworth Pinckney sat in the state legislature, as did the rest of the state's delegation to the Philadelphia convention, and the next day he rebutted Lowndes with the self-assurance of a consummate insider. Yet if Pinckney's tone was confident, the substance of his remarks was self-justifying. He opened by expressing surprise at any claim that he and his colleagues at the Federal Convention "had conceded too much" to the North given the inclusion of the three-fifths clause, which "allowed a representation for a specie of property which they have not among them." Pinckney could not honestly deny outright Lowndes's charge that the Constitution contained a potential threat to the Atlantic slave trade and therefore to South Carolina's economy. He had to admit that "the religious and political prejudices of the Eastern and middle States" as well as the opposition of Virginia had forced a compromise. That said, though, Pinckney reported that the terms of the deal could have been much worse and that, in the end, the convention had given the slaveholders concessions of their own, including the right to recover fugitive slaves, "a right we had not before." Contrary to Lowndes's sweeping denunciation, Pinckney pointed out, the new congress was not compelled to abolish the Atlantic slave trade after twenty years, and might very well decline to do so. Most important, the Constitution denied the new national government any power whatsoever to interfere with the slaveholders' existing property in man.[78]

Pinckney certainly had grounds for extolling the Constitution's proslavery features, and having personally worked so hard on them, he could do so with that much more sureness. Those features, he firmly believed, were sufficient to secure slavery's future under the new government. Still, his reply to Lowndes was remarkably defensive and at times misleading. Pinckney praised the Atlantic slave trade clause on the truthful but less than hearty grounds that things could have turned out worse—that is, though he dared not say so, the convention might well have approved a much shorter delay or even an immediate abolition of the trade. As for blocking that abolition in future, so long as Virginia continued to oppose the Atlantic slave trade, there was in fact, despite Pinckney's implication, scarce reason to believe that Congress would refuse to outlaw it at the earliest possible date, in 1808. The fugitive slave clause, meanwhile, granted the slaveholders a new right only because northern emancipation had created a new situation which the Articles of Confederation did not anticipate; and the clause secured the alleged right only vaguely at best. Pinckney's conclusion—that he and his fellow Lower South delegates had made "the best terms for the security of this species of property it was in our power to make," and that "on the whole I do not think them bad"—was more candid and no doubt sincere: if imperfect, he insisted, the Constitution—"on the whole"—offered sufficient protection to slavery. The endorsement was less than ringing, but because it came from Pinckney, it was adequate to squelch South Carolina opposition to the Constitution over slavery.[79]

In most of the other southern states, slaveholders' support for the new national union precluded much debate over slavery. Both Delaware and Georgia ratified the Constitution soon after the process began, over minimal opposition.[80] North Carolina proved much more difficult, as an initial convention adjourned by refusing either to ratify or reject, and instead produced a list of twenty-six desired amendments, but none of them was connected to slavery or the slave trade. (The state finally did ratify late in 1789, after the First Congress had approved the amendments that would become the Bill of Rights.)

One delegate to the North Carolina convention did object to the Constitution's continuation of the slave trade; another objected to the wording of the slave trade clause; and a third worried that the clause portended the abolition of slavery altogether. The eminent jurist and slaveholder (and future U.S. Supreme Court justice) James Iredell, who led the state's Federalists at the North Carolina convention, addressed all three concerns. Expressing his hatred of the slave trade, Iredell, who had not been at the Federal Convention, argued that the Constitution at least provided for the trade's potential abolition, while at the same time he assured the third questioner that it nowhere empowered the federal government to emancipate slaves already in the country. In clarifying the wording of the slave trade provision, Iredell also repeated, now as proslavery Federalist assurances, the antislavery Anti-Federalist allegations about the convention's dark meanings and motives. "The Eastern States, who long ago have abolished slaves," he claimed "did not approve of the expression *slaves;* they therefore used another that answered the same purpose."[81] Insinuations about the framers' deliberate confusion did ample work at both ends of the ratification debate.

The ratification fight in Maryland defied expectations. Two of the state's delegates to the Federal Convention, Luther Martin and John Mercer, had bolted the proceedings in Philadelphia and enlisted in the opposition, concerned chiefly with what they considered the Constitution's overcentralized framework and the powers it gave the larger states. With other state leaders uneasy about the lack of a bill of rights, Maryland's Anti-Federalists seemed likely to put up a strong fight. But the public was apathetic—it appears that fewer than one in four eligible Maryland voters participated in the election of convention delegates—and the well-organized friends of the Constitution won a sizable majority that swiftly approved ratification.

All the more ironic, then, that the state's outstanding contribution to the larger ratification struggle was an extended Anti-Federalist speech by Luther Martin, which soon circulated widely in pamphlet form. Two months after the Federal Convention ended, Martin and three other delegates addressed the state assembly with their respective impressions of the convention and its work. Martin's long-winded contribution was the most forthright, testing the limits of the convention's agreed-upon secrecy by offering some highly colored accounts of the group's inner workings while also assaulting the Constitution itself, not least over slavery and the slave trade. No other piece of commentary during the ratification struggle, whether from abolitionists or slaveholders, did more than Martin's speech to fix the image of the Constitution as unwaveringly proslavery. Indeed, one proslavery Virginia Federalist commended distributing copies of "Martin's publication," and "particularly those parts where he speaks of the slaves," as a means to persuade skeptical slaveholders to support ratification.[82]

Martin came as close as he dared to relating the details of the bargain between New England and the Lower South over the Atlantic slave trade before he condemned it as a national crime that invited God's wrath. Echoing his remarks in the Federal Convention, but with an intensity more commonly found in New England Anti-Federalist writings, he attacked slavery as *"inconsistent* with the *genius* of *republicanism."* The Constitution should have abolished the Atlantic slave trade immediately, Martin declared, and then *"authorize*[d] the general government from time to time, to make such regulations as should be thought most advantageous for the *gradual abolition* of *slavery,* and the *emancipation* of the *slaves* which are already in the States." Whereas Benjamin Rush and his fellow antislavery Federalists in the North saw great promise in the Constitution, the Anti-Federalist Martin saw glaring omissions that ought to have been corrected with an explicit antislavery affirmation—an affirmation, he knew well, the Federal Convention would never have debated, let alone approved. Martin also repeated the spreading misrepresentation about the convention "anxiously" avoiding "expressions which might be odious in the ears of Americans" while admitting "into their system those *things* which the *expressions* signified."[83]

The sharpest exchanges in the South over slavery came in Virginia. Only traces of the pro-emancipation opinion that had arisen in 1785 appeared in the Virginia press concerning ratification.[84] This still left room, though, for intense debate about the Constitution and slavery at the state's convention, most of which dealt directly with the new government's projected authority to limit or even abolish property in man. Lasting the entire month of June, the Virginia convention came at a crucial moment, after eight of the nine states required to complete ratification had agreed, but with the success of the entire project hanging in the balance. The lack of a bill of rights proved the opposition's most effective objection, and only after the state's leading Federalists, preeminently James Madison, agreed to allow the state to ratify on condition of further amendments did the convention finally assent. But, mainly because of the dissenting delegates George Mason and Patrick Henry, Madison and his allies were obliged to defend the Constitution as at once a blow against the slave trade and a firm protector of slaveholders' property rights.

Mason was one of three delegates still present at the conclusion of the Federal Convention who refused to sign the Constitution, and he now stood in all-out opposition. Although chiefly concerned about the omission of a bill of rights, he had been particularly upset by the convention's refusal to summarily abolish the Atlantic slave trade. (Until the slave trade compromise was struck, he later told Thomas Jefferson, he would "have set his hand & heart to" the Constitution, but thereafter, with the abandonment of what he saw as the convention's "great principles," he could not.)[85] Henry, the riveting patriot orator and former Virginia governor, had been selected as a delegate to the Federal Convention but feared it was rigged to consolidate national power, and so he stayed at home, famously saying (at least purportedly) that he "smelt a rat."[86] Leading the Anti-Federalist attack early in the Virginia convention, Henry charged that the proposed Constitution "squints towards monarchy."[87] As part of his broader condemnation, he went on to claim that on the matter of slavery, he smelled another rat. In tandem with Mason, he then struck to the heart of the question concerning federal authority over slavery: the absence in the Constitution of any categorical guarantee to the slaveholders of their rights to property in man.

As soon as the convention took up the slave trade provision, Mason rose to call it a "fatal section, which has caused more dangers than any other." Not only was the trade "diabolical in itself, and disgraceful to mankind," he said, recapitulating his speech in Philadelphia, but it also weakened the state by introducing a troublesome population. But Mason had a further objection: while the Constitution would permit continuation of the slave trade for twenty years, it contained no clause to secure "the property of that kind which we already have." Without an explicit assurance to the slaveholders, the national government might find some way to destroy that property, such as assessing a tax on slaves heavy enough "as it will amount to manumission." Mason proposed a course of action congenial to enlightened Virginia slaveholders: the new government should be authorized to diminish slavery's growth by closing the slave trade, but guarantee existing property rights in slaves lest a coerced manumission lead to violent chaos. The framers, Mason concluded (paraphrasing the Book of Matthew), had instead proposed precisely the opposite, "so that 'they have done what they ought not to have done, and have left undone what they ought to have done.'"[88]

James Madison knew that Mason was correct on the essential issue: the Federal Convention, partly at Madison's own instigation, had refused to validate property rights in slaves. Two months earlier, in a pair of essays for The Federalist series in New York, Madison had finessed the question of slaves as property in the Constitution, bypassing the convention's discussions of the matter in connection with the Atlantic slave trade while also registering his assent to the three-fifths clause without taking a clear stand on the issues of property and personhood that lay beneath it.[89] Mason's challenge was not so easily evaded. In his response, Madison brushed aside the Virginian's complaints about the slave trade, observing that the Constitution brought "an amelioration of our condition" over the Articles of Confederation. He dismissed the notion that, under the proposed mode of taxation and representation, the Congress would ever enact a tax tantamount to manumission. But Madison also tried to negate Mason's more unsettling contention by suggesting that the Constitution actually did what Mason claimed it had not done, pointing to the crucial clause that "secures us that property which we now possess"—the fugitive slave clause, "expressly inserted" by the convention, he said, "to enable owners of slaves to reclaim them."[90] Madison's remarks were literally accurate, but in the form that he expressed them—as a direct response to Mason—they left the impression that, with the fugitive slave clause, the Constitution fully recognized and protected property in man.

Madison's blurring of the Constitution's recognition of state property laws with protecting that property in national law—and especially his citing of the fugitive slave clause—was highly misleading. In fact, as he knew well, the convention—including the Committee of Style, on which he had served—had gone out of its way to ensure that the fugitive slave clause did not acknowledge property in man, let alone slaveholders' rights to such property. Madison's maneuver would, in the long term, prove ironic. In years to come, antislavery advocates would point to Madison's remarks at the Federal Convention to back their claims that the framers had purposely excluded property in man. At the same time, slavery's defenders would point to the fugitive slave clause as conclusive evidence that the Constitution recognized and condoned slavery in national law. Thanks to his equivocal efforts, first at the Federal Convention and then at the Virginia convention, Madison helped initiate both proslavery and antislavery interpretations of the framers' work.

In the moment, if he were candid, Madison could have conceded Mason's point but argued that it made no difference, that even without a clause that specifically guaranteed slaveholders' property rights, the Constitution offered ample security against interference with slavery by the national government. Madison certainly believed as much, just as sincerely as James Wilson believed the Constitution was antislavery, and with at least as much reason. But Madison was stuck in a dilemma that made candor impossible. Revealing to Virginia's slaveholders, even indirectly, that he and the convention majority had deliberately excluded property in man might have risked losing ratification in Virginia, which would have severely endangered the Constitution itself. (It might also have ruined Madison's political career.) Neither, though, could Madison safely leave uncontested Mason's charge that the Constitution provided slavery less than ample protection. And so Madison muddled the issue, implying that the fugitive slave provision provided the absolute protection for slavery that Mason insisted, correctly, the Constitution lacked.

Patrick Henry wasn't fooled. The fugitive slave clause, he replied, stated that "that a run-away negro could be taken up in Maryland or

New-York," but this offered "no security at all" from federal interference with slavery. That interference could come in any number of ways in view of the latitude given to the government's implied powers under the Constitution. Henry was furious over the proposed granting to the new government of the power to tax the citizenry directly, and he charged that Congress might well enact, as Mason had suggested, a "grievous and enormous" assessment that would "compel owners to emancipate their slaves rather than pay the tax."[91] In a later speech to the convention, Henry pointed additionally to the "ten thousand implied powers" embedded in the Congress's authority to secure "the general defense and welfare," which he believed would invite an immediate abolition of slavery, particularly in time of war (when abolition and conscription of the ex-slaves might be enacted as a national security measure).[92]

Like Mason, Henry professed authentically to deplore slavery while also understanding that "prudence forbids its abolition"—an understanding, he said, that eluded northerners who, though righteously opposed to slavery, also lacked "ties of sympathy and fellow-feeling" with the South. Were those northerners ever to win control over the federal government, there was every reason to believe that they would abolish slavery, one way or another. Only an explicit provision that "secure[d] us that property in slaves, which we held now" would permit the people of Virginia to live in peace and tranquility. Yet the Constitution glaringly lacked such a provision, an omission Henry said he feared had been "done with design."[93] He could hardly have known for certain, but such, precisely, had been the Federal Convention majority's design—supported by, among others, James Madison.

Mixing disdain with distraction, Madison and his allies grasped at every counterargument they could. Mason's reasoning was preposterous, one Federalist mocked, as it rejected the Constitution for being at the same time "promotive and destructive of slavery."[94] (In fact, Mason's argument was not only consistent but also, in Virginia, quite familiar.) The Lower South states most beholden to slavery, Madison asserted, were "perfectly satisfied" with the Constitution and feared "no danger to the property they now hold," which in part thanks to Charles Cotesworth Pinckney's repute was true enough. (Madison also noted the satisfaction of those northern states that still contained slaves, including New York, New Jersey, and Connecticut, which he said, inaccurately, "had made no attempt, or taken any step" toward emancipation).[95] Edmund Randolph revived Madison's misleading claim about the fugitive slave clause enshrining property in man—"when authority is given to owners of slaves to vindicate their property," he said, "can it be supposed they can be deprived of it?"—evading Patrick Henry's point as surely as Madison had. Randolph fell back on the argument that none of the state's delegates to the Federal Convention had "the smallest suspicion of the abolition of slavery."[96] Madison scorned Mason's and Henry's "unsupported suspicions" as implausible—what we today would call "paranoid"—and pleaded for the basic confidence required in any civil society, in this case meaning confidence that the national government would not "come into a measure which will strip them of their property, discourage, and alienate the affections of, five-thirteenths of the Union."[97]

When the debates concluded, slavery proved no more important in deciding the ratification in Virginia than it did anywhere else. Opponents successfully demanded twenty suggested amendments along with a bill of rights as the price of Virginia's ratification—although the convention, to the opposition's anger, made them nonbinding—but none of the suggestions touched on slavery or the slave trade. Mason's and Henry's warning that property in man lacked security went unheeded. At least for the moment, Madison's reflections on slavery and the Constitution seem to have quieted Virginia slaveholders' anxieties and helped win the victory that ensured the Constitution's ratification.[98]

In the short run, of course, Madison's defense was strong and sensible. Given the practical realities of 1788, and the safeguards for slavery built into the Constitution, it is easy to understand Madison's mounting frustration. Over the longer run, though, George Mason's and Patrick Henry's concerns would prove anything but outlandish. Madison's reassurances ultimately rested on an abstract confidence that the national government would never summarily abolish slavery even if it had the power to do so, which he insisted it did not. However, Mason and especially Henry understood much more concretely that, unless utterly and explicitly barred from doing so, a northern antislavery majority, under a national government as powerful as the one proposed in the Constitution, could pose a direct and strong threat to slavery, finding some way to destroy it or hasten its destruction without resorting to an immediate emancipation. Henry rummaged to locate the instruments such a majority might utilize—direct taxation, war powers, the preamble's remarks on the general welfare and defense—but he was certain that somewhere among the implied federal powers lay the weapons that could weaken slavery and in time eradicate it. In view of northern emancipation—whatever Madison's inexact accounting of it—there was good reason to believe that the North was turning decisively antislavery. It was thus reasonable to fear that if northerners ever captured control of the federal government, sooner or later they would find a way to commence the emancipation of all the slaves.[99] Slaveholders might reassure themselves that, thanks to the three-fifths clause—and with demographic trends looking favorable for the

South—the Constitution may have foreclosed the emergence of that northern majority. But that involved more ifs than some slaveholders would abide—and history would bear them out.

Mason and Henry, that is, understood what Madison either could not or would not admit, not even, perhaps, to himself—that by refusing to validate property in man, Madison and the other framers had created a Constitution that, under the proper circumstances, could acquire strong antislavery potential. By stifling that argument in Virginia in 1788, and by styling those dangerous circumstances as beyond improbable, Madison and his allies helped secure among the slaveholders the contrary impression, that the Constitution created a nation that was perfectly safe for slavery. But even though it would take several decades, the antislavery majority feared by Mason and Henry would eventually arrive—and with it the reckoning that brought the Civil War.

Constructions of a usable past need not distort past political arguments. As controversies over slavery deepened from the 1820s through the 1850s, Americans would develop clashing contentions about the federal government's authority (or lack of it) regarding slavery's continued existence, drawing freely and often enough promiscuously on the writings of the founding generation. Those contentions, though, were not simply inventions, twisting the words of the framers, their supporters, and their critics to fit new situations and preconceptions. Early versions of those contentions had emerged at the founding itself, during the ratification struggles of 1787 and 1788.

The fights over ratification generated views of the Constitution as essentially antislavery and essentially proslavery, backed by a variety of interpretations of specific provisions and clauses. Those views and interpretations had, at most, a marginal impact in settling ratification, but they would return over the decades to come, when their influence would be enormous. Some of the arguments made by Benjamin Rush, James Wilson, and other antislavery Federalists reappeared in claims by antislavery political leaders from the 1830s on that the Constitution had been framed to facilitate slavery's doom. So, too, the otherwise contradictory arguments of the Quaker abolitionist William Rotch Sr., the antislavery Anti-Federalist Luther Martin, and the proslavery Federalist Charles Cotesworth Pinckney resounded in the arguments of proslavery secessionists and abolitionist radicals who insisted that the Constitution validated slavery.

In the interim, antislavery advocates provoked numerous political battles that tested the federal government's authority over slavery, authority rooted in whether the Constitution regarded slaves as property. Those battles would reach a turning point during the momentous crisis over the admission of Missouri to statehood in 1819 and 1820, but they began almost as soon as the new government assembled in New York in 1789. One of the first of the battles was partly instigated, in his last public act, by a national patriarch who was also an ex-slaveholder, the president of the Pennsylvania Abolition Society, Benjamin Franklin.

4

To the Missouri Crisis

A~T EIGHTY-FOUR~, Benjamin Franklin's body was failing, but not his mind or his mordant wit. His reputation had soured in upper-class Philadelphia circles during his declining years, mainly because of his long association with France, now convulsed in revolution, and his embrace of abolitionism. At the Federal Convention, after deciding against introducing a memorial from the Pennsylvania Abolition Society, Franklin had kept his own counsel during the most contentious arguments over slavery and the slave trade. But in February 1790, with the new national government safely launched, a PAS petition above Franklin's signature arrived at the House of Representatives, along with two other antislavery petitions, and it sparked a protracted and impassioned debate. Proslavery spokesmen made a point of attacking Franklin personally: the South Carolina congressman Thomas Tudor Tucker voiced supercilious umbrage that such a "mischievous" appeal had been "signed by a man who ought to have known the Constitution better."[1]

Franklin had one last cutting retort left in him. After the House finally buried the antislavery petitions, he published a pseudonymous satire of one of the most contentious proslavery congressmen, James Jackson of Georgia, which placed Jackson's words into the mouth of a piratical, infidel, slave-owning Algerian potentate—apart from the slave-owning, a perfect monster to any southern gentleman. Franklin made a point of mocking Jackson's assertions of private property rights. "Who is to indemnify the masters for the loss?" the imaginary pirate asks, closely paraphrasing Jackson's remarks. "Can they do it? Or would they, to do what they think justice to the slaves, do a greater injustice to the owners?"[2]

Franklin was dead inside of a month, but for a quarter century thereafter, the PAS and other abolitionist groups carried on their public campaigns, while antislavery representatives instigated fights in Congress over slavery's future. Slaveholders and their allies counterattacked by ridiculing the abolitionists and denouncing Congress for even considering unconstitutional incursions on their property rights. Slavery's defenders won nearly all of these battles, opening new territories to slavery and consolidating the slaveholders' power in national politics. They did so, for the most part, without having to seriously challenge the Constitution's exclusion of property in man and Congress's consequent authority over slavery outside the existing states. Indeed, slaveholders at times showed a willingness to tolerate and even endorse congressional authority, so long as there was little chance that Congress would actually exercise it. But from time to time, antislavery advocates also pushed the matter, and occasionally they rallied considerable strength and even majorities on significant votes, reaffirming that the Constitution did not validate slavery and arousing the slaveholders' ire.

In 1819 and 1820, antislavery instigation over the impending organization of Arkansas Territory and the admission to the Union of the new state of Missouri touched off a political crisis. Faced with an unprecedented antislavery surge, angry hard-line slaveholders claimed that, in fact, the Constitution fully recognized property rights in man, and that Congress was powerless to restrict slavery in any of the lands obtained in the Louisiana Purchase. The famous compromise that followed rejected those claims, even as it opened the way for slavery's further expansion. But proslavery contentions about the Constitution had shifted the terms of debate and would not stop there, any more than the antislavery contentions that provoked them would. The storm over Arkansas and Missouri proved a turning point, after which intensifying conflicts over slavery, property, and the Constitution led toward civil war.

The first incitement over slavery came in the House in May 1789, two months into Congress's very first session, and it was relatively mild. Nearing the end of a debate over import duties, the Virginia representative Josiah Parker rankled the Lower South by proposing a tax on imports of slaves at ten dollars per head, the full rate specified in the Constitution. Parker's proposal wound up going nowhere, as would every subsequent effort to tax the Atlantic slave trade, but it elicited three notable responses. The ever-contentious James Jackson of Georgia, who praised slavery as a benevolent institution, reasonably depicted the proposal as an attack on slavery as well as the slave trade, then denounced any duty on slave imports as "the most odious tax Congress could impose."[3] Jackson could not dispute the constitutionality of the duty, but he called it nevertheless an oppressive intrusion on the slaveholders' peculiar form of property.

The other two responses came from former delegates to the Federal Convention. James Madison, now a Virginia congressman, eloquently defended Parker's proposal as a partial fulfillment of the Federal Convention's intention to express "the sense of America" on the trade's inhumanity. "It is to be hoped," he declared, "that by expressing a national disapprobation of this trade, we may destroy it, and save our-

selves from reproaches, and our posterity the imbecility ever attendant on a country filled with slaves." For decades to come, antislavery
advocates would base the legitimacy of their cause on the framers' supposed hostility to slavery as well as the slave trade. The Connecticut
congressman Roger Sherman, meanwhile, taking up a standing concern of his, opposed the bill and objected to "the insertion of human
beings as an article of duty among goods, wares, and merchandise."
The Federal Convention, he said, had drawn a clear distinction—"the
constitution does not consider these persons as a species of property;
it speaks of them as persons"—so he preferred that any duty on slaves
be considered independently. Whatever their views of the slave trade
and federal authority, everyone could agree that the framers had cat-
egorically refused to validate property in man.[4]

A year later, the well-plotted Quaker and abolitionist petition effort
involving Benjamin Franklin caught Congress and the nation by surprise, reaching the House in the midst of a momentous struggle over
Treasury Secretary Alexander Hamilton's plans to finance the public
credit. As it happened, the protracted House debate over the petitions
would also have far-reaching implications.

The petitioners—two groups of Quakers from the Middle States as
well as Franklin and the Pennsylvania Abolition Society—worded their
appeals carefully: rather than bid Congress to abolish slavery and the
slave trade summarily, or to enact any other specific legislation, they
asked representatives to do all they could within the limits of their constitutional authority. The PAS petition, by far the most sweeping of
the three, asked the House and Senate to pay "serious attention to the
subject of slavery" and "step to the very verge of the powers vested in
you" to abolish the institution itself, pointing to the powers implied by
the Constitution's promise to pursue the general welfare and blessings
of liberty. The petitioners requested that Congress lay aside its pressing

business and ascertain what the PAS confidently called the federal government's "many important and salutary powers" over the Atlantic slave trade and (in the PAS petition's case) domestic slavery itself.[5]

Lower South members in the House reacted swiftly and vehemently. Apart from the ten-dollar import duty, they asserted, the Constitution expressly barred Congress from taking any action connected to the slave trade prior to 1808, as well as any action, at any time, interfering with slavery or geared toward its abolition. The petitions were blatantly unconstitutional, the South Carolina grandee and lawyer William Loughton Smith declaimed; as Congress had no right to interfere with slavery, he said, the petitions amounted to "an attack upon the palladium of the property of our country." The House had no lawful option, Smith contended, but to reject them out of hand, thereby affirming the Constitution's compromises over slavery and protecting the slaveholders' property rights. "Perhaps the petitioners . . . did not think their object unconstitutional," he remarked acidly, "but now that they are told that it is they will be satisfied with the answer, and press it no further." Behind the dismissive rebuttals were dark and definitive threats. Were the House to shirk its obligation and as much as refer the petitions to a committee, the South Carolinian Aedanus Burke declared, it would "blow the trumpet of sedition in the Southern states." Slaveholders, James Jackson vowed, "will never suffer themselves to be divested of their property without a struggle."[6]

The intensity of the conflict stemmed from the contradictory outcomes of the ratification debates and the lack of any clear, authoritative statement about the new government's powers over slavery. Organized abolitionists and Quakers were making good on antislavery Federalists' assurances during the ratification debates and asking Congress to determine the full extent of its implied powers over both slavery and the slave trade. The Lower South, understandably, was appalled, given all that Charles Cotesworth Pinckney and the other southern Federalists had said in 1787 and 1788 about the Constitution placing slavery and, for a time, the Atlantic slave trade off-limits. Now, though, abruptly, in the second session of the very first Congress, self-confident northern Quakers and abolitionists led by the famous Franklin were petitioning the House and Senate to do everything in their power to destroy slavery as well as the slave trade. If Congress even entertained the antislavery petitions, the proslavery men concluded, it would prove that the Anti-Federalists had been correct all along and that the Constitution was a treacherous sham.

The rest of the House recoiled at the Lower South's vitriol. A few speakers expressed dismay at the southerners' apparent devotion to slavery, but most focused on the flimsiness of their constitutional arguments. Insofar as the petitions asked Congress to act within its constitutional powers, some speakers pointed out, it was nonsensical to dismiss them as unconstitutional. (To the southerners, the petitioners' claim that any such powers might exist was the true absurdity.) Other speakers directly confronted the implication that Congress lacked any authority whatsoever over either slavery or, until 1808, the slave trade. The Lower Southerners seemed to assume that because the Constitution precluded federal interference with slavery in the existing slaveholding states it barred any interference at all. To the contrary, members instructed them, Congress had ample authority, as Elbridge Gerry put it, "to intermeddle in the business," beginning with its stipulated power to regulate (though not abolish) the Atlantic slave trade. Gerry offered the hypothetical example of a plan whereby the government would purchase every slave in the Union and compensate the masters with proceeds from the sale of public lands in the West. Gerry could no more envisage a summary, involuntary, uncompensated national emancipation than most antislavery northerners could. Still, he insisted that Congress could, if it so chose, take discrete actions to end slavery as well as the slave trade, which was heresy to the Lower South slaveholders.[7]

James Madison went even further in sketching out Congress's powers, albeit in somewhat contradictory ways. Two years earlier, during ratification, Madison had placated fractious Virginia slaveholders by portraying the Constitution as a bulwark for their property in slaves. Now, however, exasperated by the Lower South slaveholders' aggressiveness, and happy to pursue additional restrictions on the slave trade, he allowed that aspects of the antislavery petitions might be unconstitutional, but that was no reason to dismiss them. He then calmly alluded to "a variety of ways" whereby Congress could "countenance" the Atlantic slave trade's restriction, including direct if limited supervision of slavery itself. Madison's view proceeded from his assurance that the federal government enjoyed explicit control over governing the western territories. At the Federal Convention, he had been the first to propose that the Constitution authorize Congress "to institute temporary Governments" in the territories before they became states.[8]

Because the Constitution had not validated property in man, it followed that Congress could deal with slavery in the territories as it saw fit. Accordingly, Madison postulated a law that would reduce the slave trade by limiting the introduction of slaves to the western Georgia cession lands, where, he said, "Congress have certainly the power to regulate the subject of slavery." That power, he said, refuted the claim "that Congress cannot constitutionally interfere in the business in any degree whatever."[9] Rendering the federal government powerless over slavery where it existed, it turned out, did not strip it of implied powers over the international slave trade or, for that matter, over slavery itself in the national territories.

The Lower South representatives, who left Madison's claims unanswered, could take comfort when the Senate brusquely rejected the antislavery petitions, virtually ensuring that no new federal law would come of the petition campaign.[10] But the Senate's rejection also focused public attention more sharply on the struggle inside the House, where, despite the three-fifths clause, the Lower South was badly outnumbered. ("Alass—how weak a resistance against the whole house," the South Carolinian Smith wrote to a friend.)[11] By a vote of 43 to 11, the House approved sending the petitions to a special committee. Virtually every northerner and large majorities from the Upper South voted aye.[12] Here was the Lower South's nightmare from the convention come to life: isolated and outmanned, their representatives could not prevent Congress from looking into the abolition of slavery as well as the slave trade. But the Lower South congressmen, possibly relieved by the Senate vote, did not blow the trumpet of sedition as they had threatened; instead they refused further cooperation in the matter and regrouped. As a result, the House special committee appointed to consider the petitions consisted of six northerners and a Virginian. To all appearances, James Pemberton of the PAS observed, the group was "favorable to the cause of humanity," and he and his associates, including the untiring Quaker abolitionist Warner Mifflin, worked closely with the members behind the scenes, at one point commenting on a draft of the report.[13] Yet the committee's chairman, Abiel Foster of New Hampshire, also expressed privately his concerns about further provoking the sullen slaveholders. Pemberton began to fear that Foster might persuade the members to "appease the South."[14]

The Foster committee's report, delivered three weeks later, appeared at first glance to smother the petitioners' demands, chiefly by acknowledging that Congress was powerless to end the Atlantic slave trade before 1808. Yet in its quiet way, the report was also explosive; indeed, it contained language that, given an antislavery reading, would have been as radical as any official congressional document on slavery composed prior to the Civil War. Specifically, while the report repeated the conventional wisdom that, "by a fair construction of the Constitution," Congress was "equally retrained from interfering with the emancipation of slaves," it stipulated that the restraint applied to slaves "who already are, or who may, within the period mentioned"—that is, before 1808—"be imported into, or born within any of the said States." Depending on how one read that last comma, it was possible to conclude that the committee was holding out the possibility that Congress possessed the power to emancipate slaves born in the United States after 1808—a staggering proposition.[15]

The report unquestionably asserted that Congress could regulate the Atlantic slave trade in specific ways not expressly granted by the Constitution and it listed several of them, including providing for the humane treatment of slaves still being transported to the United States. (The southern delegates' failure in 1787 to secure a complete ban on federal interference with the slave trade had certainly given antislavery advocates room to maneuver.) The report's conclusion, meanwhile, assured the Quakers and the PAS that Congress would pursue their "humane objects"—that is, abolition of slavery and the overseas slave trade—"in all cases" where it had authority. As much as they dared, the committee members had heeded the PAS petitioners' request and took seriously Congress's powers over slavery—creating what W. E. B. Du Bois, in a largely neglected historical appreciation, would call "a sort of official manifesto on the aims of Northern anti-slavery politics."[16]

The Lower South members, apoplectic, expounded over several days about slavery's benevolence and their rights to property in man. William Loughton Smith spoke of the "implied compact" in the Constitution that "no step should be taken to injure the property" of the southern people. In reply, the antislavery New Jerseyan Elias Boudinot denied any "claim to [slave] property vested at the time of the Constitution, and guarantied thereby." Then, suddenly, the mood inside the chamber changed, as formerly supportive northern congressmen— some dismayed, some alarmed—evinced an eagerness to return to the urgent issues concerning the nation's finances. With no sympathetic northerner taking charge of defending the report, the Foster committee's efforts seemed doomed.[17]

James Madison put aside his anger at the Lower South and stepped in to rescue what he could. With the assistance of Upper South allies, he persuaded the House to revise the report and reduce it to two simple points: first, that the federal government could neither abolish the Atlantic slave trade until 1808 nor interfere with slavery in any of the existing states either before or after 1808, and second, that Congress enjoyed the implied powers over the Atlantic trade that the Foster committee had listed.[18] Gone were the passages that most unnerved the proslavery southerners, above all any suggestion that Congress could undertake a general emancipation after 1808—an idea that, though in line with antislavery Federalist contentions about the Constitution's abolitionist leanings, was dubious on its face and politically impossible without unwavering northern support.

Yet by also fighting for expanded regulation of the slave trade, Madison incensed the Lower South representatives, notably William Loughton Smith, who charged that oversight of the trade beyond what was explicitly stated by the framers was "an indirect violation of the constitution."[19] When the debate concluded, the Lower South members restated their insistence that the House drop the entire matter immediately. At exactly that moment, more than a dozen northern and Upper South congressmen either absented themselves or defected outright. A motion to put the weakened report to a vote squeaked by with a majority of one. Then the House endorsed the report by a scant 29 votes to 25; and there the petitions controversy ended.[20]

The Lower South congressmen had rebounded remarkably thanks in part to the abolitionists' miscalculations and chiefly to northern defections, the latter reinforcing a pattern evident in the Federal Convention that would recur into the 1850s. Although they could not prevent the House from recognizing limited federal authority over the slave trade, they had in every other way thwarted the Quakers' and abolitionists' campaign. The grandest of the antislavery advocates' presumptions from the ratification debates—that the Constitution inclined toward advancing slavery's destruction—was repudiated. Proslavery presumptions that the Constitution secured for the slaveholders their property in man seemed vindicated. For seventy years to come, national debates over slavery would start by acknowledging the national government as powerless over slavery in existing states—what historians have come to know as the "federal consensus"—thereby giving the slaveholders a great tactical as well as strategic advantage.[21] It even appeared, in the immediate aftermath of the petitions battle, as if antislavery agitation had been stifled for good in national affairs. The slaveholding president George Washington—who had kept his distance from the controversy but, despite his antislavery sympathies, considered the Quaker petitions "mal-apropos"—observed with relief that the "slave business" was "at last put to rest and will scarcely awake."[22]

And so it was put to rest, but only up to a point. Over the decade to come, slaveholders would win numerous important victories in national politics, including legislation that ensured slavery's spread into territories and new states south of the Ohio River. Yet the antislavery cause, although defeated, was not destroyed. The Foster committee's close cooperation with leaders of the PAS, along with its remarkable report, revealed an antislavery presence in First Congress, or at least in the House, that was far larger and more determined than historians usually report. And that presence, outside as well as inside Congress, did not collapse or even falter after the failure of the petitions campaign. New abolitionist petitions arrived in Congress over the next two years, including one from Warner Mifflin that the House (instigated by the relentless William Loughton Smith) turned away without debate.[23] Undeterred, the state abolitionist societies, now numbering seven, stepped up their activities, confederating in 1794 as the American Convention for Promoting the Abolition of Slavery.

Moreover, although the petitions debacle affirmed the federal consensus, it did not affirm the hard-line proslavery view of the Constitution. The hard-liners contended that the framers had prohibited any federal action whatsoever regarding slavery or the Atlantic slave trade apart from what was specifically stipulated about the import duties and the trade's possible abolition in 1808. But the House, over the fierce objections of William Loughton Smith, rejected that argument and sustained, albeit by the closest of votes, Congress's implied powers to regulate the slave trade—all of which left antislavery advocates with a sliver of hope.[24]

In fact, it was more than a sliver. Congress went on to pass new laws regulating the slave trade, much as Madison had hoped it would; these including an act in 1794 prohibiting the use of any American port or shipyard for the building or outfitting of any ship to be used for the importing of slaves.[25] Although they continually adverted to their property rights, the Lower South slaveholders did not specifically argue that the Constitution recognized slaves as property, only that the Constitution blocked interference with slavery. In the absence of the property argument, and given Congress's broad powers over the nation's territories, congressmen including James Madison could claim that the

Constitution actually authorized the federal government to interfere with slavery as well as the slave trade in very exact instances and circumstances. The Northwest Ordinance, which the new Congress had rapidly reaffirmed with minor modifications in 1789, clearly supported those claims, and the petitions controversy further aroused them. Before the decade was over, antislavery House members would assert even more forcefully that Congress possessed complete authority over slavery inside its own jurisdiction, preeminently in the territories. Even as the slaveholders prevailed in one battle after another, antislavery advocates held what constitutional and political ground they could. As the petitions controversy showed, some of the ground had been cleared by the framers' decision not to grant states complete control over the Atlantic slave trade. The rest had been cleared, as would become increasingly clear, by the framers' exclusion of property in man.

At the height of the petitions controversy, the Pennsylvania Abolition Society's headquarters in Philadelphia received a request from the society's branch in Washington County, in the southwestern part of the state, about resolving a complicated matter involving a black man named John Davis. Technically freed under the state's 1780 emancipation law, Davis had been kidnapped and reenslaved in Virginia, and Pennsylvania authorities had failed to secure extradition of the three white Virginians indicted as the kidnappers. Initially flummoxed about what to advise, the PAS leaders finally petitioned Thomas Mifflin—the former delegate to the Federal Convention who was also cousin of the Quaker abolitionist leader Warner Mifflin and who was now governor of Pennsylvania. Mifflin sent a cordial note to the Virginia governor requesting extradition of the three accused men and restoration of Davis's freedom. It was only one of scores of cases in which the PAS and other abolitionist societies, unfazed by the failure of the petitions campaign in 1790, intervened to protect the rights of blacks who they believed were being unlawfully held in bondage. The Davis case, though, would prove important in ways that the PAS would bitterly regret, as it led to the passage of the Fugitive Slave Act of 1793.[26]

The Constitution's fugitive slave clause, thrown together at the last minute at the Federal Convention, offered only the vaguest provision for rendering runaways to their masters. Aggrieved slaveholders were forced to resolve cases with local courts and police, which demanded more good faith and cooperation from the authorities than could be reasonably expected. The Davis case brought the problem to a head. In time, after the case had settled into a prolonged impasse, federal officials, prodded by President Washington, finally faced up to correcting the Constitution's indirection.

The Fugitive Slave Act, approved by Congress over minimal opposition and signed by Washington in February 1793, represented the latest victory for the slaveholders. The law clarified and affirmed the federal government's role in protecting property rights in slaves as inscribed in state laws. It laid out a process whereby a master or his agent could reclaim an alleged fugitive by providing proof of ownership (including a sworn affidavit or simple oral testimony) to any federal judge, state judge, or municipal magistrate. The law also provided masters with the right to sue any person who interfered with that process, and that person would be subject to a $500 penalty as well as liable for any "injuries" caused by the interference. The law failed, as the fugitive slave clause had, to assign final responsibility for enforcement, but in doing so it left considerable leeway to slaveholders and their agents, which in turn made the law vulnerable to gross abuse, including the kidnapping of free blacks under false pretenses—precisely the alleged outrage against John Davis that had initiated the case.

A rueful Pennsylvania Abolition Society warned that the new law would be "productive of mischievous consequences to the poor Negro Slaves appearing to be calculated with very unfavorable intentions towards them." These misgivings proved prescient, especially when the number of kidnappings of free blacks mounted during coming decades. In one crucial respect, though, the misgivings were misplaced. Echoing antislavery critics during ratification, the PAS complained that the bill had been "artfully framed" with "the word Slave avoided" in order to deflect public attention.[27] In fact, Congress had simply replicated the Constitution's wording, referring to fugitives not as slaves or servants but as persons "held to labor" or "fugitive[s] from labor," while it referred to masters as persons to whom "labor or service may be due."[28]

By repeating the Constitution, the new law also affirmed, perforce, the Federal Convention's refusal to validate slavery. And although the matter did not arise in the congressional debates or public discussion, that exclusion was all the more significant given the ratification a year earlier of the Bill of Rights. Originating in promises made by Madison and others in order to thwart Anti-Federalist criticism during the ratification struggle in 1787–1788, the amendments, specifically the Fifth Amendment's due process clause, would have guaranteed slavery full federal protection had the Constitution recognized property in man. The Fugitive Slave Act, by sustaining the fugitive slave clause's stipulations about persons "held to labor," instead offered protection to slaveholders' property in state law without actually recognizing slaves as property.

Not that there was any reason in 1793 for slaveholders to challenge the Constitution's exclusion, as they were able to gain the federal security they desired without doing so. The paradox of 1787 persisted, in a Constitution that at once protected slavery and excluded it—and with respect to fugitive slaves, the paradox protected and entrenched slavery more than ever. In time, though, the balance of political forces would shift, placing slaveholders on the defensive and pushing them to advance a skewed meaning of both the fugitive slave clause and the Fugitive Slave Act. The drawn-out change came by fits and starts, chiefly in struggles over western expansion that began in 1798 with the organization of Mississippi Territory.

In 1790, Congress created, with little debate, the Southwest Territory—what would become the state of Tennessee six years later—according to the same plan as the Northwest Territory but with the restriction of slavery removed.[29] (Based on the earlier plan's precedent, the lack of any congressional stipulation meant that slavery would be permitted in the Southwest Territory where slavery already existed, giving the deceptive superficial appearance that bondage and not freedom was the presumed natural state in the territories.) Organizing Mississippi Territory would be a bit more troublesome. Situated on the nation's remote southwestern edge, the territory was a large strip of land that lay west of the Georgia border along the Chattahoochee River and north of Spanish West Florida, bounded by the Mississippi River and latitude N 32° 28'—roughly the southern half of what would become the states of Alabama and Mississippi. The United States and Spain had disputed the area until 1795, when Spain ceded it in the Treaty of San Lorenzo, although Georgia would maintain a nominal claim over the lands as part of the Georgia cession until 1802. Modestly populated mainly by Choctaw, Chickasaw, and displaced British Loyalists, the territory included a small but thriving plantation economy, newly dedicated to cotton production, on the fabulously rich Mississippi River bottomlands of what was coming to be known as the Natchez District. In 1798, the federal government sought to consolidate American sovereignty by organizing the territory, and the resident planters pressed to ensure that it would be kept open to slavery. A surprise effort arose in Congress to ban slavery from the territory, and southerners and their northern allies fought back hard.[30]

That fight began at a particularly fraught moment. The great slave insurrection in Saint-Domingue in 1791 had brought years of brutal violence that would not end until the completion of Haitian independence in 1804; and the upheaval had badly shaken American slaveholders. Thomas Jefferson, remarking in 1793 on what he saw as the inevitable expulsion of whites from the West Indies, observed that it was "high time we should foresee the bloody scenes which our children certainly, and possibly ourselves (south of the Patowmac) have to wade through, and try to avert them." While some northerners, including the Connecticut democratic firebrand Abraham Bishop, hailed the revolution as a mighty blow for freedom, slaveholders now eyed their chattel human property with heightened anxiety. The events signaled to some Americans the need to reinforce slavery where it existed and to others the imperative of halting further importation of Africans as soon as possible. Some Americans heeded both lessons.[31]

Partisan politics complicated the debate over Mississippi Territory. Since 1793, distinct party divisions had arisen out of fights over finance and foreign policy, pitting pro-administration Federalists (not to be confused with the Federalists who supported the Constitution) against opposition Republicans, led by Thomas Jefferson and James Madison. The divisions were hardening in 1798, as President John Adams, having led the country into a quasi-war with France, signed the repressive Alien and Sedition Acts. The politics of slavery, though, did not follow strict party lines. Although the Republicans' national electoral base was in the South, a core group of northern Republicans, imbued with broad egalitarian ideals—Bishop among them—voiced their opposition to slavery's expansion. Northern Federalists, meanwhile, generally lined up with the slaveholders, even as undaunted antislavery Federalists parted ways with their conservative colleagues and accused antislavery Republicans of hypocrisy for supporting a party headed by two Virginia slaveholders. When the Massachusetts Federalist representative George Thacher, a firm supporter of the Alien and Sedition Acts as well as a tireless antislavery advocate, rose to announce that he wished to make a motion "touching on the rights of man," he might have been taken to be chiding his slaveholder Republican adversaries.[32] But his motion, which called for banning slavery in Mississippi Territory, opened a debate in which Thacher's chief allies would be antislavery Republicans.

Thacher was a Harvard-educated, four-term congressman from Biddeford in the District of Maine, and a collaborator with the organized abolitionists. In effect, he was taking a step beyond even the Pennsylvania Abolition Society petitioners in 1790, bidding the House directly to eliminate slavery completely where it had the authority to do so, in a national territory. With no compunction about declaring that the national government "had the right to take all due measures to diminish and destroy slavery"—to the point of suggesting it might well interfere with existing property rights—Thacher must have known that his proposal would fail.[33] Lower South slaveholders such as the South Carolina Federalist John Rutledge (son of the delegate to the Federal Convention) could be counted upon to denounce it as an attack on the Natchez planters' rights—"we must take from you your property," Rutledge mocked—and as a broader invitation to "set your blacks at liberty to cut your throats." Robert Goodloe Harper, another leading South Carolina Federalist, would inveigh against the proposal as an unacceptable attack not just on the resident slaveholders but on all those who would "carry with them property of this kind" into Mississippi.[34]

Just as important, the slaveholding states—their numbers, even with the three-fifths clause, not nearly sufficient to carry the House on their own—enjoyed the support of influential northerners.[35] Secretary of State Timothy Pickering, a determined Massachusetts Federalist, was also an avowed antislavery man, but his report to Congress on Mississippi emphasized the necessity of satisfying the Natchez planters, which meant throwing open the territory to slavery. Northern Federalists in the House spoke as if the only right of man that mattered was man's right to property, including property in man. The estimable Harrison Gray Otis of Massachusetts, for one, insisted that "it was not the business of those who had nothing to do with that kind of property to interfere with that right," and then, sounding more like a Lower South slaveholder with his mind on Saint-Domingue, he conjured up fantasies of savage blacks slaughtering Mississippi whites. "The territory in question will be settled by people from the Southern States," he concluded, "who cannot cultivate the ground without slaves."[36]

The only representatives to speak in support of Thacher's amendment were two eminent northern Republicans, Joseph Varnum of Massachusetts and the party's House floor leader, Albert Gallatin of Pennsylvania—and they shattered the arguments of Thacher's critics. Banning slavery from Mississippi Territory on the same terms as the Northwest Ordinance, they observed, involved forbidding the admission of any more slaves, not stripping resident slaveholders of the slaves they already owned. (If the amendment stipulated that residents "should be deprived of this kind of property," Gallatin said, he would vote against it.) There was no reason to believe that excluding slavery from Mississippi Territory at this stage of its development would lead to any more unrest than had accompanied gradual emancipation in the northern states or slavery's exclusion from the Northwest Territory. At issue, they said, was the fundamental issue of slavery itself. "A proper respect for the rights of mankind," in Varnum's words, demanded halting "the existence of slavery any farther than it at present exists."

Put another way, slaveholders outside Mississippi had no rights to carry slaves with them into Mississippi Territory if Congress forbade it.[37]

Gallatin made a point of reminding his colleagues that the Constitution gave them ample power to check slavery's spread. Discounting Georgia's claim of sovereignty (previously raised in the debate by a New England Federalist), Gallatin asserted Congress' sole authority over the area. "The United States," he declared, "intend[s] to exercise jurisdiction over that Territory" as surely as it had over the Northwest Territory—and that meant with respect to slavery, as with every other matter. Congress's authority over slavery in the territories, he implied, was unambiguous, as stipulated in Article IV, Section 3 of the Constitution. The property claims of resident slaveholders would be respected, but not to the extent of overriding the will of Congress about the territory's future. "If we believe it is not conducive to the happiness of any people, but to the contrary, to legalize slavery, when we are about to form a Constitution for a Territory," Gallatin concluded, "its establishment ought to be prevented." Nobody rose to correct him. At the conclusion of the debate, Thacher, more of a radical on the issue than his supporters, declared that although destroying slavery "might injure the property of some individuals," he saw nothing wrong with forcing resident slaveholders to give up their slaves. In the end, though, he relented, saying that he would not oppose the continuation of slavery "for a limited period."[38]

The House then unceremoniously routed Thacher's motion, with only twelve members voting in favor. Even that measure of support was remarkable in view of the northern Federalist opposition.[39] To be sure, given the upshot of the Federalists' arguments, the outcome probably depended more on the urgency of consolidating American sovereignty in the unruly Southwest than with southerners' determination to open the territory to slavery. Still, proslavery forces in Congress now looked stronger than ever, having won in part thanks to forthright defenses by northern Federalists of slaveholders' property rights—rights that, with regard to resident slaveholders, even Thacher's supporters Varnum and Gallatin insisted should be respected. Combined with the Fugitive Slave Act of 1793, permitting slavery to continue to grow in Mississippi underscored how the Constitution's toleration of slavery could entail toleration of slavery's expansion.

In the long run, to be sure, Gallatin's remarks about the federal government's powers over slavery would prove equally significant. Georgia's claim to sovereignty clouded his claim that the federal government commanded sole jurisdiction; his assertion that the United States would exercise sovereignty in Mississippi initially concerned jurisdiction and then shifted into an avowal of congressional authority over slavery. More important, the constitutional matters he and Varnum raised remained moot in 1798, as the antislavery men lacked anything close to the majorities required to block slavery from Mississippi. Yet there seemed to be a basic agreement in the House that Congress at least possessed the power to legislate over slavery in the territories. Robert Goodloe Harper had opened the debate by pronouncing the Northwest Ordinance's regulation prohibiting slavery (unlike Thacher's proposal) "a very proper one," as the territory's residents came from non-slaveholding areas "and they had of course no slaves amongst them."[40] Gallatin restated with assurance Congress's authority to ban slavery in any of the territories, as if that authority was incontestable—and, indeed, no one contested him.

Still, the Mississippi Territory debates also cast a shadow of ambiguity over Congress's power to regulate slavery in the territories. Thacher, Varnum, and Gallatin spoke as if that power was absolute, short of (according to Varnum and Gallatin) interfering with slaveholders already in residence. The House majority evidently agreed. To Lower

South representatives, however, any effort by Congress to impede slave-holders from taking their slave property into territories that were suited to slavery would be wrong, as Robert Goodloe Harper observed. The claim did not directly challenge Congress's authority over slavery in the territories, let alone assert that the Constitution recognized property in man. But it did show an early uneasiness among slaveholders about Congress's authority to check slavery's expansion.

A few years later, slaveholders in the Senate explicitly allowed that Congress indeed possessed the constitutional authority to keep slavery out of the territories, including territories where slavery already existed—but only up to a point. By then, the nation had obtained vast new lands to the west—and by then, coincidentally, antislavery advocates were strong enough in Congress to build majorities on measures aimed at blocking slavery's expansion. One of these measures, connected to the domestic slave trade, unsettled the slaveholders and brought a clash over slavery, the Constitution, and property in man. That struggle was part of a turn of events in which, inside the Congress anyway, the antislavery side briefly prevailed.

Thomas Jefferson's election to the presidency in 1800–1801 coupled with the Democratic-Republicans' capture of congressional majorities preceded two momentous events connected to slavery: the Louisiana Purchase in 1803 and the closing of the Atlantic slave trade in 1807. Simultaneously, southern plantation slavery was being reborn, as the cotton revolution that was ignited in the 1790s created what would become the wealthiest and most powerful slave society in the world. National struggles over slavery, and particularly over slavery's expansion into new territories, fitfully became, as never before, struggles over the nation's future.

The Louisiana Purchase began as an effort to secure American authority over the vital port of New Orleans and wound up doubling the nation's land mass. Northern Federalists criticized such a sudden enlargement as a drain on the nation's resources. Some New Englanders attacked the purchase specifically as a cover for expanding slavery and with it the already outsized political power of the Jeffersonian South.[41] (Ironically, some of the most fervent New England nationalist defenders of the Constitution in 1787 and 1788 now suddenly decided to excoriate the framers for agreeing to the three-fifths clause; a few of them, notably the former secretary of state Timothy Pickering, plotted northern secession.)[42] Antislavery northern Republicans, meanwhile, supported the purchase but wanted to prevent any further growth of slavery in the territory, envisaging instead a land where white American farmers would prove, one Jeffersonian newspaper proclaimed, "that sugar can be produced on many plantations without slaves."[43] A few antislavery Republicans, including the aging Revolutionary hero Thomas Paine, suggested making Louisiana lands available to northern free blacks as well.[44]

In January 1804, the bill to organize the lower portion of Louisiana Territory, designated Orleans Territory, came before the Senate, advanced by John Breckinridge of Kentucky in close consultation with his ally and confidant, President Jefferson. The American Convention for Promoting the Abolition of Slavery swiftly sent a petition calling for a complete prohibition on importing slaves into the territory—and though the Senate would never go that far, there was considerable sentiment in favor of restricting slavery. The Jefferson-Breckinridge plan, anticipating the abolition of the Atlantic slave trade, included a ban on the foreign slave trade as well as on domestic trade from any state that imported African slaves. (The second part of the proposal was aimed directly at South Carolina, which had reopened its Atlantic slave trade in 1803.) For Jefferson, closing off importation of slaves from abroad while sustaining the domestic slave trade would be a vehicle for promoting the idea that defusing the slave population in the West would somehow hasten emancipation. James Hillhouse of Connecticut—a conservative High Federalist with antislavery sentiments who had voted against the purchase and joined in the New England secessionist plotting—defended the administration's proposals in the face of strong opposition from the Lower South. After two days of debate, Hillhouse moved a ban on the introduction of slaves into Louisiana from foreign ports, which passed by 21 votes to 6.[45]

The vote, in which all of the Upper South senators sided with the majority, was not entirely surprising, as the act organizing Mississippi Territory had contained a similar provision, proposed by Robert Goodloe Harper and approved shortly after George Thacher's proposal failed. Closing Mississippi to the international slave trade four years before Congress could exercise its authority to do so would not materially harm the prospects of most slaveholders; indeed, it would only increase prices in the emerging domestic slave trade. But lower Louisiana around New Orleans, with its well-established sugar plantations, had relied on the overseas slave trade far more than Mississippi had, and some Lower South slaveholders, along with resident Creole Louisiana planters, could only see the ban as a terrible blow to the development of plantation slavery in the lower Mississippi Valley.[46] Hillhouse's motion nevertheless passed convincingly, and he was prepared to push on, much further than Jefferson and Breckinridge had intended—to commence the elimination of slavery in Louisiana altogether or, short of that, to cut the territory off from the domestic as well as the international slave trade.

Over the ensuing week, senators from both parties backed three more antislavery Louisiana proposals, all presented by Hillhouse.

(Originally, Hillhouse proposed two additional amendments but the second was in time divided in two.) They included a measure that would have introduced a plan for gradual emancipation, limiting the terms of adult slaves brought into the territory to one year. "I am in favor of excluding slavery from [Louisiana] altogether," Hillhouse intoned, although he emphasized that his chief concern was that, if slavery were allowed, uprisings like the one that had devastated Saint-Domingue would follow.[47] The debate over Hillhouse's amendments in turn proved auspicious—for even though the amendments ultimately failed to check slavery's expansion, they initiated what would prove a fleeting victory for the antislavery cause.

The Senate speedily rejected Hillhouse's emancipation amendment by a vote of 17 to 11, but the margin was not quite as convincing as it looked.[48] Had four of the seven northerners who opposed the amendment voted the other way, the Senate would have approved what might well have been a historic blow against slavery's expansion. One opponent was the young John Quincy Adams of Massachusetts, who resisted all of the Hillhouse amendments not over slavery but because he saw them as part of a hasty imposition of a constitution on the people of a far-off territory without their consent.[49]

On the other two proposals, though, Hillhouse and his allies prevailed: the Senate agreed to ban from Louisiana slaves who had been imported to the United States after an unspecified date (later to be fixed at 1798), and, by a narrower margin, voted to permit only United States citizens who were bona fide settlers and owners of slaves to bring slaves into the territory, thereby indirectly closing Louisiana Territory to the domestic slave trade. The temporary absence from Washington of both South Carolina senators, who were detained and would not appear until later in the session, aided the antislavery efforts, both in the debates and in the voting tallies, but the successes were still impressive.

Quincy Adams, meanwhile, was the only northerner who opposed all four of Hillhouse's amendments, just as he would oppose every motion directly connected with the organization of Louisiana Territory on which he voted.

As it happened, though, even as he took his principled stand over an issue that had nothing to do with slavery, Adams would end up making an important antislavery contribution. Elected to the Senate a year earlier, at age thirty-six he had already served as minister to the Netherlands, Portugal, and Prussia (earning praise from President Washington as the most valuable of America's officials abroad); he had become an attorney and won election to the Massachusetts state senate; and he had also undertaken serious scholarly study that would soon lead to his being named Boylston Professor of Rhetoric and Oratory at Harvard. Although still a member of his father's Federalist Party, Adams supported the Louisiana Purchase, the first step on a road that within five years would lead party leaders in Massachusetts to brand him an apostate. Openly antagonistic to slavery, Adams was not yet an antislavery stalwart. At one point early in the Louisiana debate he remarked that "slavery is in a moral sense an evil," but nevertheless, "as connected with comer[c]e it has important uses."[50] Yet Adams was already wary of the slaveholders' sway over national politics.

Hillhouse's proposal to ban slaves imported after a specified date (aimed directly, like the administration plan, at South Carolina) carried by 21 votes to 7, although not without a passing argument over slavery and the Constitution. (Jonathan Dayton of New Jersey, who had been a delegate to the Federal Convention and was now siding with proslavery hard-liners, wondered whether the proposal interfered with the Constitution's granting to states the potential ability to import slaves before 1808; Hillhouse agreed that it interfered "& justly.")[51] But Hillhouse's final proposal, to permit only bona fide settlers to enter with slaves, rankled a number of southerners who previously had supported him, including John Breckinridge.

To this point in the debates, the consensus had held regarding Congress's authority to regulate and even ban slavery in a territory, including territories like Louisiana where slavery was already well entrenched and which were clearly hospitable for slavery's further expansion. The slaveholder Samuel Smith of Maryland, who strongly opposed interfering with slavery in Louisiana, granted that "we have a constitutional right to prohibit slavery in that country."[52] After he supported Hillhouse on blocking slaves imported after a certain date from Louisiana, Breckinridge—who though himself the owner of a considerable number of slaves, frequently proclaimed his opposition to slavery— affirmed that "we can make laws to prevent slaves, & we can carry those into effect."[53]

But Hillhouse's proposal on bona fide settlers struck Breckinridge and some other southern senators as unwise and most likely unconstitutional. By indirectly banning the domestic slave trade from the vast Louisiana Territory, it would curb slaveholders' rights in existing states to do with their property in slaves whatever they pleased, including sell them to dealers in the new territory. It would also restrict the movement of slaveholders as well as slaves considerably more than the administration had proposed, prohibiting masters, for example, from bringing inherited slaves into Louisiana. Congress might do what it wanted in governing the territories, Breckinridge and others allowed, but the moment it impinged on slaveholders in existing states, it violated those slaveholders' property rights.

Whether intended or not, these assertions carried significant and unsettling implications. In raising the constitutional issue, southerners declared that property rights in slaves were not simply creatures of state law that Congress was bound to respect, but that they extended at least in part into territories where Congress enjoyed plenary power. Once Congress decided to open a territory to slavery, they charged, it did not have the power to prevent anyone bearing slaves from settling there. To secure that point, southerners duly proposed that Hillhouse's final proposal be stricken from consideration, and soon enough, some of them, including Breckinridge, found themselves arguing that the Constitution actually did recognize and authorize property in man.[54]

David Stone, a North Carolina Republican, would state the pro-slavery case most bluntly at a later stage of the debate, rebutting Hillhouse's amendment with a syllogism: as "slaves are property" and as "the rights of property are by the Constitution guaranteed," then "why should the holders of this kind of property be prohibited from sending & selling their slaves in Louisiana[?]"[55] Breckinridge, having said that Congress could decide whether to admit slavery into Louisiana, somewhat illogically continued that, nevertheless, "our Constitution recognizes slavery—it does more[,] it *expressly* protects it." Breckinridge feared that the amendment, by barring the entry of slaves from the United States into Louisiana, would "thereby prohibit men of wealth from the Southern states going to settle in that country."[56] The Virginia Republican and slaveholder Abraham Bedford Venable backed up Breckinridge's constitutional reasoning with a conceit that had been familiar in proslavery as well as antislavery circles since the ratification debates: that although the word "slavery" did not actually appear, the Constitution "admits the *thing* and protects it—& Congress [has] uniformly acted accordingly."[57] Unspoken but implied in those remarks was the claim—foreshadowed by James Madison at the Virginia ratification convention—that the fugitive slave clause, since reinforced by Congress with the Fugitive Slave Act of 1793, provided slavery with its absolute constitutional safeguards.

Without always flatly declaring property rights in man absolute in national law, the southerners' objections took a large step in that direction, and John Quincy Adams answered the claims head-on in a rejoinder to Breckinridge. If he were forced to vote on giving a government to Louisiana, Adams said, he would vote in favor of liberty—for, he proclaimed, "the Constitution does not recognize *slavery*—it contains no such word." The framers had had to resort to "a great circumlocution," Adams admitted, in order "merely to avoid the word *slaves*," but their aim had been to exclude slavery from the Constitution.[58] It followed, Adams implied, that even if Congress chose to permit slavery in a territory, it could hinder the domestic slave trade into that territory. Adams would vote against this final Hillhouse amendment, in keeping with his opposition to any measure connected to the territory bill, but against its critics, he upheld the Constitution's exclusion of property in man. As soon as he and Venable concluded a back-and-forth on the word "slavery," the Senate defeated, by a narrow margin in a sectional vote, the southern effort to strike it down, with Adams providing a crucial nay vote.[59]

The next day, a revised version of the last of the Hillhouse amendments, limiting the category of "bona fide residents" to American citizens, passed the Senate by a vote of 18 to 11.[60] Two weeks later, at the conclusion of the Louisiana Territory debates, a clutch of senators, mainly from slaveholding states, tried once more to get the amendment stricken, but their motion failed by 19 votes to 9.[61] While approving historic restrictions of the domestic as well as international slave trade— together, the strongest limitation of slavery placed by Congress on any part of the South until slavery's abolition in 1865—the Senate sustained congressional authority, even in an area where slavery already existed to a considerable extent. The House would do the same on an even larger scale a month later, when it narrowly approved an amendment introduced by the pugnacious abolitionist and Democratic-Republican James Sloan of New Jersey. Sloan's radical proposal would have killed slavery in Louisiana by summarily prohibiting the importation of slaves "as well from the United States, as from foreign places"—basically what the abolitionist American Convention (with which Sloan was associated) had asked for in its petition, and roughly the same plan that the House had voted down decisively six years earlier with respect to Mississippi Territory.[62]

These victories, real enough in Congress, soon enough proved illusory, and antislavery advocates in the end failed miserably to keep slavery out of Louisiana. Sloan's amendment died when the Senate refused to agree to it. The Hillhouse restriction on the domestic slave trade passed the House and appeared in the final territorial organization act, but it raised a furor among resident Creole slaveholders in Louisiana and was never effectively enforced.[63] Orleans Territory—which in 1812 would be admitted to the Union as the state of Louisiana—swiftly became a haven for newcomer plantation slaveholders as well, and the city of New Orleans, tying in to the burgeoning domestic slave trade, became a thundering slave market, the largest in the nation, as well as the key entrepôt of the ever-expanding cotton boom.

Yet if the proslavery advocates eventually got their way, the debate over Louisiana at least showed that antislavery advocates were becoming a more substantial force inside Congress, one that, under the right circumstances, could now raise majorities for measures explicitly framed to block slavery's expansion. The antislavery side's passing success had instigated a claim that the Constitution expressly protected property in slaves—and that claim had been rejected. Antislavery representatives, far from discouraged, would quickly return to the fray, deepening congressional divisions over slavery.

One year after his momentary triumph during the Louisiana controversy, James Sloan introduced, as a motion in the House, a plan for gradual emancipation in the District of Columbia, effective the following Fourth of July. The federal government had moved to the District only five years earlier; both slavery and the domestic slave trade had persisted and thrived there, as permitted by the act passed in 1790 that obtained the area from Maryland and Virginia. Consequently, as the Constitution granted Congress sole jurisdiction over the District, Sloan seized an opportunity to test, in an entirely new way, Congress's implied antislavery powers. The House defeated Sloan's motion overwhelmingly, refusing even to send it to a committee, but his provocation did its work.[64] A year later, the stridently proslavery Georgia Democratic-Republican Peter Early, in a speech to the Senate on the Atlantic slave trade, likened the impact of Sloan's "celebrated resolution" to the uproar over the Quaker and abolitionist petitions in 1790: "All will recollect the height to which feelings of men were wrought on those occasions."[65] In a single maneuver, Sloan and his friends had shown that the abolitionist cause survived, as creative and disquieting as ever.

The debates over abolishing the Atlantic slave trade further strained sectional amity, and raised once more the issues of property rights and congressional authority. President Jefferson's overall record on slavery was at best contorted and self-serving, but his long-standing opposition to the Atlantic slave trade was principled and effective. In December 1806, more than a year prior to the earliest abolition date under the Constitution, Jefferson asked Congress to prepare slave trade legislation; the next day, the Democratic-Republican senator Stephen Row Bradley of Vermont announced his intention to introduce a bill; and a few days after that, the House appointed a committee to take up the matter.

Over the next two months, the House and Senate worked on their respective versions of the abolition bill. At every step, the debate shaped up the same way: despite the contrasting fears of proslavery and antislavery critics of the Constitution in 1788, strong majorities in both houses of Congress favored the basic idea of abolishing the trade. Yet there were also intense conflicts over fine points, as southern congressmen once again fought doggedly to win concessions.[66]

One of the most controversial details concerned the fate of slave smugglers and illicitly imported slaves when apprehended. The compromises finally arrived at mandated that all slaves would be forfeited to state authorities (and not simply freed) and that convicted slave traders would be liable to a heavy fine and up to four years imprisonment (and not the death penalty, as had been proposed)—both large victories for the slaveholders. Yet in granting these concessions, antislavery congressmen took care to ensure that nothing in them would smuggle into the Constitution "the false principle," in the words of Massachusetts Democratic-Republican Barnabas Bidwell, "that a property may be had in human beings."[67] On another issue, meanwhile, hard-line slaveholders fell short, to the bitter disappointment of the eccentric, implacable Virginia defender of southern rights, John Randolph of Roanoke.

The slave trade debates coincided with Randolph's greatest national prominence, just as a mounting feud with his cousin, President Jefferson, became an open schism. Alarmed at what he considered Jefferson's betrayal of strict republican principles, estranged by what he considered Jefferson's personal treachery, Randolph had now emerged as a chief spokesman of the so-called Old Republicans (or Tertium Quids), neither Jeffersonian nor Federalist—one of the nation's preeminent foes of consolidated federal power, especially as it might touch

Virginia's ruling class. A large slaveholder who denounced slavery as immoral, Randolph also defended the institution as a practical imperative. ("The question of slavery, as it is called," he wrote, "is to us a matter of life and death.")[68] Accordingly, he perceived the slightest accretion of national authority as a step toward forced emancipation and northern despotism.[69] And when he detected such authority in a provision concerning abolition of the slave trade, he worked himself up into a disunionist fervor.

The dispute began when the Senate rejected a measure approved by the House that would have preserved the interstate seaborne coastal slave trade. Randolph, incensed, extrapolated that without the exemption, slaveholders would soon be prohibited from traveling from one state to another with their slave property. A special House committee proposed a compromise that would permit abolition of the coastal trade of slaves imported after 1807 in ships weighing less than forty tons. As the coasting trade relied heavily on the lighter ships, the compromise, if passed, would be a substantial setback for the proslavery stalwarts. Randolph protested that as the proposal "touched on the right of private property," it "might be made the pretext of universal emancipation." By a healthy margin, though, the House approved the weight provision.[70]

Randolph refused to quit. If he could not stop the weight provision, he would append to it an "explanatory act" that repudiated "all Constitutional right, title, or authority, whatsoever, by any legislative act, in any wise to abridge, modify, or affect the right of property of masters of slaves not imported to the United States" after 1807. Randolph appeared to be seeking the kind of impervious protection that nothing short of a constitutional amendment could actually achieve; without this protection, he asserted, there would be nothing left for the South to do but "secede, and go home." The antislavery Pennsylvanian John Smilie made light of the threat, saying that if the southern states were "disposed" to disunion, then Congress should permit them to secede and descend into their own destruction. None of the southern states was so disposed, and Congress abolished the Atlantic slave trade with the weight provision intact, absent any explanatory act.[71]

Contrary to proslavery hopes and antislavery fears in 1787, the Constitution's twenty-year delay in authorizing abolition of the Atlantic slave trade had not doomed that abolition. Instead, abolitionists, black and white, immediately acclaimed the new law as a monumental advance. ("Hail! hail! glorious day," the Rev. Peter Williams Jr. orated at New York's celebration assembly at the city's African Church, "whose resplendent rising, disperseth the clouds, which have hovered with destruction over the land of Africa.")[72] Atop James Sloan's incitement about gradual emancipation in Washington, the slave trade battle revealed once again that northern antislavery sentiment was sizable, articulate, and far from passive—and that, as ever, it was set on affirming the Constitution's exclusion of the "false principle" of property in man. Yet the abolition of the Atlantic trade hardly cleared the way for slavery's demise, as so many abolitionists had hoped. The cotton boom, a renaissance in plantation slavery, and the rise of a vast domestic slave market had killed the prospect that closing the Atlantic trade in itself would prove slavery's coup de grâce. Even with respect to the international commerce in slaves, which did decline dramatically, the abolition law would not enforce itself, and backing that enforcement would remain a matter of hot contention for many years to come. During the fight over the abolition bill, meanwhile, proslavery southerners had once again proven themselves highly resourceful in winning concessions from their northern colleagues. They would remain just as tenacious during the ensuing fifteen years, when national political struggles over slavery reverted to the West.

In April 1812, two months before the United States went to war with Great Britain, President James Madison signed the legislation that admitted Orleans Territory into the Union as the state of Louisiana, with a state constitution that authorized slavery. Louisiana's admission stirred little controversy. Seven years later, though, Congress's debates over the admission of Missouri and the organization of adjoining Arkansas Territory, both with slavery, unleashed political pandemonium.[73]

Much had changed in the interim. The return of regular commerce with Britain in 1815 fully unleashed the cotton boom. Southern defensiveness over slavery as a necessary evil had begun to recede in favor of more pointed proslavery assertions. Mississippi Territory, enlarged to include all of the Georgia cession lands, became the new slave states of Alabama and Mississippi. The impending acquisition of the Floridas under the Adams-Onís Treaty with Spain augured a further expansion of American slavery's dominion. In the North, meanwhile, gradual emancipation brought the emergence of increasingly vocal free black communities, especially in Philadelphia and New York. Continued antislavery activities at the local and state levels led to additional reforms, most auspiciously New York's general emancipation act in 1817. A rise in the number of kidnappings of free blacks as a result of the Atlantic slave trade's abolition led northern states along the Mason-Dixon Line to enact anti-kidnapping laws. In Indiana and Illinois Territories, antislavery forces defeated, if only barely, efforts to countermand the Northwest Ordinance and reintroduce slavery.

Dramatic demographic as well as economic shifts also reversed old expectations regarding the Constitution and slavery. With the cotton boom, the expansion of the plantation economy to the southwest, and the emergence of an enormous domestic slave trade, the abolition of the Atlantic slave trade did not at all prove the death knell of the slave trade, as antislavery advocates had expected and Lower South slaveholders had feared. At the same time, however, the widely expected movement of population to favor the South and Southwest never occurred, as settlement of migrants and new immigrants disproportionately favored the North. In the House apportionment based on the 1790 census (including Kentucky), the free states had 57 representatives and the slave states had 48 representatives; in 1800, the free states had 76 representatives and the slave states had 65; in 1820, the division was 123 to 90. The three-fifths clause did keep the South from becoming a hopeless minority, but it failed to build the slaveholding majority that many had anticipated. Representation based on population, which under the terms of the Constitution seemed to some destined to give the slaveholders a virtual veto over legislation concerned with slavery, increasingly favored the free North. The same held true for the apportionment of the Electoral College.[74]

Finally, the commencement of the so-called Era of Good Feelings in 1815 had profoundly changed the dynamics of national politics. Outside of New England, the Federalist Party collapsed, creating a virtual one-party national system dominated by slaveholding southern Republicans. When the third Virginia slaveholder in a row, James Monroe, won the presidency in 1816, slavery's command of national politics seemed more certain than ever. Yet Federalism's demise also loosened the partisan bonds that had restrained antislavery opinion in both parties. The northern majority in the House, despite the three-fifths clause, became especially glaring after 1810.[75] Swelling antislavery opinion in the North lacked only an issue to make its presence felt in national politics. In April 1818, Arthur Livermore, a congressman from New

Hampshire, proposed a constitutional amendment that would ban slavery in newly organized territories and all new states. The House refused even to put it up for debate—but the antislavery forces were just getting started.[76]

Six months later, an obscure first-term congressman from Pough-keepsie, New York, James Tallmadge, tried to make a stand over Illinois. An independent-minded antislavery Republican, Tallmadge was allied with the New York supporters of DeWitt Clinton, who were increasingly disaffected over southern control of their party. Tallmadge strongly objected when, in 1818, Illinois applied for statehood with a constitution that included provisions for slavery in a limited area of the state, a draconian indenture system, and harsh restrictions on blacks' personal and civil rights. Plainly, he charged, the proposed constitution violated the Northwest Ordinance, but regardless of the ordinance, "the interest, honor, and faith of the nation" demanded that congressmen halt slavery "where they have the power to prevent its entrance." In the brief House debate that followed, the Kentuckian Richard Anderson pointed to "serious doubts" about Congress's authority to attach any conditions about slavery to admitting a new state, but he objected chiefly to Congress rejecting a constitution duly framed and approved by the citizens of Illinois. A small knot of northern antislavery Republicans rallied to support Tallmadge, but the House rejected his amendment by 117 votes to just 34.[77]

A year later, fights over the new state of Missouri and the reorganized Arkansas Territory galvanized antislavery northerners in the House and forced a major crisis. Both areas had been carved out of the southeastern portion of Missouri Territory, which itself had been created in 1812 and consisted of all the Louisiana Purchase lands north of the new state of Louisiana. Both areas had been left open to slavery. Missouri, the more populous of the two, lay on the western border of

Illinois, and had become a center for hemp production and home to upward of ten thousand slaves, roughly 15 percent of its total population. Having met all of the constitutional requirements, the white settlers applied for admission to the Union. Sandwiched between the proposed new state and Louisiana was Arkansas Territory, a rugged terrain, sparsely settled and with a smaller proportion of slaves. Given slavery's substantial presence in Missouri and given Arkansas's location, it was widely assumed that both the new state and the new territory would remain open to slavery.[78]

Tallmadge ignited his Missouri bombshell in the House in February 1819, near the end of the congressional session. His two-part amendment required, first, that the new state's constitution bar any further introduction of slavery, and second, that it include a gradual emancipation plan, in this case along the lines of New York's emancipation law of 1799. After more than two days of searing debate, the House approved both proposals by votes of 87–76 and 82–78, respectively, and sent them to the Senate. Southerners voted almost unanimously against both proposals; the northerners broke 86–10 and 80–14 in favor.[79] For the first time ever, a chamber of Congress had voted to eliminate slavery in an area under its jurisdiction including an emancipation plan for resident slaves. The day after the vote, Tallmadge's close ally from New York (and a future Speaker of the House), John W. Taylor, introduced a similar clause "to prohibit the existence of slavery in the new Territory" of Arkansas.[80]

The two sets of amendments raised different constitutional issues. Missouri was applying for full statehood, and, as the debate over Illinois showed, Congress had not yet settled whether it could refuse to admit a new state over the existence of slavery. Because Missouri's admission, though, involved slavery in the entire state, not a limited portion as in Illinois, northerners were aroused as they had not been a year earlier. Southerners contended that the Constitution did not empower Congress to block a new state over slavery. Northerners replied that until Missouri was formally admitted, it remained a territory over which Congress could exercise complete authority.

Arkansas Territory seemingly presented a more straightforward situation. As recently as the admission of Louisiana Territory in 1804, slaveholders had conceded Congress's authority over slavery in the territories. Proslavery advocates had beaten back efforts to ban slavery in Mississippi and Louisiana Territories, but not on the grounds that Congress was prohibited by the Constitution from doing so. Under the pressure of the debates over Missouri, though, some slaveholders—"the zealots," John Quincy Adams called them—counterattacked by contending that Congress was powerless over slavery in the territories as well, or at the very least those territories, including Arkansas, obtained in the Louisiana Purchase.[81] As justification, they advanced new claims that the Constitution actually recognized property in man, which precluded any congressional restrictions.

The initial southern ripostes to Taylor's Arkansas amendment, to be sure, ran an erratic gamut, ranging from accusations that Taylor was slandering the South to denunciations of his proposal as "an entering wedge" for national emancipation. (Speaker Henry Clay accused Taylor of Negrophobia, which elicited a prickly reply from Taylor that the debate over Arkansas in fact revealed that fear of blacks prevailed not in the North but the South, where "it haunts its subjects in their dreams, and disturbs their waking hours.") Hugh Nelson of Virginia shifted the debate to constitutional grounds. Had their predecessors proposed the principles embodied in Taylor's amendment, Nelson asserted, "the Federal Constitution would never have been formed"; and if the antislavery men persisted, he warned, the Union would be dissolved. Taylor was incredulous, insisting that the Constitution gave Congress "full and undisputed sovereignty" over the territories: "Has it then come to this? Is the preservation of our Union made to depend on the admission of slavery into a territory not belonging to the States when the Constitution was adopted?"[82]

Felix Walker of North Carolina and Louis McLane of Delaware rose to say, in effect, that it *had* come to this, and their remarks pressed what would become a full-scale proslavery counteroffensive over property and congressional authority. Walker charged that "the great and radical objection" to Taylor's amendment was its denial of "the people of this territory the natural and Constitutional right of legislating for themselves." Here was the germ of an argument that, thirty years later, would become known as the doctrine of "popular sovereignty," but Walker had further constitutional objections. The proposed amendment, he claimed, violated the framers' great compromise of 1787, which, he asserted, "conceded that the slaveholding States were to hold an equal portion of policy, and enjoy the same advantages as other States in the Union," with respect to the territories as with anything else. As the Louisiana Purchase had been paid for with national funds—with the southern states contributing "their full share"—so slaveholders were "morally and politically entitled to equal advantages of the soil" in Arkansas.[83]

Walker made no case for the institution of slavery, which he called "an evil we have long deplored but cannot cure"; he upheld a notion that had gained popularity in the Upper South and Border States—and was favored most famously by Thomas Jefferson—that diffusing slavery into the territories would ameliorate the slaves' condition and actually hasten their emancipation. Congress, however, could do nothing to keep slaveholders from settling in Arkansas, or, by implication, in any other territory formed out of the Louisiana Purchase lands. Nor could Congress bar the new territory's residents from establishing slavery under a new territorial government.[84]

McLane, representing a border state, protested even more his dislike of slavery—an evil, he said, "unfortunately entailed on us." He then adverted to the existence of slavery prior to the Louisiana Purchase in the lands now being organized as Arkansas (as well as in Missouri), and to the subsequent removal of slaveholders with their slaves to the territory. The 1803 Louisiana Purchase treaty with France, he noted, expressly guaranteed all extant residents "free enjoyment" of their property, which obviously included slaves; thereafter, those residents were to enjoy all the rights, advantages, and immunities secured United States citizens by the Constitution. These rights, McLane insisted, included "the right of holding slaves if they please to do so."[85]

Quite apart from the Louisiana treaty, meanwhile, McLane argued that to deprive resident slaveholders of their slaves would plainly violate the masters' property rights—and no less importantly, the rights of slaveholders who henceforth wanted to enter the territory "with the bona fide intention of residing permanently therein." To prohibit any further introduction of slavery would be to deny those who chose to inhabit the territory "the right and privilege of deciding for themselves" whether the territory ought to be open to slavery. With a territory no less than with a newly admitted state, Walker concluded, the Constitution posed "an insuperable barrier" to congressional restriction of slavery. And though, for the moment, he limited himself to talking about Louisiana lands, it was an argument that, abstractly, could be applied to any future territory obtained by the United States—or, for that matter, to anywhere that fell under Congress's jurisdiction.[86]

At the root of the matter, for both Walker and McLane, was the imperative of protecting the slaveholders' property rights. A less radical strategy might have led them to point to ambiguities in the Constitution's wording that other southerners interpreted to mean that Congress's authority over the territories did not include authority over slavery.[87] But Walker and McLane took a stronger stand, based on the alleged inviolability of property in man. Apart from levying taxes, Walker contended, Congress had "no legitimate power to legislate on the property of the citizens" including property in slaves. Were Taylor's amendment approved, he said, Congress would have the power to "prohibit other species of property from crossing the Mississippi."

McLane was even more precise in asserting that outside of states where slavery was prohibited, property rights in slaves were absolute. The Constitution of the United States, he said, no less than the laws of the slaveholding states, "recognize[s] the interest of the owner of his slave as property." Indeed, McLane declared that "the Union is founded upon this principle," as disclosed by the Constitution's fugitive slave clause, which he represented as authorizing a master "to reclaim his slave on the ground of property." The citizens of a territory, he allowed, could choose to prohibit slavery, but for Congress to do it for them was a gross usurpation. Above all, in McLane's words, the Constitution guaranteed to "citizens of the United States, the right to possess slaves"—a right that was "unquestionable."[88]

McLane's reading of and reliance on the fugitive slave clause was erroneous but, by this time, not at all peculiar. The view that the fugitive slave clause somehow assured absolute protection against government interference dated back at least as far as Madison's ambiguous remarks to the Virginia ratification convention in 1788. Although not affirmed by Congress, that view had spread over the decades as a kind of popular, commonsense conception of the Constitution. It was not at all confined to the South: ambivalent northern courts, when dealing with fugitive slaves, generally held, first, that the Federal Convention had recognized slaveholders' property and, second, that this recognition had been an essential concession to the South in 1787–1788, without which the slaveholders would have spurned the Union. It was "well-known," the chief justice of the Pennsylvania Supreme Court William Tilghman declared in 1819, that the southern states would not have approved the Constitution "unless their property in slaves had been secured."[89]

Lacking Madison's notes on the Federal Convention, it was impossible to appreciate how far the framers had gone to preclude such a reading of the fugitive slave clause, let alone to show that the proslavery delegates had never presented it as a sine qua non. Close scrutiny of those notes (as we shall see) would produce a more accurate understanding, but without them there was enough plausibility to the idea for it to stick. As one historian has written, the "proslavery constitutional myth" about the fugitive slave clause "fortified the self-justification of more than one northern judge caught between the obligations of duty and the appeals of conscience."[90] A southern version of that myth almost certainly lay behind southern senators' claims about the Constitution and slavery during the Hillhouse amendment debates in 1804. Embroiled in the Arkansas controversy fifteen years later, McLane, taking the myth at face value, commenced turning it into a crucial argument in favor of extending slavery into the territories.

Sharp debate over Taylor's Arkansas amendment continued for two days, and the contest was extremely close. During the second day, the House twice narrowly rejected the proposed ban on introducing slaves to Arkansas, but it approved, also narrowly, Taylor's gradual emancipation plan. Only after further parliamentary maneuvering—including a tie-breaking vote by Speaker of the House Henry Clay on a crucial procedural motion—were both parts of the amendment barely defeated and Arkansas Territory declared organized with no restrictions on slavery.

It seems unlikely that these outcomes stemmed mainly from congressmen's concerns about congressional authority. House majorities, after all, simultaneously and repeatedly backed Tallmadge's amendment on Missouri, where Congress's powers were far less clear-cut. The new territory's location, with its southerly portion bordering Kentucky and Tennessee, probably swayed more votes than did questions about property rights and the Constitution. Yet congressmen Nelson, Walker, and McLane had directly challenged Congress's constitutional authority over slavery, to the point where a Massachusetts congressman, Ezekiel Whitman, felt it necessary, late in the struggle, to rebut them. A surviving Federalist, Whitman opposed restricting slavery as far south as Arkansas (though he supported doing so in Missouri), and he wanted to make clear that he did not question Congress's power to ban slavery in the territories if it so chose. "We certainly have this power," he declared. "The Territories are under the absolute control of the United States."[91] Whitman may have sensed a shift was under way inside Congress, as the continuing Missouri debates showed that a growing minority of southerners now flatly denied Congress's authority in either new states or the territories.

The Senate, where the slaveholders enjoyed a small but solid working majority, quickly rejected Tallmadge's Missouri amendment, but the House refused to concur. The Senate insisted and again the House refused, so the Missouri statehood bill was laid over until the next Congress, which would not assemble until the end of the year. Hopes that the interim months would temper passions over the bill died in late summer when northern antislavery advocates organized an impromptu and energetic Free Missouri campaign—an effort which, in calling for enactment of Tallmadge's amendments, insisted that, as one Delaware abolitionist group put it, "Congress can impart no right to citizens of the United States in regard to slavery."[92] State legislatures as well as mass meetings from Vermont to Delaware prepared Free Missouri memorials and petitions. Anti-extension pamphlets and commentary poured off northern presses, much of it distributed by the American Convention, which also coordinated antislavery strategy with the restrictionist forces in Congress. Beginning in January 1820, the House debated the amendment anew, which turned into an unusually rigorous and extended clash over the Constitution. Both sides were prepared to fight over every detail and nuance, and they did so at length, but without reaching any resolution. As the deadlock continued, it revealed a new and fundamental division about slavery's place in the Constitution.

Speaker after speaker from the slaveholding states hammered on a few key points. First and foremost, as Alexander Smyth of Virginia announced early in the debate, "the Constitution recognises the right to the slave property, and it thereby appears that it was intended, by the [Federal] Convention and by the people, that that property should be secure." Interference with that property by the federal government or any other body in any way was a violation of the slaveholders' guarantee of due process under the Fifth Amendment.[93] Several southerners had stated their willingness to concede that banning slaves in the territories, including Arkansas, was, as Charles Mercer of Virginia observed, "within the fair scope" of congressional power.[94] More hardline proslavery advocates, however, objected, insisting that the right to property in man was unconditional—"absolute and unqualified, as much so as to any property a man can possess," in the Kentuckian Benjamin Hardin's words—and that it was "unequivocally recognized by the Constitution."[95] The slaveholders asserted that the framers had supposedly made that explicit in the three-fifths clause and, even more clearly, in the fugitive slave clause, which, by upholding a master's right to reclaim his slaves, recognized those slaves as property. It was perfectly obvious to them that the wording of those clauses indisputably established property in man: "A person 'held to service of labor' is the constitutional and legal definition of the word 'slave,'" Smyth observed, in a neat tautology. Congress's authority over the rules and regulations of the territories did not extend to slavery any more than its authority over admitting new states did. "The whole nation sanctioned the right of slavery by adopting the Constitution," Smyth concluded.[96]

As the debates continued, a substantial element among the southerners supported this absolutist line, and its proponents spoke with rising assurance. "Rail at slavery as much as you please," Congressman (and future president) John Tyler of Virginia declared in a major speech, "I point you to the Constitution, and say to you that you have not only acknowledged our right to this species of property, but that you have gone much further, and have bound yourselves to rivet the chains of the slave." As the fugitive slave clause recognized slaves as property (or so Tyler imagined), as individual property rights were inviolable, and as the Louisiana lands, "purchased out a common purse," were the common possession of all the states, then any restriction of slavery's expansion, "even in regard to an unsettled territory," he said, "I should deny to be Constitutional."[97] (Several other southerners emphasized the point about common possession, asserting that as the territories carved out of the Louisiana Purchase were, as Richard M. Johnson of Kentucky had proclaimed in the Senate, "a common property, purchased with the money of the whole people," then slaveholders could not be prevented from settling there with their property in man.)[98] As if to settle once and for all any doubts about framers' intentions, Charles Pinckney of South Carolina, the aging proslavery leader from the Federal Convention and now a congressman, addressed the House with a lengthy and meandering excursus that bypassed the property matter but restated the key point, that Congress was powerless to inhibit slavery in either a new state or territory.[99] Other proslavery men advanced another of Pinckney's charges, that as the Confederation Congress lacked any power whatsoever over the territories, the clause on slavery in the Northwest Ordinance of 1787 was either of no effect or an outright usurpation, a "nullity," with "not the least color of Constitutional authority over its subject."[100]

Antislavery northerners rebutted these proslavery arguments point by point. "Slavery, sir, I repeat, is not established by our Constitution," Arthur Livermore proclaimed at the outset of the struggle.[101] The anti-restriction argument, Daniel Cook of Illinois observed, rested on the fallacy that "the right to hold slaves is guarantied by the Federal Constitution" and was thus immune to congressional interference. Slavery, Cook said, existed before the Constitution was framed, and the Federal Convention, in order to secure the Union, merely "provided against the invasion of that right in such of the then existing States" where slavery was legal. "The right to hold slaves, therefore, is not created by the Constitution," he said; nor did the Constitution elevate slavery into a "federal right," outside Congress's control. "It is a State right," he said, "or, in other words, a State wrong." None of the Constitution's compromises over slavery either created or recognized property in man, least of all the fugitive slave clause, which was "a necessary regulation that grew out of slavery's previous existence." The Northwest Ordinance, far from unconstitutional, was approved while the Federal Convention was still in session and was certainly known to and approved by the delegates, none of whom called it in violation of their own work; and the first Congress meeting under the new Constitution quickly affirmed it.[102] The evil of slavery was sufficiently strong in 1787 that the Constitution had to take it into account, William Hendricks of Indiana observed, "but, being an evil, the provisions of the Constitution never meant to foster and cherish it in the Government."[103]

The antislavery Vermont Republican Charles Rich delivered a full refutation of the slaveholders, and with it a summation of an emerging antislavery constitutionalism.[104] Although it pained him to oppose his longtime southern Republican allies, Rich said, he found it impossible to square the first principles of either the Declaration of Independence or the preamble of the Constitution with slavery. Although slavery existed at the nation's founding, this misfortune hardly necessitated slavery's continued existence. "By what charter of a national character," he asked, "[has] a right to hold a human being in slavery . . . ever been recognised?" The absence of the word "slavery" in the Constitution signaled that, although "for obvious reasons, [the framers] were obliged indirectly to admit the fact of its existence, they purposely, and very carefully, avoided the use of any expressions from which, by fair construction, even an argument could be derived in favor of its legitimacy." Any justification for slavery would have to be derived "by a reference to the laws of nature and natural rights, and not to the Constitution."

As slavery was strictly an unfortunate local institution, Rich asserted, Americans had an obligation, in accord with the laws of nature and natural rights, to prevent its extension, The Missouri question presented to the nation an irrevocable choice:

> Hitherto, slavery has not been so recognized by the General Government, as to cause our national character to be materially affected by it; for, although there are States in the Union which, from the necessity of the case, may be termed slaveholding States, it cannot, with truth, be alleged that, as a nation, we have permitted slavery. But if, under present circumstances, Congress shall solemnly decide that it cannot restrain the unlimited extension of it, and that a want of power to do so results from an unqualified recognition of it by the Constitution, our national character will become identified with it; and instead of its being, as heretofore, a

local malady, and susceptible of cure, it must henceforth be regarded as affecting the whole system, and past the hope or possibility of a remedy.

Rich bade his colleagues and countrymen to join in limiting "an evil which cannot at present be removed" or "diminished by dispersion"— hemming it in and keeping it a local institution "till removed, and our national character thereby preserved."[105]

By the time they concluded, the Missouri debates opened a breach that had been developing since 1787. With their compromises over slavery, the framers had created their terrible paradox, writing a Constitution that protected slavery but did not sanction it. For decades thereafter, through sporadic national fights connected to slavery, that paradox more or less held, until the debates over Arkansas and the crisis over Missouri shook it badly. Responding to a rising, aggressive antislavery insurgency, hard-line slaveholders now denied that the paradox had ever existed; the Federal Convention, they charged, had purposefully validated rights to property in man and rendered those rights absolute under the Constitution, which meant that the federal government could do nothing to restrict slavery in any new state or any territory—or at least any territory formed out of what had been Louisiana Territory. Antislavery advocates stuck by the paradox and insisted that the framers had purposefully excluded property in man from national law, which meant that the federal government could halt slavery's existence in any new state as well as any territory. Regarding Arkansas, the antislavery side could not quite win sufficient support to sustain its argument in Congress. Regarding Missouri, however, the restrictionists created an impasse. The crisis deepened in the Sixteenth Congress when the House approved an even stronger version of Tallmadge's amendment.

It required all of Speaker Henry Clay's enormous political skill to fashion a two-pronged compromise. The first part, pairing the admission of Missouri with that of the newly created state of Maine, made it possible to maintain parity between slaveholding and non-slaveholding states in the Senate. The second part had its origins in the debates over Arkansas. The pro-extension congressman Louis McLane floated a suggestion that the North and South might avoid future struggles by agreeing to fix a line of latitude above which slavery would not be permitted. (That McLane's proposal would also affirm Congress's authority over slavery in the territories obtained in the Louisiana Purchase apparently bothered him not at all.) John Taylor picked up the idea and, after his antislavery Arkansas amendment was finally defeated, he proposed setting a demarcation at latitude 36° 30′ across all of the Louisiana Purchase lands—a line that would have permitted slavery in Arkansas but banned it in Missouri. The proposal went nowhere, with some congressmen grumbling that it still sanctioned slavery and others that it gave too much to the North.[106]

As the Missouri stalemate worsened, the anti-restrictionist Illinois senator Jesse B. Thomas seized upon Taylor's proposal, altered it to permit slavery in Missouri (which lay above 36° 30′), and presented it to the Senate as a compromise amendment. In exchange for admitting Missouri with slavery, Congress would repudiate the southern zealots' absolutist view of property in slaves under the Constitution and acknowledge its own authority over slavery in the territories obtained in the Louisiana Purchase. The proposal showed how far the hard-liners had pulled the debate in their own direction, offering to antislavery northerners a concession on the exercise of a specific congressional power that until the Missouri debates had not been seriously challenged. Yet the most determined hard-liners, now convinced of the righteousness as well as the constitutional correctness of their position, also rejected the bargain as, in the words of the Old Republican senator Nathaniel Macon of North Carolina, "acknowledging too much."[107]

Macon and a handful of recalcitrants held out as long as they could—Macon until the bitter end—but the Senate approved the Thomas proposal handily with virtually universal northern support. Then it approved the amended bill by a much smaller margin—the latter vote a mark of how deeply the Missouri issue divided the sections.[108] Speaker Clay and his lieutenants immediately went to work in the House. Seeing the closeness of the final vote in the Senate, which was 24 to 20, Clay now shrewdly divided the two halves of the compromise. After a touch-and-go negotiation, the House finally approved, by a three-vote margin, Missouri statehood without restriction of slavery, then passed Thomas's 36° 30' amendment by a much larger margin. As if to add an exclamation point to Thomas's amendment, the House and Senate agreed to specify that its purpose was "to prohibit slavery in certain Territories."[109]

The so-called Missouri Compromise was really more of a well-managed bargain, breaking the logjam while allowing the most determined antislavery and proslavery forces to vote their beliefs. On the constitutional issues at the heart of the fight, Congress appeared to split the difference, abjuring the authority to block a state's admission over slavery while affirming its authority over slavery in the territories—including, contrary to the "equal advantages" argument, Louisiana Territory. In effect, the compromise shored up the paradox of 1787 by protecting slavery as a local institution while also denying it protection in national law. Yet the sectional differences remained deep: despite crucial defections, northern congressmen had voted 87 to 14 against slavery in Missouri, while only a bare majority of slave state congressmen had supported Thomas's amendment.[110] The crisis had also altered the political as well as the constitutional map: while antislavery northerners had threatened the slaveholders as never before, proslavery hard-liners had managed to make the affirmation of long-acknowledged congressional authority over slavery in the territories look like an indulgence—an indulgence they despised.

Both sides harbored their fear and loathing of each other; neither side abandoned its principles. Whatever else it hoped to accomplish in the future, the nation's political leadership would need to continue containing the furies unleashed in 1819 and 1820. But that would require suppressing a widening and essential breach about slavery and the nation itself, and whether the Constitution validated property in man.

Public reaction to the compromise was generally one of relief, but antislavery northerners expressed deep frustration at slavery's extension into Missouri. The New York *Daily Advertiser,* edited by the formidable ex-Federalist and ardent restrictionist Theodore Dwight, typified their disappointment, calling the compromise "a mere farce" that would fool no one "with sense enough to keep out of the fire."[111] At the other end of the spectrum, ardent anti-restriction southerners rejoiced when the Missouri statehood bill passed. John Randolph of Roanoke boasted that he and his allies could have pulled in as many votes as they needed from northerners he mocked as "doughfaces" to ensure Missouri's admission with slavery.[112] Charles Pinckney called the compromise a "great triumph" for the slaveholding states, in which they lost nothing except access to "a vast Tract, inhabited only by savages and wild beasts."[113] For many southerners, the real goal all along had been securing Missouri as a slave state, with the 36° 30′ restriction serving as, in one historians' words, "a consolation prize" to the North, useful (or so it was surmised) in giving some political cover to Randolph's "doughfaces."[114] Yet there was also a great deal of proslavery displeasure at the result, as well as measured antislavery satisfaction.

For some southerners, permitting Congress to prohibit slavery in any of the territories was too much to bear. In the southern press, conforming to the voting pattern inside the House, opposition to Thomas's amendment was loudest in Virginia, where the *Richmond Enquirer* described it as a disaster that left "a constitution warped from its legitimate bearings, an immense region of territory closed for ever against the Southern and Western people." The *Enquirer's* editor, Thomas Ritchie, had never believed the Union was seriously endangered, and he mourned the outcome: "We scarcely ever recollect to have tasted a bitterer cup. . . . What is a *territorial* restriction to-day becomes a *state* restriction to-morrow." A Norfolk editor wrote that he would have preferred no settlement to seeing constitutional guarantees "set at naught by congressional usurpation." Elsewhere, a constituent of one Kentucky congressman, not a slaveholder, called the compromise a swindle in which the South had exchanged "the restriction on the Territory [above 36° 30′], for a right to which Missouri was entitled without it."[115] The reaction may well have proved costly to those congressmen whom Clay persuaded to back Thomas's amendment: more than two-thirds of the inflexible southerners who voted against it were reelected in 1822, compared to only about two-fifths of those who supported it.

Antislavery northerners for their part expressed disgust at the House turncoats who had either "fled the field on the day of battle" or "betrayed us to the lords of the South" by voting to admit Missouri with slavery.[116] Northern antislavery mobs burned offending congressmen in effigy; William Plumer Sr. of New Hampshire wrote to his son, a member of the Senate, that for any northern member of either house of Congress to tolerate slavery's expansion was "political suicide."[117] Like the compromising southerners, the northern defectors and absentees seem to have paid dearly at the polls: only five of the eighteen would still be in Congress after the 1822 elections. Yet if outrage predominated, some antislavery advocates looked beyond the statehood settlement and embraced the 36° 30′ line as a partial victory on which they could build. Most conspicuously, the Pennsylvania Abolition Society—Benjamin Franklin's old group, whose members had commenced the congressional wrangling over slavery thirty years earlier— found reason for a cheer or two. Still very much at the center of the antislavery cause, the society had campaigned hard to restrict slavery in Missouri and was deeply saddened at the result, and yet, the society told its fellow abolitionist groups, it was not a total loss. "Limits have been set to the extension of that evil in our Western territories," the society observed, "and if the same spirit which dictated the late resistance to Slavery shall continue to be exerted, the shores of the Pacific, and a large extent of territory on the Missouri and Mississippi, will be saved from this scourge of humanity."[118]

The 36° 30′ concession would never make up for the loss of Missouri, but it would soon help buttress the antislavery constitutionalism that Charles Rich and others had begun to articulate during the congressional debates in 1820. Disgruntled slaveholders, meanwhile, would turn their frustration into a new departure. Once they had formulated their absolutist view of the Constitution and slavery, proslavery hard-liners would not abandon it. Over the coming decades, as the nation expanded far beyond the Louisiana Purchase lands, they would proclaim that view and toughen it in renewed fights over slavery's future. At every step, they would be provoked and battled by antislavery campaigners who continued to take inspiration and guidance from the framers' exclusion of property in man.

5

Antislavery, the Constitution, and the Coming of the Civil War

Secretary of State John Quincy Adams supported the Missouri Compromise, but he perceived great omens in it. Appointed by James Monroe in 1817, Adams was in the middle of his distinguished eight-year tenure at the head of the State Department. Although his personal sympathies were entirely with the restrictionists, he understood the slaveholders' alarm. "Here was a new party ready formed . . . terrible to the whole Union, but portentously terrible to the South," he wrote in his diary, "threatening in its progress the emancipation of all their Slaves." With the compromise, Adams said, "this contest is laid to sleep"—but only, he said, "for the present."[1]

The conflict resumed sooner rather than later. Antislavery advocates, disappointed but not destroyed, returned to the offensive at the end of the decade and took off from there with a new militancy, provoking political debates that escalated for thirty more years, revolving, as ever, around the constitutional paradox of 1787. When, in 1857, the Supreme Court's ruling on the enslaved Dred Scott's freedom suit affirmed the absolutist proslavery interpretation of the Constitution, antislavery politicians and agitators denounced the decision largely on the grounds that the framers had purposely excluded property in man. The issues and even the words were familiar; and the conflict was in some ways the same as it had been for seventy years; but now it would no longer sleep.

The Missouri Compromise subdued the political furor but neither quashed antislavery politics nor calmed southern nerves. In October 1821, the American Convention for Promoting the Abolition of Slavery addressed a new memorial to Congress bidding it to halt slavery's expansion once and for all. Two years later, Ohio lawmakers approved a set of general emancipation resolutions that elicited support from across the North and rebukes from nine southern legislatures. "By what authority can we be divested of *our whole property*," the young South Carolina political leader Whitemarsh Seabrook protested, "for, deprive us of our slaves, and you render our lands valueless?"[2]

The Missouri crisis had lasting effects on national politics. The fragmented presidential election of 1824 pitted against one another four sectional candidates, including the eventual winner—Secretary of State John Quincy Adams. Slavery was not explicitly at issue in the campaign, but as the only non-slaveholder in the race, Adams inevitably aroused antislavery hopes and proslavery fears. Once he was elected, his opponents seized every opportunity to alarm slaveholders, revealing, one pro-administration editor wrote, "the cloven foot of negro slavery and southern dominancy."[3]

In fact, President Adams trod very carefully, wary of provoking southern disunionism and convinced that he would need some southern electoral votes to win reelection in 1828. The antislavery stalwart James Tallmadge would look back twenty years later and accuse Adams of having "*betrayed* his friends in expectation to have gained the South for his re-election."[4] To the slaveholders and their allies, though, Adams merely gave respectable cover to the schemes of self-aggrandizing abolitionist misfits such as Tallmadge.

Playing to slaveholders' susceptibilities, the New York master politician Martin Van Buren famously laid out a vision in 1827 of a new opposition party that would ally "the planters of the South and the plain republicans of the north" in order to marginalize the malcontents and shut down "the clamour against Southern Influence and African Slavery."[5] That party, headed by the slaveholder candidate Andrew Jackson, would trounce Adams in 1828 and usher in a political world purposely made safe for slavery, dominated by Jackson's Democrats and their Whig Party adversaries. Not that either the Democratic or Whig Party was, per se, proslavery or antislavery: although northern Whigs were always far more prone to condemn slavery and protect black rights than the Jacksonians, the northern wing of both parties included supporters who believed slavery a moral as well as political outrage, just as both parties had the backing of powerful slaveholders. Accordingly, leaders of both parties agreed, out of expediency as well as principle, to prevent antislavery campaigns from touching national politics, a stance that perforce reinforced the slaveholders' regime. The rise of the well-connected American Colonization Society, dedicated to voluntary manumission conditional on free blacks emigrating to Africa, further threatened the existing abolitionist societies, which by decade's end were struggling to survive.[6]

Their political influence waning, antislavery forces regrouped. In northern cities, free black communities enlarged by northern emancipation protested the American Colonization Society as a racist threat, a "many headed hydra," as one Boston abolitionist put it.[7] The American Abolition Convention considered and then rejected colonization. One of the convention's most spirited adherents, Benjamin Lundy, urgently propagated his own gradualist antislavery program. Finally, Lundy's young associate William Lloyd Garrison came to personify a new abolitionist militancy, hostile to colonization and gradual emancipation schemes, committed to working closely with defiant free blacks, and dedicated to the immediate commencement of a general emancipation.

Garrison's establishment in Boston of his newspaper, the *Liberator*, in 1831 and the founding two years later, under his strong influence, of the American Anti-Slavery Society (AA-SS) marked a major radicalized departure in antislavery agitation, which would renounce the Constitution itself as a proslavery compact. Yet for all of their combativeness, Garrison and the immediatists also built on, at least initially, the established antislavery political agenda, with its commitment to exhorting and even collaborating with elected officials. The AA-SS's founding declaration, far from condemning either the Constitution or political action, committed the group to work, "in a constitutional way," to persuade Congress to outlaw the domestic slave trade and "to abolish slavery in all those portions of our common country which come under its control, especially the District of Columbia."[8] As their central political endeavor, the new militants undertook the latest version of the public campaign that the Pennsylvania Abolition Society and its Quaker allies had pioneered in 1790, petitioning Congress to act to the fullest extent of its powers and hasten slavery's destruction.

It was the immediatists' aggressive tone, mass-based appeals, and expert organizing that from the start most distinguished them from earlier abolitionists. Hurled against a hardened, bipartisan, anti-abolitionist consensus, those appeals would stir, in 1835 and 1836, the decade's most momentous struggle in Congress over slavery. The catalyst, in line with the AA-SS's declaration, was the long-familiar issue of slavery and the slave trade in Washington, D.C. With their agitation, the immediatists once again raised abiding issues surrounding congressional authority and the Constitution's meaning regarding property in man. The fight originated in an effort that involved Benjamin Lundy's and William Lloyd Garrison's first collaboration.

Slaves made up a declining portion of the population of Washington in the 1830s, but that figure was deceptive. Over the first quarter of the century, the proportion of slaves had risen sharply, underscoring symbolically but also in everyday reality that the United States was a slaveholders' republic. Above all, the thriving local slave trade was an odious and ubiquitous assault: numerous critics disgustedly reported witnessing slave coffles being driven along Pennsylvania Avenue, destined to be sold like cattle. For abolitionists, meanwhile, Washington was strategically vital. In the absence of any impending contests over slavery in new states or territories, the capital was the one place in the nation where slavery and the domestic slave trade could be attacked head-on, because the District of Columbia fell wholly under Congress's jurisdiction. James Sloan's antislavery provocation of a quarter century earlier might now become a great public cause.[9]

The idea of building public support with mass petition drives, as opposed to polite memorials from particular organizations or constituencies, was fairly new in the United States. The Missouri crisis did bring a brief wave of petitions to Congress from across the North. But in 1826, Benjamin Lundy turned his attention to slavery in Washington and undertook what would evolve into an enormous and continuing petition protest. Over the next two years, Lundy escalated the battle, in time obtaining more than a thousand signatures from citizens inside the District on a "monster petition" calling for gradual emancipation. While on a New England tour, Lundy sought out Garrison, then editing a newspaper in Bennington, Vermont, with the intention of persuading him to become his assistant in Baltimore; failing in that for the moment, he got Garrison to join in circulating petitions. More auspiciously, the Pennsylvania House of Representatives also urged an end to slavery in the District. Based on the petitions, Lundy's congressional ally, Charles Miner of Pennsylvania, successfully moved a series of resolutions bidding the House to inquire into ending both slavery and the slave trade in the capital. Although Miner's colleagues soon enough buried the resolutions in committee, the fact that the House consented, by sizable margins, even to consider them was a flicker of hope.[10]

An emboldened Lundy now foresaw swamping the Congress with petitions on the District—"teaze the members with importunities, until they are *provoked* to deeds of *justice,*" he wrote—and Garrison, having briefly joined Lundy in Baltimore before striking out on his own, helped turn the idea into the abolitionists' most effective campaign.[11] The very first issue of the *Liberator* featured on its front page an appeal to "the 'earthquake voice' of the people," calling for a massive and systematic petition campaign to demand that Congress rid the capital of slavery and the slave trade.[12] The AA-SS took up the petitioning in earnest in 1835, and the impact was stunning: antislavery petitions, one South Carolina senator remarked, "do not come as heretofore, singly, and far apart; from the quiet routine of the Society of Friends, or the obscure vanity of some philanthropic club, but they are sent to us in vast numbers, from soured and agitated communities."[13] Two years later, when Congress convened for its regular session late in 1837, antislavery petitions signed by more than 400,000 Americans deluged Capitol Hill.[14]

The famous drive in the House to silence the protestors with a gag rule marked at once a reprise of previous confrontations and an intensification of the struggle. Between the beginning of Lundy's petition effort in 1827 and the acceleration of the AA-SS campaign eight years later, a series of dramatic events had rubbed nerves raw, including Nat Turner's uprising in Virginia in 1831, the nullification crisis of 1832–1833, and an AA-SS campaign that inundated the southern mails with abolitionist literature beginning in the summer of 1835. Clearly the major political parties were having trouble clamping down on agitation over slavery. The abolitionist petitions, if permitted a hearing, would bring that agitation directly into the halls of Congress.

Thanks to the immediatists, meanwhile, abolitionism had become a passionate popular movement unimaginable to earlier generations of antislavery advocates. The petition campaigns, as hoped, made the vocal abolitionist minority look gigantic—and by trying to thwart them, slaveholders in Congress called into question their respect for citizens' basic rights to petition their government. Yet if the scale as well as the stakes were vastly enlarged, the gag rule controversy also involved the perennial struggle over Congress's powers to regulate and abolish slavery outside the states where slavery existed. As ever, that struggle turned on clashing interpretations of property, slavery, and the Constitution. And once again, as in 1790, it arose over slaveholders' efforts to block what they deemed unconstitutional abolitionist petitions to Congress.[15]

Over the course of the petitions controversy, southerners in the House proposed two basic versions of the gag rule. The harsher of them, initially proposed by John C. Calhoun's South Carolina protégé James H. Hammond, would reject the petitions out of hand as unconstitutional, on the grounds that the Constitution, having "recogni[zed] slaves as property," guaranteed that property to its owners under the Fifth Amendment's due process clause.[16] To the hard-liners' chagrin, though, the House majority rallied around a "soft" gag, proposed by another South Carolinian, Henry Pinckney (and approved by Vice President Van Buren), and the House passed it in May 1836. The Pinckney version would receive the petitions but automatically table them and take no further action, on the grounds that while slavery in the states was untouchable, Congress "ought not" to legislate on slavery in the District of Columbia.[17] The distinction made no difference to antislavery advocates—repression was repression—but it outraged proslavery hard-liners, who thought it quietly surrendered to Congress the constitutional authority to abolish slavery in the District. Hammond and the militants initially gave way, but they did not give up. A year after the House adopted the Pinckney resolutions, the hard-liners expanded the rule to cover petitions concerning slavery in the territories and the domestic slave trade; a year after that, the House passed a rule that explicitly denied Congress constitutional authority to interfere with slavery anywhere. Finally, in 1840, the House approved a version of Hammond's original "hard" gag.

The hard gag's proponents restated the militant proslavery arguments from the Missouri crisis: as slaveholders' property rights in man preceded the Constitution, and as the Constitution affirmed and guaranteed those rights, Congress was utterly powerless to meddle with slavery.[18] The issue was particularly clear-cut, they said, respecting the District of Columbia, where slavery had existed for years with Congress's express approval, and where slaveholders held their human property with the assurance that it was protected by national as well as local law.

The hard-liners did their utmost to prove that the Constitution recognized property in man. Hammond gestured to the fugitive slave clause, by now a familiar move, and then asserted that the

Constitution acknowledged "slaves as property, entitled to representation only as three fifths, and not as persons entitled to full representation," a curious reading of the three-fifths clause.[19] James Bouldin of Virginia claimed that the framers drew no distinction between slaves and any other kind of property, and on that basis, he claimed (as did Hammond) that the Fifth Amendment provided absolute protection for slave property. The South, Bouldin declared, would never have assented to a Constitution that entrusted their rights "to those who they knew believed, or professed to believe, that property could not be held in a slave."[20]

Other hard-liners simply asserted what proslavery advocates were beginning to regard as truisms. "Congress cannot declare any thing designated and held as property not to be property, without express grant," James Garland of Virginia claimed. "In relation to slaves, the constitution regards them as property, and guaranties its security."[21] There was some slight precedent for the proslavery position, as Congress, in organizing the territories, had consistently rejected all proposals that would have touched the property claims of resident slaveholders. But the hard-liners' absolutism denied the federal government any authority whatsoever over slavery in the District, and that view was quickly gaining support outside as well as inside the capital. "Congress has no more power to legislate on the subject for the District of Columbia than it has for South Carolina," a correspondent wrote to the *Charleston Courier*.[22]

Some of the more pointed hard-line House speeches—although not always the most extreme—came from yet another Virginian, the Whig congressman Henry A. Wise, who would for years be one of the hard gag's chief proponents. Slavery in the District of Columbia, Wise charged, was the exclusive concern of citizens of the District; abolitionist outside agitators had no business even speaking up. More important, Congress had no express constitutional power to legislate about slavery, and its implied authority over slavery in the District was restricted by the Constitution's protection of private property. No one could doubt, Wise averred, that this restriction included slaves, as the Constitution recognized property in man as surely as any other form of property. Would Congress dare to challenge the fugitive slave clause, Wise asked, "a most important provision, one of the sacred compromises of the Union," with its "guarantee of slave property"? Would the petitioners, in addition to destroying the District's existing slavery laws, also absolve the District's residents of their obligations to return runaway slaves? Wise conceded that some northern states had abolished slavery on the post-nati principle, which, by implication, he tolerated.[23] Militants such as Bouldin strongly demurred, thinking it was ridiculous to forbid the owners of slaves from owning their slaves' children: "It is property, or not," Bouldin inveighed. But no state, as far as Wise knew, had "taken slave property against the consent of the owners, and without compensation," as he claimed the petitioners proposed that Congress do inside the District.[24]

The most prominent northern opponent of the gag, former president John Quincy Adams, now a congressman, responded over an entirely different set of constitutional concerns. Thoroughly depressed by his defeat in 1828, Adams had kindled his spirits by winning election to the House in 1830, momentarily under the sway of the popular Anti-Masonic movement. Although he retained his antislavery views and despised the slaveholding interest more than ever, he had little use for the abolitionists, whom he considered reckless incendiaries. The proposed gag rule, however, offended him as a violation of citizens' rights to petition their governments freely. As long as the gag was in force, Adams was its bitterest and most resourceful enemy in Congress, leading a small band of northern Whigs in a kind of parliamentary guerrilla warfare.[25]

A few of Adams's allies stood up for what the abolitionists had to say as well as for their right to say it. William Slade was a Middlebury, Vermont, lawyer and newspaper editor, a Jeffersonian Democratic-Republican turned Anti-Mason who had served as Vermont's secretary of state before he entered Congress nearly a decade later, in 1831. Like Adams, he joined the Whigs, and he would be one of Adams's steadiest allies in resisting the gag rule. But Slade was a committed antislavery advocate, an immediatist in the sense that he believed in immediately enacting gradual emancipation wherever possible. In a remarkable speech early in the struggle, he dared to announce that he supported the petitions' abolitionist aims, and then prodded the question of property in man as a moral and philosophical issue as well as a constitutional one.[26]

The abolitionists had purposely framed their petitions in an ambiguous manner, asking Congress (in a typical example) "to pass without delay such laws, as to your wisdom may seem right and proper for the entire abolition of slavery and the slave trade in the District of Columbia."[27] This might be construed as favoring either immediate and unqualified or gradual emancipation in Washington, either with or without compensation to resident slaveholders. With that in mind, Slade went on the offensive. Holding aside momentarily the issue of slavery, he called for the instant and absolute abolition of the District's slave *trade*, a matter proslavery advocates preferred not to address. He dismissed the claims by some slaveholders that slavery was Christian as well as constitutional, saying that he was not prepared to hear "that religion justified the holding of human beings as property."[28]

Slade then took direct aim at Wise's defense of the gag. Far from disinterested, the petitioners, like all American citizens, had a large stake in the laws of the nation's capital. The District would certainly be bound by the Fugitive Slave Act, but this did not disqualify Congress from abolishing slavery in the District any more than it exempted those northern states which had abolished slavery from adhering to the law. Slade favored gradual over immediate emancipation as better suited to the interests of the slaves and society at large, but the normal laws and customs of property, he explained, made no distinction between stripping a master of his slave and stripping him of the right to own the children of that slave. How, then, could Wise tolerate gradual emancipation while condemning immediate emancipation as a gross violation of "the great principle of vested rights"? On this point, if nothing else, Slade agreed with the more extreme proslavery advocates: any form of emancipation denied the legitimacy of property in man.[29]

Slade struck hardest over the character of slaves as property. He might have pointed out that, contrary to Wise's claims, the petitioners were not stipulating an instant abolition of slavery in the District. Instead, Slade drove to the heart of the matter, denying the legitimacy of human chattel under any circumstances. The petitioners, he declared, were not asking Congress "to take private property" but rather wanted Congress "to free the African from the unnatural condition of being the property of another" and allow him to become "the proprietor of himself."[30] Abolition of slavery had nothing at all to do with property, except to restore to the slaves their stolen natural right of self-ownership. Under the Constitution, slaveholders' aberrant claims to vested interests in their slave property had to be respected inside existing slave states, but nowhere else. Emancipation outside of those restrictions and jurisdictions, including the emancipation of slaves held by resident masters, could not be challenged or curtailed by assertions of property rights in man. Outside of those restrictions and jurisdictions, such claims had no force whatsoever. Regardless of whether

Congress sought to abolish slavery gradually or summarily in the District of Columbia, no assertion of slaveholders' private property rights could prevent it.

The Senate largely avoided the gag controversy by adopting a rule, over the repeated objections of its own southern hard-liners, whereby the petitions would be read before senators voted simply to ignore them. For eight years more, though, the House regularly rejoined the battle, ostensibly over the question of petitioning rights but with the underlying struggle over slavery always near or at the surface. Finally, in 1844, Adams and his band of resisters turned rising northern resentment at the domineering slaveholders into a House majority that killed the gag for good. Throughout the struggle, in and out of Washington, public debate intensified concerning Congress's powers over slavery. Positions hardened at both extremes, leaning toward James Hammond and Henry Wise's arguments on one side and William Slade's on the other.

The most exacting, coherent, and influential defense of Congress's authority came in a pamphlet by the extraordinary abolitionist radical Theodore Dwight Weld. A onetime protégé of the abolitionist Charles Stuart, Weld had been a student rebel at Lane Theological Seminary before he enlisted as an agent in the American Anti-Slavery Society in 1834. A tireless organizer and writer, he recruited to the cause the likes of Henry Stanton and Harriet Beecher Stowe, edited the abolitionist newspaper the *Emancipator,* and toured the North giving speeches until he had lectured himself hoarse. With his wife, the formidable abolitionist and women's rights advocate Angelina Grimké, and her sister Sarah, Weld would go on to assemble a pivotal abolitionist propaganda compendium, *American Slavery as It Is,* in 1839, before relocating to Washington, where he would attach himself to John Quincy Adams as a combination advisor, researcher, and legislative assistant. A year before *American Slavery*, working out of the AA-SS national headquarters in New York, Weld composed *The Power of Congress over the District of Columbia*, crafted out of a series of articles he had published in the Democratic New York *Evening Post*.[31]

Weld's basic premises were the same as those that Slade had proclaimed in the House two years earlier, and which had been central to abolitionist pronouncements since the Revolution. Slavery, he wrote, was the artificial creation of *"positive legislative acts,* forcibly setting aside the law of nature, the common law, and the principles of universal justice."[32] Abolishing slavery did not violate property rights; it restored to the slaves the self-ownership from which all legitimate property rights originated. In support of these points, though, Weld supplied a formidable array of evidence culled from congressional debates, state laws, judicial decisions, and virtually every other public record that touched on the character of slaves as property and on Congress's power to interfere with slavery.

Weld expounded the core antislavery argument that the Constitution deliberately refused to recognize property in man. Although he lacked Madison's notes on the Federal Convention, which would not appear in print for another two years, he presented a concise and strikingly accurate summary of the framers' exclusion and all that it implied:

> The constitution of the United States does not recognize slaves as "PROPERTY" any where, and it does not recognize them in *any sense* in the District of Columbia. All allusions to them in the constitution recognise them as "persons." Every reference to them points *solely* to the element of *personality;* and thus, by the strongest implication, declares that

> the constitution *knows* them only as "persons" and *will* not recognise them in any other light. If they escape into free States, the constitution authorizes their being taken back. But how? Not as the property of an "owner" but as "persons;" and the peculiarity of the expression is a marked recognition of their *personality*—a refusal to recognize them as chattels— "persons *held* to service." Are *oxen* "*held* to service?"[33]

Wherever the Constitution alone was sovereign, Weld concluded, natural rights to self-ownership negated false claims to property in man. By giving Congress full authority over the District of Columbia, the Constitution empowered the federal government to abolish slavery in the capital however it saw fit.

The formulations contained in Weld's pamphlet would prove essential for antislavery advocates over the next two decades—and in the months before it appeared, Senator John C. Calhoun began to reformulate forcefully the essential arguments of slavery's strongest defenders. Having returned to the vice presidency and then angrily departed it under Jackson, whereupon he entered the Senate, Calhoun had become the foremost champion of slaveholders' interests, first during the nullification crisis of 1832–1833, then even more vigorously in responding to the abolitionist agitation. In 1836, he joined other proslavery militants in contending that the due process clause of the Fifth Amendment denied Congress power to interfere with slavery in the District any more than in the states. "Are not slaves property?" he demanded. "And if so, how can Congress any more take away the property of a master in his slave, in this District, than it could his life and liberty?"[34] A year later, he delivered an oft-cited speech to the Senate in which he upheld slavery not simply as an established interest but as a positive good, for slaves and masters (and civilization) alike—but that speech originated in yet another denunciation of the abolitionists and the unconstitutionality of their petitions. Congress, he charged, "had just as good a right to abolish slavery in the States as in this District."[35]

As the gag controversy wore on in the House, Calhoun pushed even harder to get the Senate to reject the petitions out of hand, and he expanded his claim that rights to property in man were absolute. Late in 1837, he introduced six resolutions renouncing attacks on slavery, one of which stated that Congress was powerless to regulate slavery in the territories as well as the District of Columbia. Some Upper South members balked at that, among them Henry Clay, now a major power in the Senate, who tried to insert language that implicitly upheld the 36° 30′ restriction in the Missouri Compromise. Calhoun rejected the change, admitting that he had agreed with that part of the compromise in 1820 but now considered it "a dangerous measure" that had "done much to rouse into action" the current abolitionist spirit. Calhoun linked his defense of slave property to his emerging theory of state sovereignty, which itself amounted to a rehash of proslavery positions advanced at least as early as the debates over Arkansas Territory twenty years earlier: as the Constitution intended to give every state in the nation equal access to its bounties, he said, so banning property in slaves from the territories was unconstitutional.[36]

The Senate, not yet prepared to repeal the second half of the Missouri Compromise, approved the diluted version of Calhoun's resolution; the on-and-off battling over the abolitionists continued; and in 1840, Calhoun gave his fullest remarks yet on the matter. "The presentation of these incendiary petitions," he declared, "is itself an infraction of the constitution." Everyone, he said, acknowledged "that the property, which they are presented here to destroy, is guarantied by the Constitution." He continued: "Have we not a right, under the

Constitution, to our property in our slaves? Would it not be a violation of the Constitution to divest us of that right? Have we not a right to enjoy, *under* the Constitution, *peaceably and quietly, our acknowledged rights guarantied by it,* without annoyance?"[37]

Calhoun's speech at once echoed the proslavery polemics from the 1790 petition controversy and reached the logical conclusion of what had become the absolutist position—and for the moment, that position appeared to have triumphed inside Congress. Only one senator, the antislavery maverick Thomas Morris of Ohio, challenged Calhoun's presumption about constitutional guarantees to property in man. (For his troubles, Morris was excommunicated from the Democratic Party, making him the first political martyr of the antislavery cause.)[38] Antislavery voices were stronger in the House, but not strong enough to prevent the imposition, in 1840, of the hard gag rule. For all of its fervor, meanwhile, the immediatist agitation had failed to break through the bipartisan accord to keep slavery out of national debates. With their radical incitement, the abolitionists had certainly broadened and sharpened public debate over slavery, congressional authority, and the Constitution. But for abolitionism to matter in American politics and law would require the collapse of the party system whose very existence depended on suppressing debates over slavery. In 1840, amid the tumult of the Log Cabin presidential campaign that elevated the Whig William Henry Harrison to the White House, that system looked stronger than ever. Other events that same year, though, would augur the system's collapse.

By complete coincidence, 1840 saw the publication of the first edition of James Madison's notes on the Federal Convention. After he departed the presidency in 1817, Madison had continued to shift back and forth in his stated views on slavery and the Constitution, sometimes shading his own past pronouncements. In a private exchange in 1819 over the Missouri crisis, for example, he affirmed that "some of the States" had prevented the Constitution from "acknowledging expressly a property in human beings," but he also omitted his own role in the exclusion while implying (much as he had during the Virginia ratification debates) that the Constitution somewhere *implicitly* acknowledged property in man. Madison cast doubt on Congress's authority over slavery in the territories and denied any such congressional authority over incoming states; he also made it clear that he shared his friend Jefferson's opinion that expanding slavery would have an ameliorative, diffusing effect that would improve conditions for slaves and hasten gradual emancipation. Over the years, meanwhile, Madison had quietly edited and revised his original notes from the Federal Convention; at one point, as we have seen, he may have augmented his opposition to extending non-interference with the Atlantic slave trade to 1808 in a way that emphasized his disagreements with the proslavery hard-liners in 1787. Hedging all the way, Madison tried his best to adapt his thinking to the new political realities surrounding slavery without contradicting his past record—to the point, perhaps, of touching up that record.[39]

Madison had wanted to keep the notes private until all of the delegates were dead, including himself, and as it happened, he lived the longest of them all, until 1836. The following year, Congress allocated $30,000 to purchase the manuscript from Madison's widow, Dolley, and it appeared in print three years later, in a three-volume edition that also included Madison's earlier notes on debates in the Confederation Congress. Hailed as a definitive record of the nation's founding, Madison's transcriptions and observations would promise to raise constitutional interpretation to a new level, above and beyond the exegeses in the *Federalist* essays, not least on slavery.[40]

Much of the antislavery interpretation would stem from another of the year's important developments, the rise of the antislavery Liberty Party. In 1839, a group of New York abolitionists, frustrated by the limits of moral suasion, initiated independent political efforts that a year later produced a schism within the abolitionist movement. Only by engaging in electoral politics, the Libertyites thought, could antislavery advocates break the partisan hammerlock over slavery issues. The Liberty leaders persuaded the stalwart but uncharismatic Ohio abolitionist editor James G. Birney to run for president, an effort that received a paltry 7,000 votes—a minor sideshow amid the Log Cabin campaign. But the party would soon enough generate powerful lines of antislavery argument that, unlike the radical Garrisonians' immediatism, gave antislavery an appeal well beyond the abolitionist faithful. The most important formulator of these arguments would be Birney's friend Salmon P. Chase.[41]

Chase was in political transition. A Cincinnati lawyer who had already shifted unsteadily from pro-bank Whiggery to sympathy with Jacksonian financial policies—becoming "a sort of independent Whig with Democratic ideas," he later recalled—he was also a devout and resourceful antislavery activist whose legal work led opponents to dub him the "Attorney General of Fugitive Slaves."[42] Since the mid-1830s, he and Birney had been discussing their ideas about the constitutional status of slavery, similar to those stoked by the petitions controversy. Breaking entirely with the prevailing view of the fugitive slave clause, Birney reasoned that it in no way made slavery anything more than a creature of local law and that slavery could not exist outside of the jurisdiction that created it. Chase agreed, and in 1837 he pressed the argument, unsuccessfully, in a freedom case involving a fugitive named Matilda. A man of considerable personal political ambition, Chase was less swayed by Birney's upstart Liberty Party, and in 1840, nauseated by President Martin Van Buren's abject subservience to the slaveholders, he voted for another Ohioan, William Henry Harrison, who he thought would at least be less proslavery than the incumbent. But Harrison died after a month in office, bringing in the slaveholder John Tyler, and at the end of 1841, fed up with both major parties' resistance to the slavery issue, Chase threw in with the political abolitionists, who quickly made him one of their chief strategists and spokesmen. As the Liberty Party would prove the germ of the Republican Party, so Chase would emerge as the Liberty Party's, and then the Republicans', most influential thinker about slavery and the Constitution.[43]

Chase expanded upon existing antislavery arguments, claiming that the framers not only excluded slavery but deliberately geared the Constitution toward eradicating it. The founding generation, he argued, was essentially hostile to slavery, a conclusion he based heavily on a skewed reading of the career and writings of Thomas Jefferson. Chase granted that the Federal Convention—lacking any model for a rapid emancipation, and intent on circumscribing its new, expansive national government—had not sought to abolish slavery, but he insisted that at every step the framers limited it with an eye to its eventual demise. "Their policy," he would later write, "was one of repression, limitation, discouragement; they anticipated with confidence the auspicious result of universal freedom."[44] Chase, like almost all antislavery advocates, venerated Jefferson's Declaration of Independence as the egalitarian taproot of American politics, but he presented the Constitution, more tendentiously, as another thoroughgoing expression of the nation's supposed antislavery founding.

By these lights, the Fifth Amendment, far from protecting property in man, as the proslavery hard-liners presumed, aimed to prohibit Congress from sanctioning slavery anywhere inside its jurisdiction. The fugitive slave clause amounted to no more than an agreement between the states, which individual states might implement however they pleased. Proslavery hard-liners' claims that the clause recognized slaves as property were nonsensical; instead, the Fugitive Slave Act, by arrogating to Congress power not stipulated in the fugitive slave clause, was unconstitutional. The intentions of the framers, Chase charged, had been perverted by a sinister slave power consisting of slaveholders and their northern lackeys, who had seized control of the federal government over the previous thirty years. But the Constitution, he insisted, provided the means whereby the slave power could be overthrown, vindicating the framers' antislavery purposes.

Chase pushed his antislavery interpretation as hard as he could, but most of his key points had already emerged in antislavery speeches and writings, including Weld's pamphlet, and were widely shared in antislavery circles. Like earlier commentators, Chase claimed that the Constitution left slavery a local and not a national institution—"the creature and dependent of state law," he wrote in 1841, "wholly local in its existence and character."[45] The framers, he repeated, had deliberately worded the Constitution so that the federal government would treat all men as "persons," as Madison's notes affirmed. With no constitutional protection in national law, slavery was subject to regulation and abolition wherever Congress held jurisdiction, including the territories and the District of Columbia. And at the foundation of Chase's more radical interpretation was the familiar insistence that the framers had insisted on excluding slavery from national law. "The Constitution," he wrote to Joshua Giddings, the front-line antislavery Whig congressman, in 1842, "must be vindicated from the reproach of sanctioning the doctrine of property in men."[46]

Other abolitionist radicals agreed that the Constitution was antislavery but thought that Chase was far too cautious. In 1837, the New York abolitionist Alvan Stewart declared that the Fifth Amendment empowered the federal government to abolish slavery everywhere, including the states where it existed. The idea shocked the AA-SS, but by the mid-1840s, a number of radicals, including the Boston druggist George W. F. Mellen, the Liberty Party organizer William Goodell, and the anti-statist writer Lysander Spooner, presented variations on the argument that, as Goodell had it, the Constitution authorized Congress to declare every person held in bondage "yet *not* 'deprived of liberty, by due process of law,' *to be free.*"[47] Some years later, the great black abolitionist Frederick Douglass issued a scalding rebuke to the hypocrisy of the Declaration of Independence that nevertheless described the Constitution as "a GLORIOUS LIBERTY DOCUMENT," citing the work of Goodell and Spooner among others. "Now, take the constitution according to its plain reading, and I defy the presentation of a single pro-slavery clause in it," Douglass declared. "On the other hand it will be found to contain principles and purposes, entirely hostile to the existence of slavery."[48] These more radical renderings—what one historian has described as political abolitionism—denied the federal consensus that Chase and his allies accepted, but they still advanced the broad idea that the Constitution neither condoned nor enshrined property in man.[49] It would fall to the immediatists around William Lloyd Garrison to attack that idea root and branch, and interpret the Constitution almost exactly as Calhoun and the proslavery militants did.

Garrison himself had long regarded the Constitution as a pact with evil which vitiated American politics, but the contempt intensified amid heightened conflicts over fugitive slaves. Efforts by abolitionist lawyers such as Chase to test the constitutionality of the Fugitive Slave Act had come to nothing; northern jurists continued to fall in line with the view expressed by Supreme Court associate justice Henry Baldwin, who in a charge to a circuit court jury in 1833 spoke of property in man as one of the "cornerstones" of American government.[50] The issue exploded—and threw the Garrisonians into furious despair—in 1842, when the Supreme Court issued a landmark ruling (with Baldwin in the majority) in the case of *Prigg v. Pennsylvania.*

Writing the majority opinion in *Prigg,* Associate Justice Joseph Story, a premier authority on the Constitution, declared unconstitutional a pair of Pennsylvania laws designed to prevent kidnapping of blacks, on the grounds that they violated both the fugitive slave clause of the Constitution and the Fugitive Slave Act. Although Story's ambiguous opinion opened the possibility that local officials could refuse to cooperate with the rendition of slaves, it consistently described the fugitives as property. It also proclaimed the proslavery myth that the fugitive slave clause was so vital to southern interests that "it cannot be doubted that . . . the Union could not have been formed" without it.[51] Eight months after the ruling, the seizure in Boston of an alleged runaway slave, George Latimer, touched off huge public protests, and the Garrisonians, all the more appalled after Story's opinion, now directed their wrath against the Constitution itself. "The fault is in allowing such a Constitution to live an hour," the Garrisonian orator Wendell Phillips proclaimed to a mass rally at Faneuil Hall. "I say, my CURSE be on the Constitution of the United States."[52]

Redoubling their radicalism, the Garrisonians had decided it was not simply foolish but wicked to attack slavery in line with a Constitution that they now proclaimed, especially in light of the *Prigg* decision, was proslavery to its very core. To a new slogan of fractious defiance, "No Union with Slaveholders," they added denunciations of the framers and of the deluded, self-styled abolitionists who had invented what Phillips mocked as "this new theory of the Anti-slavery character of the Constitution."[53] Phillips pulled together an influential compendium of antislavery attacks on the Constitution along with copious official records, including the relevant passages from Madison's convention notes—the most extensive use of the notes by any commentator at the time, proslavery or antislavery.[54] All of it, especially the notes, supposedly proved beyond cavil that the convention had willingly made a pact with evil. The Garrisonians were hardly the only ones who viewed Madison's notes as an indictment of the framers' work: Phillips's pamphlet quoted John Quincy Adams speaking of how "the deadly venom of slavery was infused into the Constitution of freedom."[55] But for Phillips and the Garrisonians, there was not the slightest trace of freedom in the proslavery Constitution—a compact "formed at the expense of human liberty" and "cemented with human blood"—and there could be no hope of redeeming it.[56]

A distant echo of the more severe of the New England antislavery condemnations from the ratification struggle, the Garrisonians' hostility to the Constitution focused on the framers' compromise over the Atlantic slave trade, as exposed in Madison's notes. For the Garrisonians, morality dispelled context and bred certitude; anything short of revulsion at that compromise, rendered as condoning evil for the sake of commercial profit, signified grotesque complicity in slavery. The Constitution's other compromises affirmed how willfully and selfishly the framers had bargained away the nation's soul by establishing a government (the AA-SS declared) "expressly designed to favor a slaveholding oligarchy."[57] The slave power did not, as the Libertyites claimed, arise from a corruption of the framers' intentions; the slave power was the framers' very own creation, the spawn of their unholy union with slavery.

The Garrisonians did not rebut the antislavery constitutionalists' arguments over property in man as much as scorn them. Drawing a distinction between slavery as a national institution and a local institution was ridiculous to the immediatists: to tolerate slavery in any way, they believed, was to sanction and enshrine it. But even were the distinction granted, the Garrisonians asserted, the constitution-alists were wrong, as the Constitution actually did formalize slavery as a national institution in the fugitive slave clause, just as the proslavery militants—and Justice Story—claimed. According to the immediatists' logic, sophistry about how the Constitution refused to admit slaves as property showed nothing more than that the framers honored slavery by using other words. There was, the AA-SS confessed, something "paradoxical" embedded in the Constitution, as in slavery itself, whereby slaves were recognized "not merely as property, but also as persons." The paradox, however, could not be resolved, only repudiated as the pretext for a tyranny "more fierce and cruel than any whose atroci-ties are recorded on the pages of history or romance."[58]

With all of their fame and notoriety, the Garrisonians still repre-sented a minority opinion among the abolitionists, and despite the immediatist denunciations of antislavery constitutionalists, the Liberty Party survived and grew into the mid-1840s. James Birney ran for pres-ident again in 1844, on a platform written by Chase, and the party improved its showing, especially in New England. The results were weaker, however, than the Libertyites had expected, and the practical effect of their campaign may only have been to tip the election to the pro-expansion Democrat James K. Polk, who owed his ascension to the political machinations of John C. Calhoun. Although not himself a proslavery hard-liner, the Jacksonian Polk's pursuit of Manifest Destiny would run roughshod over the protests of even the mildest antislavery advocates.[59] That pursuit would in turn reopen the questions suppos-edly settled by the Missouri Compromise about Congress's constitu-tional authority in the territories, and in time they would reopen the battle over the remanding of fugitive slaves. All of these fights would be inseparable from the perennial issues connected to the framers' handling of property in man.

The resumption of territorial expansion in 1845 doomed the sectional compromise essential to the parties and the political system itself. The annexation of Texas, hastened by Polk's election to the presidency, badly fractured the Democrats and signaled the further ascendancy of the more militant slaveholders inside the party. The war with Mexico that predictably followed, whatever its precise origins, very quickly turned into a war for territorial conquest, which in turn produced the boldest northern effort yet to assert congressional authority over slavery.

The radical features of the Wilmot Proviso—the measure, first passed by the House in 1846, that would ban slavery in all territories conquered during the war with Mexico—are now virtually forgotten. That the men behind it, including its namesake, Pennsylvania congressman David Wilmot, were northern Jacksonians, some of them antislavery racists, partly accounts for the neglect. So does the fact that the proviso's sweep would only became fully apparent after the war was over, when the nation contemplated a Mexican cession nearly as large as the entirety of the Louisiana Purchase lands. Still, Wilmot and his allies knew from the start that theirs would be a large proposal, perhaps the largest of its kind since the failed congressional effort in 1784 to ban slavery from the western territories. It was also the first major proposal since 1787 to restrict slavery's expansion without also making any concessions to slavery. And because Mexico had long been free soil (following Mexico's abolition of slavery in 1829), there could be no claims made on behalf of resident slaveholders as there had been with respect to Mississippi, Louisiana, and Arkansas Territories.[60]

It took several months, but once its implications became clear, everything about the proviso was alarming, especially to the South. The initial House vote approving it marked a complete breakdown of party allegiances: every southerner, of both parties, opposed the proviso, whereas virtually every northern Whig supported it—as did, remarkably, the vast majority of northern Democrats, by a margin of 52 to 4.[61] By presenting it for a second vote and then a third the following February, the proviso's supporters made clear they had no intention of backing down. It had been a quarter century since the antislavery "party" that John Quincy Adams detected during the Missouri crisis had arisen with such force and tenacity. Fervent support for the proviso was nearly universal in the northern press, prompting southern talk of secession if the measure was ever enacted. Even devoted Whig nationalists such as Georgia congressman Alexander Stephens got caught up in the disunionist passion. "Would you have us submit to aggression upon aggression?" Stephens asked the House. "I would rather that the southern country should perish."[62] The pro-proviso side—which is to say pretty much all of Stephens's northern colleagues—gave no quarter. "It cannot be supposed," Preston King of New York proclaimed, "the people of the free States will approve the exertion of the power of the Federal Government to extend indefinitely the institution of slavery over territory which is now free."[63]

The acrimony belied a clear-cut reality: like Tallmadge's amendment on Missouri, the Wilmot Proviso never had much hope of clearing the Senate, which was evenly divided between free and slaveholding states. Still, the North's ability to prolong and intensify debate over slavery's extension initiated a transformation of the politics of slavery and antislavery. Liberty Party supporters, heartened by the disruption, edged closer to allying with dissident Democrats and antislavery Whigs. (The Garrisonian immediatists held back, wary as ever of impure politics—a stand that raised doubts in the mind of one of their outstanding spokesmen, the fugitive slave Frederick Douglass.)[64] Southern militants further stiffened their arguments on slavery and the Constitution, encouraging an anti-Wilmot stampede that began looking like an organized proslavery, southern rights movement, standing outside the national parties.

At the center of the controversy, in new configurations, were the enduring clashes over property rights and congressional authority. Picking up from where the gag rule fight had ended two years earlier, proslavery advocates rejected the proviso as unconstitutional, on the grounds that Congress could not interfere with slave property in the territories. Anti-proviso speakers insisted that the Constitution recognized and sanctioned property in man absolutely. "If any of these rights can be invaded, there is no security for the remainder," Congressman Franklin Welsh Bowden of Alabama said of the protections for slavery.[65] "I shall not stop to inquire whether slavery is a blessing or a curse," Arthur Bagby, also of Alabama, told the Senate, in one of the more temperate proslavery speeches. "The Constitution guarantees it to those who think proper to hold it; and while the Constitution exists, they cannot be deprived of it."[66] Jacob Collamer, a congressman from Vermont, spoke as if in direct reply: "This is untrue; their slaves are not property but in slave States. It is true they may reclaim them when they flee into free States, but they must be *taken back* to be held."[67]

John C. Calhoun responded to the proviso by making the proslavery hard line a little harder. In a pair of Senate resolutions, he rehashed his earlier reworking of proslavery arguments into what became known as the "common property" doctrine. The territories, according to his latest articulation, did not fall under the federal government's authority but were the "joint and common property" of the several sovereign states. Congress, which was merely a "joint-agent" of the states, could neither prevent the citizens of any state from "emigrating with their property," including slaves, into the territories, nor prevent the citizens of the territories from deciding on slavery for themselves. The Constitution, far from authorizing slavery's exclusion from the territories, bound the federal government to protect slaveholders' rights to property in man wherever Congress oversaw the states' common property, including the territories. In what amounted to an anti–Wilmot Proviso, Calhoun verged on denying the very existence of the nation as an entity with distinct powers, while he turned the antislavery constitutionalist arguments inside out.[68] Far from excluded by the framers, he later inveighed as his central contention in a major speech, property in slaves was "the only property recognised by [the Constitution], the only one that entered into its formation as a political element . . . the only one that is put under the express guarantee of the Constitution."[69]

As Congress sought futilely to find some compromise between the Wilmot supporters' contentions and Calhoun's, a third solution emerged, in yet another recasting of old ideas. In its earliest measures permitting slavery's expansion, from organizing the Southwest and Mississippi Territories though to the Missouri Compromise, Congress did not stipulate that any areas be open to slavery; rather it refused to prohibit slavery in those areas. Formally, settlers in these territories would determine for themselves whether slavery would be permitted—a policy that, in view of both geography and the prior existence of slavery, virtually ensured slavery's spread. During the Arkansas and Missouri crisis, proslavery advocates tried to turn that policy into a political principle. The "great and radical objection" to Congress's barring slavery in Arkansas, the North Carolinian Felix Walker had said, "is taking away from the people of this territory the natural and Constitutional right of legislating for themselves, and imposing on them a condition which they may not willingly accept."[70]

By the late 1840s, with the potential conquest of Mexican lands, it was no longer so clear that leaving the matter up to a territory's voters would automatically lead to the expansion of slavery. Accordingly, it became possible to turn tacitly proslavery policy into a principle that could be sold to northerners as an eminently just and democratic doctrine. And so, in 1847, conservative northern Democrats, squeezed between the Wilmot supporters and the proslavery hard-liners, repackaged the old practice under the slogan of "popular sovereignty," described by its original proponent, Vice President George M. Dallas of Pennsylvania, as "leaving to the people of the territory to be acquired the business of settling the matter [of slavery] for themselves."[71] By remaining conveniently ambiguous about the stage of organization at which the settlers would make their decision, the idea of popular sovereignty rejected congressional authority over slavery without endorsing Calhoun's claims about "common property."

Over the next three years, supporters of popular sovereignty would battle antislavery exclusionists and proslavery expansionists in the events that produced the famous Compromise of 1850. In February 1847, an expanded version of the Wilmot Proviso effort lost the support of a vital number of northern Democrats and died. A year later, an attempt to attach the proviso to the treaty that concluded the war failed. Antislavery forces, undaunted, formed the Free Soil Party, uniting Liberty Party abolitionists with dissident Democrats and antislavery Whigs around a platform, co-authored by Salmon Chase, proclaiming that the "settled policy" of the framers had been "to limit, localize, and discourage Slavery."[72] The Democrats, rejecting the proslavery hardliners, nominated the Michigan Jacksonian Lewis Cass on a platform endorsing popular sovereignty; the Whigs obfuscated and won the election for their nominee, General Zachary Taylor, a slaveholder war hero with no clear political convictions. The Free Soil ticket, headed by the former doughface Van Buren, wound up winning some strong statewide totals, but its overall showing fell short of expectations: established party connections still proved sturdy. As president, though, Zachary Taylor turned out to be a southern man with northern principles, and he opposed the admission of any more slave states. Serious talk of secession resumed until Taylor's sudden death brought to the presidency Millard Fillmore, a conservative northern Whig more amenable to southern demands.[73]

The 1850 compromise over the Mexican cession lands engineered by Henry Clay and the popular-sovereignty Democrat Stephen A. Douglas looked superficially like a series of trade-offs. California joined the Union as a free state, while Utah and New Mexico Territories were organized under the popular-sovereignty rule; the slave trade was abolished in the District of Columbia, while a new, more draconian fugitive slave law took effect. On closer inspection, though, the compromise was a damaging rebuke to the antislavery proponents of congressional authority over slavery and the constitutional exclusion of property in man. The arrangement repudiated the Wilmot Proviso principle of non-extension of slavery. Apart from California, it extended the old principle of non-intervention as far north as possible in the remaining cession lands, well above the 36° 30′ Missouri Compromise line for the Louisiana Purchase lands. While it removed the offensive slave trade, it retained slavery in the District of Columbia, thereby affirming in practice if not in principle the resident slaveholders' property claims. Above all, the new Fugitive Slave Act greatly fortified federal involvement in enforcing what proslavery hard-liners upheld as the Constitution's surest guarantee of their property rights in national law.[74]

The new law on fugitive slaves, it needs noting, did nothing to validate property in man under the Constitution. The paradox of 1787, for the moment, survived: the new Fugitive Slave Act did not once mention slaves or slavery but instead employed, like the original 1793 law, the Constitution's term, "person held to service or labor."[75] Ironically—and unwittingly—the act encapsulated precisely the principle that antislavery advocates were now seizing upon, that the Constitution excluded property in man. Yet the act also showed once again how the Constitution's paradox could lead in powerfully proslavery directions, if Congress so willed it. What remained to be seen, as the strains over slavery and the Constitution intensified, was how much longer the paradox could endure, and with it the nation.

Despite resolute antislavery protests and palpable northern discomfort, opposition in Congress to the Fugitive Slave Act proved futile. Salmon Chase, elected to the Senate as a Free Soiler in 1849, had continued his attack on the constitutionality of the 1793 Fugitive Slave Act, most notably as the attorney for the defense in the case of *Jones v. Van Zandt* in 1845, but no court ruled in his favor. He fared no better in the Senate. With the framers' exclusion of property in man on his mind, Chase declared that he was "unwilling to make a supplement to the Constitution, for the sake of erecting a bulwark for slavery."[76] Regardless, the new law passed the Senate comfortably, and its sponsors rammed it through the House three weeks later by a vote of 109 to 75. Yet twenty-three senators did not vote, and in the House, where every southerner present supported the bill, only about one in five northerners did so, with thirty-three northerners not voting. Once again, a small minority of the northern representatives provided the margin in the House in slavery's favor, but the overall sectional divide was stark.[77]

News of the Fugitive Slave Act's passage provoked fierce protests in the North, including spectacular efforts to protect runaway slaves, and it famously inspired Harriet Beecher Stowe to write her galvanizing novel *Uncle Tom's Cabin*. A counterreaction by northern moderates, however, quieted the initial protests and seemed for a time to reinstate respect for law and order, private property, and the primacy of Union. "The patriotic obligation of obeying the Constitution and the laws," Henry Clay observed in October 1852, "is now almost universally recognized and admitted."[78] Southerners supporting the compromise made clear that its reinforcement of their property rights was now essential to sectional peace. "Should Congress at any time exhibit its intentions to war upon our property," a widely endorsed southern pro-unionist statement warned, "we stand ready to vindicate those rights *in the Union* so long as possible, and *out of the Union,* when we are left no other alternative."[79] Political abolitionists felt disoriented as well as marginalized: "The organization of [the] movement is broken up and I do not think is practicable or desirable to renew it," one New York Free Soiler wrote in despair.[80] The Free Soil Party's presidential vote dropped by half from 1848 to 1852.

With the creation of a law that in effect obliged the entire northern population to join in the capture and return of fugitive slaves, the sanctity of slaves as property superficially seemed more ensured than ever. Yet the quieting of antislavery protests was deceptive and proved short-lived. In 1854, a display of federal might to enforce the Fugitive Slave Act in Boston, regarding the captured escaped slave Anthony Burns, provoked massive demonstrations of outrage. Building on the antislavery constitutional arguments of Chase and others—and picking up on the *Prigg* decision's opening for local officials to refuse to cooperate with the rendition of slaves—between 1854 and 1860 lawmakers in ten northern states enacted a fresh round of defiant personal liberty laws designed to obstruct enforcement of the new federal law. Alongside contests over slavery in the territories, the fugitive slave issue would remain a hot point of political struggle over property in man and the Constitution. And at the very moment in 1854 that the Burns affair exploded, Congress shockingly reopened the territorial conflict.

The Kansas-Nebraska Act of 1854, a product of Stephen A. Douglas's collaboration with proslavery hard-liners, instantly destroyed the awkward pact reached in 1820 over property in man. By explicitly repealing the second half of the Missouri Compromise, the act completed the renunciation of congressional power over slavery in the territories, as desired by southern militants ever since the compromise's approval. Without saying so explicitly, it thereby bolstered proslavery contentions that the Constitution guaranteed slaveholders' property rights in their slaves as absolute. By shrouding the renunciation in the billows of popular sovereignty, Douglas hoped to contain what he knew would be a convulsive reaction in the North. Instead, the Kansas-Nebraska Act destroyed the existing party system by bringing the final collapse of the Whig Party and, with the first stirrings of the Republican Party, the transformation of schismatic antislavery politics into a major political organization.

Salmon P. Chase and a small group of antislavery congressmen prepared in advance to frame the Kansas-Nebraska debate on their own terms. Their inflammatory manifesto, *Appeal of the Independent Democrats in Congress* (published the day after the Kansas-Nebraska Act's introduction to the Senate), denounced the measure as the opening gambit of an "atrocious plot" to spread slavery throughout the western territories. Designed to revive and unite every strand of northern antislavery opinion, the *Appeal* offered no constitutional exegesis but emphasized what had become the central antislavery assertion: that "the original settled policy of the United States" had been "non-extension of slavery."[81] The experienced political abolitionists were seriously back in the fray, once again agitating the issue of congressional authority over slavery in the territories.

Just as the Kansas-Nebraska Act revived antislavery veterans such as Chase, so it shook northerners across the political spectrum, including the Illinois ex-congressman Abraham Lincoln. A dedicated Whig for his entire political career, Lincoln had spent his one term in the House in close connection with the most outspoken antislavery Whigs, rooming at the boarding establishment known informally as Abolition House, stoutly opposing the Mexican War, and devising a plan, never formally proposed, for compensated gradual emancipation in the District of Columbia. Years later he remarked that he had always been "naturally anti-slavery," but the Kansas-Nebraska Act jolted him into understanding that the future of slavery was now the "paramount" national question.[82]

At Peoria in October 1854, in direct reply to a speech by his long-time political nemesis Stephen Douglas, Lincoln explained his revised views on slavery in the longest speech he would ever deliver. Lincoln's main conclusion, that Congress ought to restore the Missouri Compromise, was tepid compared to the political abolitionists' protests. The speech's remarks conciliatory of the South, its denial of racial equality, and its insistence that the Constitution's compromises over slavery be respected—including, if only grudgingly, the fugitive slave clause and with it the new Fugitive Slave Act—sounded positively conservative. But at the heart of the speech lay propositions with distinctly abolitionist overtones, filled out with the logic—not yet fully coherent in Lincoln's mind—of what would become the antislavery politics of the Republican Party.

At bottom, Lincoln declared, the nation faced a moral issue that could not be evaded: slavery was a "monstrous injustice" because it denied blacks their natural right to self-government. ("There can be no moral right in connection with one man's making a slave of another," he said.) The founding generation, he said, was basically antislavery, its egalitarian ideals proclaimed by the Declaration of Independence. The Constitution, of necessity, contained compromises with slavery that could not now be wished away, but the framers had gone no further than those compromises. Instead, they had purposely refused to use the word "slave" or "slavery," referring instead to "a person held to service or labor." As slavery could not be eliminated in 1787 without destroying the Union, Lincoln claimed, the framers had hidden slavery away in the Constitution, with the promise that it would be destroyed at a later date. And while the compromises made in 1787 had to be respected with regard to where slavery existed, they had no force in the territories, where the Constitution gave Congress complete authority. The second half of the Missouri Compromise, based on that authority, had been struck in keeping with the framers' view that slavery should be "hedged and hemmed . . . in to the narrowest limits of necessity." Now, with the Kansas-Nebraska Act, the Congress had broken faith with the framers and vaunted a bogus principle of "popular sovereignty" that professed complete indifference to the despotism of slavery.[83]

Like Chase and the Libertyites and Free Soilers before him, Lincoln at Peoria exaggerated the concerted antislavery motives and deeds of the founding generation. He had not worked out for himself fully the connections between the exclusion of slavery and the politics of preventing slavery's extension. (In this, he lagged behind some of the political abolitionists.) Nor, as he confessed, did he have a clue about how slavery would actually be destroyed. But in explaining his opposition to the Kansas-Nebraska Act, Lincoln grasped how the Federal Convention had gone only so far in compromising with the proslavery southerners. He understood how, by referring to slaves as persons, not property, the framers had refused to recognize slavery as a national institution. He sensed how the framers, with their refusal to go any further than political necessity demanded, offered his generation the instruments to cut out what he called the "cancer" of slavery before it killed the Republic.[84]

The turmoil of the next three years would clarify to the entire nation the struggle's contours, above all with respect to the Constitution and property in man. Thereafter, the issues made plain, Lincoln and the Republicans would force them to a point where they could no longer be ducked or compromised.

The *Dred Scott* decision in 1857 brought the property issue into sharp focus and placed the authority of the Supreme Court behind the absolutist proslavery claims that had been evolving for nearly forty years. It came at a startling moment of political truth.

In the 1830s, Dred Scott, born a slave in Virginia, was taken by his owner, Dr. John Emerson of Missouri, to reside first in the free state of Illinois and then in Wisconsin Territory, where slavery was barred under the Missouri Compromise. While in Wisconsin, Scott married an enslaved woman, Harriet Robinson, and in time they had two daughters. In 1846, having returned to Missouri, the Scotts lodged a suit claiming that their residence on free soil had set them free. The case eventually landed on appeal in the Supreme Court, where Chief Justice Roger B. Taney, backed by all but two of the eight associate justices, ruled, that as black persons, the Scotts had no standing in court, and that as the Constitution "distinctly and expressly affirmed" the right of property in a slave, masters could take their slaves into free states and federal territories without fear of granting them freedom. Thus, the Court decided, the second part of the Missouri Compromise, repealed three years earlier, had been unconstitutional all along.[85]

The political stakes attached to the decision could not have been higher. It had been apparent for some time that demographic trends had turned features of the Constitution that originally seemed likely to favor the slave South into advantages for the free North, above all the allocation of representation in the House of Representatives and the Electoral College by population. The bonus given by the three-fifths clause, which southerners had supposed would secure them a majority in the House and the Electoral College, had long since failed to keep pace with a relative rise in northern population, and the disparity kept getting worse. In 1820, the non-slaveholding states (including those that had commenced emancipation) held 123 seats in the House, compared to 90 held by the slave states; in 1850, the respective figures were 147 and 90.[86] In 1856, the Electoral College favored the non-slave states by a margin of 176 to 120. Since the dawn of the republic, southerners had proven adept at peeling off enough northern votes to get their way on sectional issues, including issues directly related to slavery, but especially after the tempest that followed the Kansas-Nebraska Act, it would be harder to overcome the gap in numbers. With the Constitution's political safeguards for slavery looking feeble, it fell to a proslavery majority on the Supreme Court to rewrite the Constitution.

Party political developments greatly heightened the sense of urgency. The demise of the Whig Party in the aftermath of the Kansas-Nebraska debates smashed one of the crucial intersectional bonds that had protected slavery since the Arkansas and Missouri crisis. The new Republican Party's success in the 1856 elections, winning eleven of the fifteen non-slave states for its presidential candidate, John C. Frémont, showed that the antislavery party foreshadowed in Congress in 1820 and 1846 might soon be in a position to win national power. Simultaneously, the continuing fallout from the Kansas-Nebraska Act, leading to civil war and competing claims to sovereignty in Kansas, embroiled the Democrats in fractious conflicts between northern advocates of popular sovereignty, led by Stephen A. Douglas, and southern hard-liners including James H. Hammond, now a senator. The incoming doughface president James Buchanan backed the southerners. By affirming the longtime proslavery position on property in man as absolute, the *Dred Scott* decision effectively declared the Republicans' cardinal political principle unconstitutional, while it cast a dark shadow over the vague concept of popular sovereignty.

The ruling was in fact several rulings, including Taney's majority opinion as well as the six concurring opinions and two dissents. Two of the majority opinions added little of substance; the others offered different routes to reach the same conclusions. For the most part, though, on the crucial matter of slavery in the territories, each opinion amounted to an emphatic restatement of proslavery arguments that dated back at least as far as the Arkansas and Missouri crisis. Justices Peter V. Daniel and John A. Campbell, for example, as well as Taney, cited the same narrow interpretation of the Constitution's territory clause that southern hard-liners had advanced during the Missouri debates, denying that the clause (as Alexander Smyth put it in 1820) contained any "grant of power [to Congress] to legislate over persons and private property within a territory."[87] Justice Taney reformulated the idea floated by Felix Walker, Louis McLane, and John Tyler (among others) during the Arkansas and Missouri debates that all territory obtained in the Louisiana Purchase belonged to all of the states; Taney extended the idea to cover any territories obtained by the United States after 1789. Justice Daniel relied heavily on the more forceful so-called common property doctrine formulated by John C. Calhoun, and contended that the Northwest Ordinance as well as the second part of the Missouri Compromise were illegal. Justice Catron revived an old claim that restricting slavery in the purchase lands violated the original purchase treaty with France. Above all, each of the majority opinions insisted that the right to property in man was as absolute as the right to any other form of property—that, indeed, the nation had been founded, as Louis McLane had proclaimed in 1819, on "the interest of the owner of his slave as property," and that the framers, as Calhoun had pronounced, had provided an "express guarantee" for slavery.[88]

While they rehashed hard-line proslavery doctrines, the justices, Taney in particular, also pushed them beyond the point of credibility, as the dissenting justices Benjamin Curtis and John McLean pointed out in their own opinions. To state, for example, as Taney did, that the Constitution "distinctly and expressly" guaranteed rights to property in man may have become commonplace proslavery doctrine thanks largely to Calhoun, but it was also plainly false: at no point, not even in the fugitive slave clause, did the framers explicitly affirm anything about slavery as a property right. Remarkably, though, the glaring imprecision and illogic in the opinions accompanied points of congruence with what had become conventional judicial thinking about the status of slaves as property.

If, for example, so eminent a constitutional scholar as Justice Joseph Story (who had died more than a decade earlier) could write consistently of slaves as property and of the fugitive slave clause as a foundation of the Union, as Story had in his *Prigg* opinion, who could dismiss that view in connection with the slaves Dred and Harriet Scott? Arguments to the contrary, notably Salmon P. Chase's in the fugitive slave cases he undertook, had gained no purchase in any American court. Even in Congress, where antislavery constitutionalism had been a major force for decades, the Kansas-Nebraska Act had battered claims about congressional authority over slavery and the key underlying contention about the Constitution's exclusion of property in man. With all of its excesses, the *Dred Scott* decision carried with it enough precedent as well as widely accepted proslavery mytholog, about the Constitution that it could be hailed by its defenders as a legitimate ruling by the nation's supreme legal authority, the disobedience of which, in one New York newspaper's words, was "rebellion, treason, and revolution."[89]

The emerging northern Republican majority, though, was appalled, not simply by the Court's attack on its principles and program but by what Republicans perceived as the decision's larger constitutional implications. Before *Dred Scott*—no matter the numerous concessions made to the slaveholders, and no matter even the mythology surrounding the fugitive slave clause—slavery had been deemed a legal institution only where it was so authorized by local law. That is, slavery had been tolerated by but not sanctioned in national law, just as the framers had decided in Philadelphia. In *Dred Scott,* though, the Taney Court declared that slavery was legal everywhere *except* where it was *prohibited* by local law, with Congress powerless over the matter. The decision, as Republicans saw it, turned the Constitution inside out: whereas the Federal Convention had implicitly rendered slavery local and freedom national, from now on, by judicial decree, freedom would be local and slavery national. Not only would Congress be prohibited from constraining slavery's expansion into the territories, but the prospect loomed that, with property rights in slaves deemed absolute, the courts might erode and overturn even state laws prohibiting slavery. The American house, divided over slavery since 1780, would cease to be divided, as Abraham Lincoln would famously declare a year later. Unless slavery was extinguished, Republicans were coming to believe, the United States in its entirety would become a true slaveholding republic.

Dred Scott posed different difficulties for the northern proponents of popular sovereignty, above all Stephen A. Douglas, which in turn raised further questions about the Court's ruling. His ambitions now fixed on winning the presidency, Douglas could not afford to reject the *Dred Scott* decision out of hand lest it thoroughly alienate southern Democrats. Yet the Court's ruling that slaveholders' property rights were inviolate raised serious questions about whether a territorial government had any more power to ban slavery within its jurisdiction than Congress did. (Taney explicitly asserted that it had no such power.) Three months after the Court handed down its ruling, Douglas tried to square the circle by claiming that rights to property in man would prove "worthless" unless supported by "appropriate police regulations and local legislation" enacted by a territorial government. Douglas, for the moment, carved out some middle ground on slavery—but in doing so pushed proslavery hard-liners to wonder whether their property rights could only be fully secured with national legislation that guaranteed slavery in the territories, regardless of any territorial majority. Such a federal slave code for the territories, one Chicago Republican newspaper observed, would be "a logical sequence of the Calhoun dogmas respecting the federal constitution and of the decision of the Supreme Court in the Dred Scott case, both of which Senator Douglas indorses."[90]

Lincoln and Douglas joined the issue in 1858, in their famous debates contesting Douglas's Senate seat. During the second debate at Freeport, Lincoln got Douglas to restate his well-known opinion that territorial legislatures could effectively ban slavery with local legislation, a position that came to be known at the Freeport Doctrine. In subsequent debates, Lincoln pushed hard on the issue of property in man, and on the contradictions between Douglas's position and the Court's. How, he asked at Jonesboro, could Douglas support the Court's ruling that property rights in slaves were absolute and still assert that territorial governments could ban slavery even indirectly? If any territorial legislature attempted to abridge those absolute rights, would Congress not be obliged to intervene? Would Douglas support such intervention, Lincoln demanded, if it came before the Senate?

Douglas tried to evade Lincoln's questions by insisting that territorial legislatures could regulate property as they saw fit and that Congress could pass no law whatsoever about slavery in the territories—thereby preserving the idea of popular sovereignty, but only by backing off the hard-line proslavery view of property in man expressed in *Dred Scott*. Having made his point about the political implications of a constitutional right to property in man—and now concerned that Douglas's evasions might confuse and satisfy voters—Lincoln shifted, in the final two debates, to the moral ground on which antislavery constitutional arguments had always rested, and on which he had decided finally to define his differences with Douglas.

Douglas's popular-sovereignty idea, Lincoln proclaimed, arose from a vast indifference to the idea that some men could own other men as chattel. Proposing, as Douglas did, that the federal government could not halt slavery's expansion might stand, Lincoln said, if there was no difference between property in humans and property in hogs or horses. But if there was a difference, he continued—if one form of property was right and the other was wrong—"then there is no equality between the right and wrong."[91] As the Constitution did not endorse property in slaves as an absolute right, no matter what the Supreme Court majority had ruled, Congress could decide that slavery was a perfect wrong and take steps toward hastening its abolition.

By 1858, Lincoln's final, pivotal proposition about the Constitution and property rights required no explication; it was already on people's minds. Early on during the Lincoln-Douglas debates, for example, the pro-Lincoln *Chicago Press and Tribune* declared, as a fundamental principle, "We do not believe that there is or can be, by virtue of the Federal compact, such a thing as *property in man*."[92] Over the next two

years, Lincoln and his Republican allies would turn that pronounce-
ment into the core of their political program—and they would force a
national confrontation that proved irresoluble.

The *Dred Scott* decision did not in itself spark the Civil War, but it drove
to the center of national politics the issue that would: the constitutional
status of property in man. In 1857, distinct from but related to the
Court's decision, unfolding events in Kansas surrounding slavery and
the so-called Lecompton Constitution sharply divided Douglas from
the pro-southern president, James Buchanan, which in turn threatened
a rupture inside the Democratic Party. As the 1860 election approached,
proslavery militants, who rejected Douglas's version of popular sovereignty as no more constitutional than Republicanism, began to rally
around demands for a federal slave code for the territories—a measure
that, in their view, the *Dred Scott* decision's absolutist claims about property in man virtually demanded. In his annual message, delivered on
December 19, 1859, President Buchanan fully endorsed the militants,
declaring that, in accord with *Dred Scott*, property in slaves was a "vested
right" protected "under the Federal Constitution," which "neither Congress nor a Territorial legislature nor any human power has any authority to annul or impair." One month later, Albert Gallatin Brown
of Mississippi laid before the Senate a pair of resolutions calling for a
territorial code that would protect "property recognized by the Constitution of the United States."[93] Two weeks after that, Brown's fellow
Mississippian Jefferson Davis presented an even more elaborate set of
related proposals, which soon won the backing of the Democratic
Senate caucus and the Buchanan administration.

By the end of June 1860, the slave code issue had torn the Democratic
Party in two, pitting the party's proslavery southern wing, which

nominated Vice President John C. Breckinridge for the presidency, against the northern popular-sovereignty Democrats, who in a separate convention nominated Douglas. All along, Douglas had been venting his anger at the southern hard-liners and their administration supporters. In September 1859, three months before Brown and Davis presented their resolutions to the Senate, Douglas published in *Harper's New Monthly Magazine* a 20,000-word essay explaining and defending his idea of popular sovereignty—a piece that, though exceptionally ponderous, had an electrifying political effect.

Douglas's main purpose was to establish beyond dispute that although Congress was powerless to establish or prohibit slavery in the territories, territorial legislatures very much possessed the authority to do so. It was a daunting assignment given the ricketiness of Douglas's proposition. It was all the more daunting because, with the presidential election approaching, Douglas was required to reconcile popular sovereignty with his avowed support of the *Dred Scott* decision. Despite all of his industrious verbiage, Douglas failed. At one point, amid a jumbled commentary on *Dred Scott*, he tried to refute the proslavery hard-liners' interpretation of the decision by charging that if the Constitution established slavery in the territories "beyond the power of the people," then there was nothing to prevent slavery from being similarly established in every state of the Union.[94] That is, if the proslavery hard-liners' position was correct, so was the Republican charge that the decision paved the way for the nationalization of slavery— precisely the Republicans' charge against *Dred Scott*. It was an irresistible conclusion—but to southern Democrats it was political heresy.

And there was more. In attempting to salvage popular sovereignty from the implications of *Dred Scott*, Douglas finally argued himself into a position he had worked hard to avoid in his debates with Lincoln. Whereas earlier he had simply backed off from an absolutist view of slave property, he now explicitly endorsed the long-standing antislavery contention that property in man was solely a creation of state law—authorized "not under the Constitution of the United States, nor by the laws thereof, nor by virtue of any Federal authority whatsoever."[95] Although slaves could be considered property the same as any other in local law, slavery was entitled to no special protection from the federal government, except with regard to fugitive slaves. In all, under the pressure of *Dred Scott* and the continuing political crisis in Kansas, the author of the Kansas-Nebraska Act now found himself compelled to deny flagrantly what had long been the keystone of proslavery politics—the inviolability of property in man under the Constitution. Southern militants instantly understood as much; the Richmond *Enquirer* denounced the *Harper's* essay as "an incendiary document."[96] The Democratic divisions deepened, on the way to the party's collapse nine months later.

Abraham Lincoln, preparing in the autumn and early winter of 1859 to launch his bid for the Republican presidential nomination, lightly mocked the *Harper's* essay as the strongest of Douglas's "explanations explanatory of explanations explained," but he also studied it closely.[97] In October, Lincoln accepted an invitation to deliver a major address at the famed abolitionist minister Henry Ward Beecher's church in Brooklyn. (The venue would later be moved across the East River to the larger Cooper Institute.) He knew it would be a crucial occasion to win over a large assembly of influential, skeptical New York Republicans. Douglas's essay was something of a godsend, excellent fodder for blasting the illogic of popular sovereignty, and Lincoln pored over it, as he did with the Court's various *Dred Scott* opinions, plumbing the constitutional issues they raised.

Lincoln needed to accomplish two things above all at the Cooper Institute: first, to refute the claim, made by both wings of the Democratic

Party, that Congress was powerless to legislate on slavery in the territories; and second, to refute the proslavery argument underlying that claim that the Constitution affirmed an absolute right to property in man. Put together, these points would cut directly to the fundamental issue in the campaign, explode the constitutional rationale behind the proslavery position on the territories, and then prove to any doubters the depth of Lincoln's antislavery commitment. The second point, about property in man, would additionally expose the incoherence of Douglas's popular-sovereignty doctrine in light of *Dred Scott*.

Lincoln opened by approvingly quoting Douglas on how the framers of the Constitution understood the matters at hand just as well as their descendants, if not better. He followed with historical discourse on how, for decades, Congress had repeatedly exercised its authority over slavery in the territories, with the full knowledge and in some cases the blessings of men who had been delegates to the Federal Convention. Beginning with the prohibition of slavery in the Northwest Ordinance in 1787, Lincoln explained how Congress, short of banning slavery, used its constitutional powers to "interfere with it—take control of it," citing some of the debates over Mississippi Territory in 1798 and over Louisiana Territory in 1804. In all, Lincoln calculated, twenty-one of the thirty-nine signers of the Constitution at some point endorsed federal efforts to constrain slavery in the territories, while only two of the thirty-nine voted against congressional prohibition of slavery in the territories.[98] Lincoln carefully avoided turning his exercise into blind worship of the framers' intentions, which, he said, "would be to discard all the lights of current experience—to reject all progress."[99] But because Douglas himself had invoked the authority of the framers, Lincoln said, it was important to understand correctly what the framers had actually said and done. At all events, there was abundant precedent for Congress to interfere with slavery in the territories.

On rights to property in man, Lincoln stuck to the text of the Constitution itself (with assistance from Madison's notes) and made quick work of demolishing the proslavery hard-liners' constitutional contentions, as proclaimed by the *Dred Scott* decision. Southerners had reached the point, he charged, where some had vowed to break up the Union rather than forsake what he called "an assumed Constitutional right of yours, to take slaves into the federal territories, and to hold them there as property."[100] Northerners insisted that no such right existed in the Constitution, even implicitly; in response, the proslavery side had recklessly vowed to destroy the national government unless allowed to interpret and enforce the Constitution however it pleased.

What, though, of the *Dred Scott* decision? Whatever northerners thought, had the Supreme Court not decided the issue of slavery in the territories once and for all in the slaveholders' favor? In view of the decision, weren't the antislavery northerners, and not the southerners, subverting the Constitution and the rule of law? Lincoln demurred. The badly divided court, he said, had decided *Dred Scott* in, at best, a "sort of" way. Even the majority of justices disagreed about the decision's meaning. Above all, the decision was "mainly based upon a mistaken statement of fact," namely that the Constitution "distinctly and expressly" affirmed the right of property in a slave.[101] The implication was clear: it would be absurd to let stand any Court decision, let alone one of such magnitude, which turned on a falsehood, especially if that falsehood concerned a fundamental point of constitutional law. And here, calmly and methodically, Lincoln went for the jugular.

Plainly, he remarked, the Constitution does not "distinctly and expressly" affirm any right to property in slaves. It was inarguable that *Dred Scott* rested on a fabrication, and hence was vulnerable to being overturned by a later, less biased Supreme Court. The justices, he suggested, would have been wiser to claim that the Constitution only implicitly affirmed property in man, but here, too, they would have quickly run into trouble. The words "slave" and "slavery," he pointed out, never appear in the Constitution; neither does the word "property" "in any connection with language alluding to the things slave, or slavery." Wherever alluded to, slaves appeared as persons owing service or labor to another—a usage, Lincoln asserted, that "contemporaneous history" revealed "was employed on purpose to exclude from the Constitution the idea that there could be property in man." Lincoln had by now, if not earlier, closely studied Madison's notes, which he took to show incontrovertibly that the framers had rejected not just the word "slave" in national law but the legal reality behind the word, the condition of property in man. With that single revelation, the entire rationale behind *Dred Scott* collapsed, as did the proslavery militants' constitutional claims. "To show all this," Lincoln concluded, "is easy and certain."[102]

Lincoln's Cooper Institute address has been described as the speech that made him president, and it was certainly the speech that made him a serious contender for the Republican nomination, which he secured in mid-May.[103] The fraught campaign rhetoric that followed on all sides never reached the same level of exposition and exhortation that Lincoln did in New York. Yet even when it went unsaid, everybody knew that the heart of the matter was slavery, and that the main political issue was the future of slavery in the territories. That issue turned on a fight over the Constitution and property rights.

In various forums, advocates from across the antislavery political spectrum—except the Garrisonians—returned in 1860 to this crucial point. A month after Lincoln's speech, the radical Frederick Douglass, who had fled to Britain months earlier in the wake of John Brown's failed insurrection, addressed an antislavery meeting in Glasgow with a strong defense of the Constitution as an antislavery document, an extended reprise of the conclusion to his famous speech eight years earlier on the hypocrisy of the Fourth of July. Douglass remained a constitutional abolitionist, contending, unlike the Republicans, that the Constitution empowered the federal government to abolish slavery everywhere, including states where it legally existed. But Douglass hit many of the same chords as Lincoln and the Republicans did, and he counted on his remarks making their way home where they might goad the abolitionist rank and file to vote.

The Garrisonians, Douglass said, believed the Constitution was a slaveholding instrument, and they denounced anyone who voted or held office, no matter how strong the voter's or officeholder's anti-slavery views. "I, on the other hand, deny that the constitution guarantees the right to hold property in men," he told his audience, "and believe that the way, the true way, to abolish slavery in America is to vote such men into power as will exert their moral and political influence for the abolition of slavery. This is the issue plainly stated, and you shall judge between us." (Douglass did not need to explain which candidates and which party would exercise the right interest.) A slaveholding oligarchy, he acknowledged, had long ruled the nation by perverting the intentions of the framers, but that tyranny was losing its grip. "If the South has made the Constitution bend to the purposes of slavery," Douglass concluded, "let the North now make that instrument bend to the cause of freedom and justice."[104]

Congressman John Sherman of Ohio could in most ways hardly have been more unlike Frederick Douglass and still be an antislavery Republican. A political moderate (and brother of soon-to-be general William Tecumseh Sherman), Congressman Sherman, as chairman of the House Ways and Means Committee, had begun an ascent that would lead him in the future to become a sound-money treasury secretary and, finally, President William McKinley's secretary of state. But Sherman was a brave and outspoken antislavery advocate, and his campaign speeches in 1860 hit the property question squarely and hard. "The radical difference between the Republicans and both wings of the democratic party is on a question of constitutional law," he told an enormous rally in Philadelphia. "It is this: are negroes, held as slaves in the southern States, regarded by the Constitution of the United States as property in the same sense in which, by universal law, horses, cattle, oxen, and other chattels are held[?]" Sherman denounced the doctrine of slaves as constitutionally protected property, calling it the false founding principle of "the Calhoun school of politicians," at odds with the Constitution itself and the framers' express statement "that the idea that men should hold property of other men was carefully excluded."[105]

The appeals proliferated; another came from a writer with a distinguished background that included a unique personal connection to the Constitution, James Alexander Hamilton, Alexander Hamilton's third-born son. Hamilton had embarked on a career as a lawyer in upstate New York when in 1829, thanks to his friend Martin Van Buren, he joined the inner circles of Andrew Jackson's White House. There Hamilton served briefly as interim secretary of state, and he advised the president closely during the war against the Second Bank of the United States—the successor bank to his father's brainchild—as well as the nullification crisis. After a stint as U.S. attorney for the Southern District of New York, Hamilton assumed the role of urbane elder statesman, a trusted counselor to political leaders across party lines as well as to foreign dignitaries.

In 1858, Hamilton had a strange shipboard encounter, as he recalled in his memoirs. Bound home from Europe, he struck up a conversation with a fellow passenger—Charles Cotesworth Pinckney, the nephew and namesake of the proslavery mainstay who had served with Hamilton's father at the Federal Convention. Leaving the convention aside, Hamilton brought up the subject of John C. Calhoun and the nullification crisis of 1832. Hamilton vividly remembered that President Jackson had believed the affair was a treasonous ploy for southern se cession, worked up by slaveholders who feared northern power, with slavery "at the bottom of the whole subject." Pinckney confirmed as much to Hamilton and said that, with the air once more thick with talk of southern secession, not much had changed in twenty-five years. "My dear Sir," he averred, "we do not mean to submit to the popular control of the North." Back then, he allowed, the slaveholders weren't willing to fight the federal government explicitly in the name of slavery, but this time they would proudly proclaim their cause. "We intend to establish a great Southern Empire, with slavery as a basis," Pinckney said, "we only wait our opportunity."[106]

The episode shook Hamilton into undertaking what he called "an examination of the Constitutional questions connected with slavery," and he went on to compose a six-thousand-word essay, "Property in Man." The *New York Times* prominently published the piece in full on Independence Day in 1860, just as the presidential campaign began in earnest. Hamilton's argument struck hard, and he expressed hope that it had stirred discussion of the question that was "at the bottom of the party differences of the country."[107]

Hamilton was not perfectly reliable about the historical record, making it appear at one point, for example, that the framers had unanimously passed a resolution striking out the words "slave" and "slavery."[108] Yet the essay accurately related and ably interpreted other speeches at the convention and in the First Congress. Hamilton adeptly parsed the meaning of key texts such as the fugitive slave clause. Above all, he cut through the misreading that had accumulated for decades about the framers' wording, concluding that the convention aimed "to exclude from the Constitution, not only the hated word *'Slave,'* but the detested thing *'Slavery.'*"[109] His least likely note was his last: he hoped that, should the Republicans capture the presidency, the South would resist calls to follow the "fratricidal and suicidal" course of secession and instead revert to "the principles which guided those who formed the Constitution."[110]

On November 20, twelve days after Lincoln's victory, Hamilton wrote directly to Thomas Cotesworth Pinckney, the son of the departed framer Charles Cotesworth Pinckney, in a last-ditch gesture to rekindle their fathers' shared principle of compromise. The national government, Hamilton pleaded with Pinckney, was "the palladium of our liberty." Dissolving it would only bring warfare between two bordering nations. He beseeched the South Carolinian to trust and respect "our common memories of the past and hopes for the future."[111]

Exactly one month after Hamilton wrote his letter, a special state convention approved and announced South Carolina's ordinance of secession. Over the next five weeks, six more southern states seceded. Hamilton never received a reply "other than two pamphlets written with the clear intent, by gross exaggeration, to 'fire the Southern heart.'"[112]

Outside South Carolina, secession was not a foregone conclusion, even in the Lower South, but the clash over the issue of property in man had long since passed the point of compromise. Either the Constitution affirmed property rights in slaves, with regard both to fugitive slaves and the territories, or it did not. Proslavery southerners made it perfectly clear in 1860 that they considered this the nub of the conflict, and that they would not yield over it any more than Lincoln or the Republicans would.

In June 1860, the southern Democrats supporting John C. Breckinridge approved a campaign platform that declared, first, that all American citizens had an equal right to settle in the territories "without their rights, either of person or property, being destroyed or impaired by Congressional or Territorial legislation," and, second, that the federal government had a constitutional duty to protect property rights in the territories "and wherever else its constitutional authority extends." This was no surprise: proslavery militants, including Breckinridge, had been presenting property rights in slaves as the central issue of the campaign even before the campaign began. "Did not the Constitution languish in the [Federal] convention, until stipulations were inserted to guard and protect our rights?" Breckinridge demanded in an address at the end of 1859, later reprinted as a campaign pamphlet.[113] A federal slave code to secure that property, he later observed from the stump, far from "hostile to the Constitution or the union of States," preserved the very soul of the framers' work by protecting property in man.[114] It was the abolitionist Republican Party and not the proslavery side that threatened to desecrate the Constitution, by abrogating property rights that the Federal Convention had rendered inviolable.

When Lincoln won and South Carolina seceded, the property issue duly dominated the secessionists' call to arms. To be sure, South Carolina's declaration justifying secession began with a lengthy defense of state rights and the compact theory of the Constitution. But that opening section concerned the legitimacy of secession; the fundamental cause for secession, the declaration explained, was the North's unconstitutional attacks on "the right of property in slaves."[115] The declaration singled out the antislavery personal liberty laws passed by numerous northern states to counter the Fugitive Slave Act of 1850, which had become a particularly powerful source of resentment, but the offenses, the declaration said, ran deeper, touching the territorial issue as well.

In explaining its case, the South Carolina declaration offered a summary of the hard-line proslavery arguments (with some fresh twists) that had developing gradually since 1787 and come to govern southern political and constitutional thinking about slavery. The Constitution, the declaration asserted, had established

> a Federal Government, in which each State was recognized as an equal, and had separate control over its institutions. The right of property in slaves was recognized by giving to free persons distinct political rights, by giving them the right to represent, and burthening them with direct taxes for three fifths of their slaves; by authorizing the importation of slaves for twenty years; and by stipulating for the rendition of fugitives from labor.
>
> We affirm that these ends for which this Government was instituted have been defeated, and the Government itself has been made destructive of them by the action of the non-slaveholding States. Those States have assumed the right of deciding upon the propriety of our domestic institutions; and have denied the rights of property established in fifteen of the States and recognized by the Constitution.

After a quarter century of agitation, a sectional party had elected to the presidency a man who had declared that "the public mind must rest in the belief that slavery is in the course of ultimate extinction." Rather than submit, South Carolina would secede.[116]

The South Carolinians' claim that the three-fifths clause somehow affirmed property in slaves was not unprecedented, but it was unusual; their claim that the Atlantic slave trade clause did the same thing was even more unusual. But if the reasoning was slightly different, the conclusion was the same one that proslavery hard-liners had been proclaiming for decades. The paradox of 1787 had finally collapsed. What, as early as 1790, a South Carolina congressman had threateningly called "the trumpet of sedition" now resounded in the slaveholding states.[117]

On March 11, in Montgomery, Alabama, representatives of the seven states that had already seceded signed the Constitution of the Confederate States of America, the supreme law of the rebel government until the end of the war. Largely a word-for-word duplication of the U.S. Constitution, the document included a few crucial changes regarding slavery—and the changes involved precisely the clauses that had been so troublesome in 1787. Everywhere that the Federal Convention excluded property in man, the Confederate constitution pointedly included it.

The Confederate version of the three-fifths clause, for example, referred explicitly to "slaves," not "persons." The Confederate clause banning the international slave trade (as a boost to the dominant domestic slave trade) likewise struck the word "persons" and specified "negroes of the African race." The Confederates' privileges and immunities clause now included wording along the lines that Charles Cotesworth Pinckney apparently desired at the Federal Convention, stating that citizens could travel to any state "with their slaves and other property; and the right of property in said slaves shall not be thereby impaired." The clause on fugitives now spoke of any "slave or other person held to service or labor." As if to remove any ambiguity, the Confederate framers added two new provisions. The first guaranteed that "the institution of negro slavery, as it now exists in the Confederate States," would be protected in all territories, and that inhabitants would have the right to carry with them into the territories "any slaves lawfully held by them." The second, attached to the clause banning bills of attainder and ex post facto laws, flatly prohibited any law "denying or impairing the right of property in negro slaves."[118]

The secessionists could not have been plainer about their motivations, and about the nation they intended to create—a new version of the United States in which slavery would at last exist as a national institution. "We have now placed our domestic institution, and secured its rights unmistakably, in the Constitution," the Alabama politician Robert Hardy Smith pronounced. "We have called our negroes 'slaves,' and we have recognized and protected them as persons and our rights to them as property."[119]

Embedded, though, in all of these declarations, and in the constitution the declarations celebrated, was a stark admission that the U.S. Constitution of 1787 was not, in fact, what the secessionists had claimed it was—or, indeed, what slaveholders, in various ways, had been claiming it was since the nation's founding. Beginning in the very first Congress, proslavery advocates, in defending the "palladium" of their property in humans, had asserted their fidelity to the actions and intentions of the framers. From then on, slavery's defenders had accused their adversaries, from the Pennsylvania Abolition Society to the Republican Party, of brazenly flouting the Constitution. Yet to create the slaveholders' nation they desired required a new slaveholders' constitution that repudiated precisely the provisions from 1787 that excluded property in man. To secure that constitution in 1861 required treason in the form of secession. And secession, as the incoming President Lincoln made clear, meant war.

Epilogue

THE WAR CHANGED EVERYTHING, but even a brief sketch shows that the old issues of property in man continued to reverberate as slavery reached its doom.

As soon as fighting began, the status of slaves as property became dependent on the existing military situation, but as neither side anticipated a protracted conflict, the issue was not immediately pressing. Still, late in 1860 and early in 1861, as southern secession turned into civil war—and well before slaves began escaping en masse to Union lines—Republican leaders pronounced that disunion would enable the North, now free from the constraints of the Constitution's federal consensus, to initiate abolition. Once the fighting turned, as it quickly did, into an extended and relentless conflict, the politics of emancipation became a point-counterpoint between decisions and debates in Washington and events on the battlefield.

Long before the firing on Fort Sumter, dating back to the aftermath of the Revolution, a broad American consensus held that it was legitimate under the laws of war to free enemy slaves, especially in exchange for military service, and that once emancipated, those freedmen could not be reenslaved. John Quincy Adams, who as secretary of state had aggressively taken the opposing position, came, as a congressman, to endorse the idea that under the Constitution's treaty powers, Congress could actually abolish slavery in the existing states. (Adams thereby affirmed, though with opposite aspirations, the broader concerns voiced by Patrick Henry in 1788.) Even radical antislavery congressmen balked at that idea. But once Union armies on southern soil encountered swelling numbers of masterless slaves—some abandoned by their owners, and some who had escaped—army officers had to decide how the laws of war applied and whether to handle the slaves as persons or as property. Thus began an uneven and contested process that President Lincoln called "practical emancipation."[1]

The process evolved and expanded fitfully during the first two years of the war. In July 1861, from Fortress Monroe, Virginia, General Benjamin Butler informed Secretary of War Simon Cameron that although the thousands of slaves who had come inside his line were property under the laws of the state from which they had escaped, "we do not need and will not hold such property, and will assume no such ownership." A week later, Congress passed and Lincoln signed the First Confiscation Act, which stipulated (as Cameron informed Butler) that escaped "persons held to service . . . employed in hostility" would be "discharged" from that service—that is, emancipated.[2] By the middle of 1862, the Union had broadened its policy to embrace universal military emancipation. Finally, on January 1, 1863, Lincoln's Emancipation Proclamation declared that all slaves in rebellious states were "henceforth and forever free," thereby turning the war to crush the slaveholders' rebellion into a war of liberation. In effect (or so some Union leaders believed), the proclamation returned to the slaves the most fundamental of property rights—the right to self-ownership—which slavery had viciously denied them. Securing the key moral precept of abolitionists dating back to the Revolution was now, by those lights, federal government policy.[3]

To the Confederacy, military emancipation as formalized by Lincoln's proclamation was barbaric. President Jefferson Davis condemned it as an outrageous attack on civilian property and a clear incitement to slave insurrection. At the same time, though, the Emancipation Proclamation, according to Davis, vindicated secession, commencing the revolution in property relations that the slaveholders had charged the North with planning all along. Davis retaliated by decreeing that all ex-slave Union soldiers, along with their white officers, should be handed over to state authorities as insurrectionists, subject to execution. And though that policy never took effect, the Confederacy's determination to defend property in man remained its overarching purpose, affecting even mundane military transactions.[4]

On September 2, 1864, Atlanta fell to William Tecumseh Sherman, a turning point that foretold Union victory. One month later, an increasingly beleaguered Robert E. Lee, hunkered down in Virginia, proposed to Ulysses S. Grant an exchange of soldiers captured outside Richmond. Grant had decided to suspend exchanges, believing that at this point in the conflict they could only help the Confederacy, but he pressed Lee on whether the exchange would include black Union soldiers "as have escaped from Southern Masters." When Lee refused point-blank, Grant spurned the deal. Two weeks later, Lee followed up with a long, stiff letter explaining that his government's proper obligations "to the owners of this species of property" were the same as those he said had been long respected by the Constitution of the United States. It was as if Lee could not see or admit that secession had effectively voided the Fugitive Slave Act; he not only had his orders but would stand by them righteously and let his opposing number know as much. Emancipated soldiers would be reenslaved; indeed, according to Lee and his superiors, they had never been emancipated. Lee has been vaunted by many in later generations as a man who disliked slavery and disunion but whose loyalty to Virginia compelled him to lead the secessionist army. His response to Grant, however, shows that his loyalty to the Confederacy—and thus to the right to property in slaves—ran deeper than that.[5]

As the fighting pounded on mercilessly into its final months, the Thirteenth Amendment to the Constitution, abolishing slavery, lay before the House of Representatives, where it would finally win passage in January 1865. As Lincoln understood well, a concluding Union victory would not in itself ensure emancipation, whatever the effects of his proclamation; the cessation of war would leave the defeated states with the authority, under the existing Constitution, to carry on with slavery as they always had. The framers' work still contained its central paradox about slavery: just as the secessionists had had to write a new constitution in order to launch a nation of slavery, so the Union would have to rewrite the U.S. Constitution, beginning with an abolition amendment, in order to secure a nation of freedom.

The previous April, on the day when the Thirteenth Amendment passed the Senate, Senator Charles Sumner of Massachusetts had delivered a lengthy speech, later published as a pamphlet entitled *No Property in Man*. Sumner had been at the forefront of antislavery politics for nearly twenty years; in 1856, one of his more acidulous speeches had led an infamous South Carolina congressman to cane him within an inch of his life on the Senate floor. Ardent, impulsive, and at times almost morbidly self-involved, Sumner projected a hauteur that he compounded with florid rhetoric. But no one (least of all President Lincoln) doubted Sumner's political skills and consuming devotion to the abolition of slavery, and in 1864, he was one of the most powerful men in the United States.

In 1852, Sumner had delivered a celebrated speech accompanying a motion to repeal the Fugitive Slave Act in which, citing chapter and verse from Madison's notes, he rehearsed the idea that the Federal Convention had acted purposefully "to exclude from the Constitution all idea that there can be property in man." Although he acknowledged that Congress could do nothing to abolish slavery in an existing state, he insisted that the framers had rendered slavery purely a local institution and thereby rendered freedom national.[6] Now, with slavery's abolition in view, he had shifted to the radical position of the constitutional abolitionists, claiming that by excluding "the unnatural pretention of property in man," the Constitution actually did empower Congress to abolish slavery everywhere. Yet Sumner also weighed the courts' past willingness to justify slavery as well as the Congress's reluctance to exercise its full authority, and so while he thought the amendment superfluous, he backed it in order to "give completeness and permanence to emancipation and bring the Constitution into avowed harmony with the Declaration of Independence."[7]

Sumner's readings of the Constitution and the framers' intentions were partial. So were Lincoln's and Chase's and William Slade's, as well as those of the entire procession of antislavery constitutionalists and constitutional abolitionists before them, stretching back to Benjamin Franklin and the Pennsylvania abolitionists in 1790. However much the antislavery framers in 1787 believed that slavery was dying out, however much they expected that by one day abolishing the Atlantic slave trade their new government would seal the institution's fate, they conceded too much to the proslavery framers to make the Constitution simply an engine of emancipation. But like the others, Sumner grasped that the Constitution did not foreclose pushing for emancipation and that it even provided the national government with means to constrain slavery's growth and thus hasten its doom.

James Madison may not have been a stalwart antislavery champion when he told the Federal Convention that it would be wrong to admit into the Constitution the idea that there could be property in man. "Of course it was wrong," Sumner exclaimed to the Senate. "It was criminal and unpardonable. Thank God! it was not done."[8] That it was not done, though, made all the difference. Despite all the slaveholders won in 1787, despite all the ways the Constitution reinforced human bondage and thwarted its abolition, that exclusion would help inspire and legitimize the politics that, within a long lifetime's memory, brought slavery to its knees.

NOTES

INDEX

NOTES

AC   Joseph Gales and William W. Seaton, *The Debates and Proceedings in the Congress of the United States* [otherwise known as *Annals of Congress*], 42 vols. (Washington, DC, 1834–1856).

CG   Francis P. Blair and John C. Rives, *Congressional Globe*, 46 vols. (Washington, DC, 1833–1873).

Farrand   Max Farrand, ed., *The Records of the Federal Convention of 1787*, rev. ed., 4 vols. (1911; New Haven, CT, 1966).

Jensen   Merrill Jensen et al., eds., *The Documentary History of the Ratification of the Constitution*, 29 vols. to date (Madison, WI, 1976–).

Kaminski   John P. Kaminski, ed., *A Necessary Evil? Slavery and the Debate over the Constitution* (Madison, WI, 1995).

RD   Joseph Gales and William W. Seaton, *Register of Debates in Congress,* 14 vols. (Washington, DC, 1825–1837).

INTRODUCTION

1.   The charge that the Constitution "enshrined" slavery appears regularly in a wide range of scholarly writings across several disciplines, as well as in more popular accounts. (Some authors use different words to the same effect, including "approved," "ratified," and "sanctioned.") It has by now become common to see the charge invoked as a truism. For a random

and by no means exhaustive sampling from recent years about slavery being "enshrined," see Henry Wiencek, *An Imperfect God: George Washington, His Slaves, and the Creation of America* (New York, 2003), 270; Lucius J. Barker and Katherine Tate, "The Dynamics of Race and Governance in American Politics: Problems in Search of Theory, Leadership, and Resolution," in *The Evolution of Political Knowledge: Theory and Inquiry in American Politics,* ed. Edward D. Mansfield and Richard Sisson (Columbus, OH, 2004), 263; Richard Beeman, *The Penguin Guide to the United States Constitution: A Fully Annotated Declaration of Independence, U.S. Constitution and Amendments, and Selections from the "Federalist Papers"* (New York, 2010), 159; *The American Civil War: The Essential Reference Guide,* ed. James R. Arnold and Roberta Wiener (Santa Barbara, 2011), 201; Alan Gilbert, *Black Patriots and Loyalists: Fighting for Emancipation in the War for Independence* (Chicago, 2012), 243; Ruthann Robson, *Dressing Constitutionally: Hierarchy, Sexuality, and Democracy from Our Hairstyles to Our Shoes* (Cambridge, 2013), 154; Mathias Möschel, *Law, Lawyers, and Race: Critical Race Theory from the US to Europe* (Abingdon, 2014), 11.

2. Farrand, II:417.

3. Ibid., II:372.

4. Ibid., II:416.

5. Historians disagree on the degree to which the convention's secrecy was intended chiefly to insulate the delegates from outside interference, or to help ensure that the meanings attached to the Constitution would arise from the understanding of the ratifiers and not the intentions of the framers. For a provocative discussion in connection with the flaws of originalism, see Jack N. Rakove, *Original Meanings: Politics and Ideas in the Making of the Constitution* (New York, 1996), 339–365. For a broader consideration of secrecy and politics in the Atlantic world during this era, see Katlyn Marie Carter, "Practicing Politics in the Revolutionary

Atlantic World: Secrecy, Publicity and the Making of Modern Democracy," Ph.D. diss., Princeton University, 2017.

6. Farrand, II:443.

7. John Dickinson, "Notes for a Speech, July 9–14(?), 1787," in James H. Hutson, "John Dickinson at the Federal Constitutional Convention," *William and Mary Quarterly* 40 (1983): 280.

8. David Waldstreicher, "How the Constitution Was Indeed Pro-Slavery," *Atlantic*, September 19, 2015; David Waldstreicher, *Slavery's Constitution: From Revolution to Ratification* (New York, 2009), 98.

9. Paul Finkelman, *Slavery and the Founders: Race and Liberty in the Age of Jefferson* (New York, 2001), 6.

10. Paul Finkelman, "Slavery in the United States: Persons or Property?," in *The Legal Understanding of Slavery: From the Historical to the Contemporary*, ed. Jean Allen (New York, 2012), 118.

11. Farrand, I:561. See, for example, Douglas R. Egerton, *Death or Liberty: African Americans and Revolutionary America* (New York, 2009), 246.

12. Farrand, II:415.

13. Luther Martin, "Genuine Information VIII," *Maryland Gazette*, January 22, 1788, in Kaminski, 173.

14. Dayton quoted in David Brion Davis, *The Problem of Slavery in the Age of Revolution, 1770–1823* (Ithaca, NY, 1974), 127–128. Dayton was almost certainly recalling Sherman's and Clymer's remarks over a motion advanced but quickly withdrawn by Gouverneur Morris.

15. Farrand, II:416.

16. Philadelphia *Independent Gazetteer*, November 8, 1787, in Jensen, XIV:61.

17. Nor did the wording confuse antislavery northerners who *supported* the Constitution. Some of them praised the framers' omission of words like "slave" and "Negro" because, as the abolitionist Benjamin Rush surmised, "it was thought the very words would contaminate the glorious fabric

of American liberty and government." But Rush and his allies were perfectly clear that the provisions on slavery referred to slaves. They believed, with reason, that the wording employed excluded the thing itself from national law—racial slavery, property in man—and not merely the offensive words. Rush to John Coakley Lettsom, September 28, 1787, in Kaminski, 117. See Chapter 3.

18. On these flaws, and especially Madison's tampering with his manuscript notes after 1787, see Mary Sarah Bilder, *Madison's Hand: Revising the Constitutional Convention* (Cambridge, MA, 2015).

19. *The Collected Works of Abraham Lincoln,* ed. Roy C. Basler (New Brunswick, NJ, 1953), I:545.

20. See, in particular, Ira Berlin, *The Long Emancipation: The Demise of Slavery in the United States* (Cambridge, MA, 2015); Patrick Rael, *Eighty-Eight Years: The Long Death of Slavery in the United States, 1777–1865* (Athens, GA, 2015); and Manisha Sinha, *The Slave's Cause: A History of Abolition* (New Haven, CT, 2016). Garrison's critics and adversaries within the antislavery movement held him and his disciples responsible for manufacturing the myth that before him, as one abolitionist put it, "there was hardly a ripple of excitement about slavery in any part of the nation." See Leonard Woolsey Bacon, *Anti-slavery before Garrison* (New Haven, CT, 1903), quotation on 10.

21. "Garrison sees in the Constitution precisely what John C. Calhoun sees there," Douglass wrote in 1850 (*The North Star* [Rochester, NY], April 5, 1850). At the time, Douglass was still a Garrisonian, though wavering; in time, he would change his mind about slavery and the Constitution, which helped prompt his break with Garrison. The modern literature on the Constitution as proslavery commenced forcefully with Staughton Lynd, "The Abolitionist Critique of the United States Constitution," in *The Antislavery Vanguard: New Essays on the Abolitionists,* ed. Martin Duberman (Princeton, NJ, 1965), 209–239, and Staughton Lynd, "The Com-

promise of 1787," *Political Science Quarterly* 81 (1966): 225–250. The most influential statement of the neo-Garrisonian position is Paul Finkelman, "Slavery and the Constitutional Convention: Making a Covenant with Death," in *Beyond Confederation: Origins of the Constitution and American National Identity*, ed. Richard Beeman, Stephen Botein, and Edward C. Carter II (Chapel Hill, NC, 1987). See also William Wiecek, *The Sources of Antislavery Constitutionalism in the United States, 1760–1848* (Ithaca, NY, 1977), 62–83; and Waldstreicher, *Slavery's Constitution*. Recent studies that either endorse or are sympathetic to all or part of the neo-Garrisonian view include James Oakes, "The Compromising Expedient: Justifying a Proslavery Constitution," *Cardozo Law Review* 17 (1995–1996): 2023–2056; George William Van Cleve, *A Slaveholders' Union: Slavery, Politics, and the Constitution in the Early American Republic* (Chicago, 2010); and Berlin, *Long Emancipation*, 62–63. Often, the fact that the Constitution tolerated slavery gets translated into the Constitution favoring slavery, which in turn comes to mean that the Constitution was proslavery. The most direct and extended challenges to the neo-Garrisonian interpretation appear in Earl M. Maltz, "The Idea of the Proslavery Constitution," *Journal of the Early Republic* 17 (1997): 37–59; and Don E. Fehrenbacher, *The Slaveholding Republic: An Account of the United States Government's Relations to Slavery*, completed and ed. Ward M. McAfee (New York, 2001), esp. 3–47, but see also Howard Albert Ohline, "Politics and Slavery: The Issue of Slavery in National Politics, 1787–1815," Ph.D. diss., University of Missouri, 1969, 22–125, which, though it preceded the modern controversy, also anticipated much of it. See as well William W. Freehling, "The Founding Fathers and Slavery," *American Historical Review* 77 (1972): 81–93, although cf. Freehling's essay "The Founding Fathers, Conditional Antislavery, and the Nonradicalism of the American Revolution," in his collection *The Reintegration of American History: Slavery and the Civil War* (New York, 1994), 12–33, which offers a harsher view of the subject. A recent assessment by

Patrick Rael comes closer than many to the interpretation in this book: "This, then, became the Constitution's slavery, as well as its antislavery: chattel bondage as an acknowledged and legal practice, but not a social good, and one that might at some point in the future be eradicated" (Rael, *Eighty-Eight Years,* 78–79). Rael allows the Constitution its antislavery dimension; still, a basic disagreement remains over the extent to which the Constitution actually acknowledged slavery and affirmed slavery's legality. Another balanced interpretation which emphasizes the Constitution's proslavery features appears in Michael J. Klarman, *The Framers' Coup: The Making of the United States Constitution* (New York, 2016), 257–302. The key Garrisonian polemic on the Constitution, Wendell Phillips, *The Constitution a Pro-Slavery Compact* (New York, 1845), helped inspire and still informs neo-Garrisonian historical writing.

22. Of course, the framers were not at all unanimous in their views about how thoroughly federal power ought to be circumscribed. As originally presented to the convention, for example, the so-called Virginia Plan, projecting a powerful national government, gave Congress the power to veto state laws "contravening in the opinion of the National Legislature the articles of Union." James Madison then passionately seconded a motion by the proslavery South Carolinian Charles Pinckney expanding that veto to cover any state law that Congress deemed "improper." The Pinckney-Madison proposal quickly failed, and the convention soon enough excised the more modest proposal from the Virginia Plan. With Pinckney and Madison at the forefront, plainly neither version intended to empower Congress to negative state laws regulating slavery. Still, it is interesting to contemplate what might have happened to the future course of antislavery and proslavery politics had the Constitution included either proposal. See Farrand, I:162, 164, 168; Alison L. LaCroix, "What If Madison Had Won? Imagining a Constitutional World of Legislative Supremacy," *Indiana Law Review* 45 (2012): 41–59.

23. John Jay to the English Anti-Slavery Society, June [?], 1788, in *The Correspondence and Public Papers of John Jay*, ed. Henry P. Johnston (New York, 1890), III:342.

24. Berlin, *Long Emancipation*, 70.

25. *Hampshire Gazette* (Northampton), June 4, 1788, in Kaminski, 111.

26. Another speculation holds that had the northern delegates stood firm on the three-fifths clause and the Atlantic slave trade, the Lower South, its economy badly deranged by the Revolution, would have backed off and joined the new union anyway. This presumes that Lower South slaveholders, in order to obtain a Constitution they hoped would better secure national commerce, would have committed, as they saw it, economic suicide.

27. *United States Chronicle* (Providence), July 17, 1788, in Kaminski, 114.

28. It is too easily forgotten that while the fugitive slave clause gave slavery vague new security, it did so in response to the emancipation laws and judicial rulings in the North that had appeared since 1780. Slavery's defenders would call it a major advance over the Articles of Confederation—but nothing like it appeared in the Articles because it was nothing that would have occurred to anyone to include. During the colonial period, return of runaway slaves and servants was presumed across county and colony jurisdictions, according to the common law of recaption. The Continental Congress first addressed the issue while negotiating the peace treaty with Britain that secured American independence, when it sought the return of slaves who had run to British lines. The wartime experience, as well as the beginning of emancipation in the North, alerted slaveholders to the need for greater legal security. Slaveholders were also concerned about the possible effects of the famous *Somerset* decision in England in 1772, which declared Britain free soil to any slaves, even though no northern state in close proximity to the slaveholding states had shown any inclination to declare itself free soil for fugitive slaves. See

Fehrenbacher, *Slaveholding Republic,* 206–207; Steven Lubet, *Fugitive Justice: Runaways, Rescuers, and Slavery on Trial* (Cambridge, MA, 2010), 11–22.

29. See, for example, Ohline, "Politics and Slavery," 64–65; Fehrenbacher, *Slaveholding Republic,* 44.

30. On the rise of antislavery constitutionalism, see Wiecek, *Sources,* esp. 106–287; James Oakes, *Freedom National: The Destruction of Slavery in the United States, 1861–1865* (New York, 2013), 1–48; and James Oakes, *The Scorpion's Sting: Antislavery and the Coming of the Civil War* (New York, 2014).

31. Douglass, "The American Constitution and the Slave: An Address Delivered in Glasgow, Scotland, on 20 March 1860," in *The Frederick Douglass Papers,* series one, *Speeches, Debates, and Interviews,* ed. John W. Blassingame (New Haven, CT, 1985), III:352. Garrison, it needs saying, was not as thoroughgoing in his renunciation of the political abolitionists as he sometimes sounded. Despite the division, he continued to publicize their efforts and regard them as allies in the larger antislavery cause. Yet the division was real and could provoke intense sectarian clashes. For an excellent reassessment of Garrison and his supporters, emphasizing their links to British and European liberals, see W. Caleb McDaniel, *The Problem of Democracy in the Age of Slavery: Garrisonian Abolitionists and Transatlantic Reform* (Baton Rouge, LA, 2013).

32. Lincoln, *Works,* II:461.

33. For still-relevant consideration of the constitutional origins of the war, though without direct reference to the property question, see Arthur Bestor, "The American Civil War as a Constitutional Crisis," *American Historical Review* 69 (1964): 327–352. On the question of property rights as the central issue that sparked the war, see also James L. Huston's powerful pioneering article, "Property Rights in Slavery and the Coming of the Civil War," *Journal of Southern History* 65 (1999): 249–286.

34. On the seventeenth-century background, see Holly Brewer, "Slavery, Sovereignty, and 'Inheritable Blood': Reconsidering John Locke and the Origins of American Slavery," *American Historical Review* 122 (2017): 1038–1078.

35. See, above all, Huston, "Property Rights," and James L. Huston, *Calculating the Value of the Union: Slavery, Property Rights, and the Economic Origins of the Civil War* (Chapel Hill, NC, 2003).

36. For a largely complementary view of Madison, concerned as much with race as slavery, see Noah Feldman, *The Three Lives of James Madison: Genius, Partisan, President* (New York, 2017).

37. As, indeed, some historians and constitutional scholars assert it was; see, e.g., Paul Finkelman, "The Union Wasn't Worth the Three-Fifths Compromise," *New York Times*, February 27, 2013.

I

SLAVERY, PROPERTY, AND EMANCIPATION IN
REVOLUTIONARY AMERICA

1. The most thorough study of northern emancipation remains Arthur Zilversmit, *The First Emancipation: The Abolition of Slavery in the North* (Chicago, 1967). See also Ira Berlin, *Many Thousands Gone: The First Two Centuries of Slavery in North America* (Cambridge, MA, 1998), 228–255. On early emancipation efforts in the South, see, for a recent overview, Manisha Sinha, *The Slave's Cause: A History of Abolition* (New Haven, 2016), 85–96. On South Carolina, see Philip Morgan, "Black Society in the Low Country, 1765–1810," in *Slavery and Freedom in the Age of the American Revolution*, ed. Ira Berlin and Ronald Hoffman (Charlottesville, 1983), 114–115, 124–125. On the ideas and legal doctrines that informed early American antislavery and emancipation, see above all William M. Wiecek, *The Sources of Antislavery Constitutionalism in the United States, 1760–1848* (Ithaca, NY, 1977), 20–39.

2. David Brion Davis, *The Problem of Slavery in Western Culture* (Ithaca, NY, 1966), 248. See also the second volume of Davis's magisterial trilogy, *The Problem of Slavery in the Age of Revolution, 1770–1823* (Ithaca, NY, 1975), which has strongly shaped my thinking about the entire subject.

3. Elihu Coleman, *A Testimony Against the Anti-Christian Practice of Making Slaves of Men* (1733; New Bedford, 1825); Philadelphia Yearly Meeting Minutes, [July 23], 1696, ms., Quaker and Special Collections, Haverford College, at http://triptych.brynmawr.edu/cdm/ref/collection/HC _QuakSlav/id/11713. On the English background, see above all John N. Blanton, "This Species of Property: Slavery and the Properties of Subjecthood in Anglo-American Law and Politics, 1619–1783," Ph.D. diss., Graduate Center of the City University of New York, 2016.

4. [Sewell], *The Selling of Joseph: A Memorial* (Boston, 1700), 1; [Saffin], *A Brief and Candid Answer to a Late Printed Sheet, Entitled,* The Selling of Joseph (1701), in George Moore, *Notes on the History of Slavery in Massachusetts* (New York, 1866), 252. On the Sewell-Saffin exchange, see Zilversmit, *First Emancipation,* 58–61; Larry E. Tise, *Proslavery: A History of the Defense of Slavery in America, 1791–1840* (Athens, GA, 1987), 16–19; Wendy Warren, *New England Bound: Slavery and Colonization in Early America* (New York, 2016), 221–246.

5. Quotation in Richard D. Brown, *Self-Evident Truths: Contesting Equal Rights from the Revolution to the Civil War* (New Haven, CT, 2016), 9.

6. David Waldstreicher, *Slavery's Constitution: From Revolution to Ratification* (New York, 2009), 21–56.

7. Thomas Jefferson, *A Summary View of the Rights of British America* (Williamsburg, [1774]), 16–17.

8. The classic study by Benjamin Quarles, *The Negro in the American Revolution* (Chapel Hill, NC, 1961), has inspired an important literature on black quests for freedom in the Revolutionary era. For a recent overview, see

Douglas R. Egerton, *Death or Liberty: African Americans and Revolutionary America* (New York, 2009), esp. 41–92.

9. The implications of this clause for slavery would prompt a brief debate in 1787. See Chapter 2.

10. *Journals of the Continental Congress, 1774–1789,* ed. Worthington Chauncey Ford et al. (Washington, DC, 1904–1937), VI:1080.

11. *The Public Statutes at Large of the United States of America* (Boston, 1845–1875), VIII:83. On the Treaty of Paris and its subsequent importance to antislavery politics, see James Oakes, *The Scorpion's Sting: Antislavery Politics and the Coming of the Civil War* (New York, 2013), 104–165.

12. Although it should be noted that abolitionists did occasionally push for national reforms. Above all, in 1783, the Quaker abolitionist leader Anthony Benezet led a small delegation to the Confederation Congress, then meeting in Princeton, with a petition, signed by more than 500 Quakers, reminding the Congress of their "solemn declarations often repeated in favour of universal liberty," and asking for a prohibition on the importation of slaves. The Congress referred the petition to a committee, which three months later recommended that the individual state legislatures "enact such laws as to their wisdom" might seem best suited to ending the trade. Split along sectional lines, the Congress did not approve even that mild proposal. Any national effort against the slave trade, let alone slavery itself, was out of the question. Thus, however, was begun a line of agitation about congressional authority over slavery that would revive in 1790 and return even more powerfully in the 1830s. Kaminski, 26–27. On abolitionism more generally during the Revolution, see Sinha, *Slave's Cause,* 34–47.

13. The Constitution of Vermont (1777), at www.sec.state.vt.us/archives -records/state-archives/government-history/vermont-constitutions /1777-constitution.aspx.

14. Zilversmit, *First Emancipation,* 109–124.

15. Ibid., 124–153.

16. *Acts and Laws of the State of Connecticut in America* (New London, 1784), 233–235.

17. Recent studies that have emphasized the limitations of gradual emancipation include Gary B. Nash and Jean R. Soderlund, *Freedom by Degrees: Emancipation in Pennsylvania and Its Aftermath* (New York, 1991); Shane White, *Somewhat More Independent: The End of Slavery in New York City, 1770–1810* (Athens, GA, 1991); Joanne Pope Melish, *Disowning Slavery: Gradual Emancipation and "Race" in New England, 1780–1860* (Ithaca, NY, 1998); David Menschel, "Abolition without Deliverance: The Law of Connecticut Slavery 1784–1848," *Yale Law Journal* 111 (2001): 183–222; Richard S. Newman, *The Transformation of American Abolitionism: Fighting Slavery in the Early Republic* (Chapel Hill, NC, 2002); David N. Gellman, *Emancipating New York: The Politics of Slavery and Freedom, 1777–1827* (Baton Rouge, LA, 2006); Berlin, *Many Thousands Gone,* 228–255; Christy Mikel Clark-Pujara, "Slavery, Emancipation and Black Freedom in Rhode Island, 1652–1842," Ph.D. diss., University of Iowa, 2009; and James J. Gigantino, *The Ragged Road to Abolition: Slavery and Freedom in New Jersey, 1775–1865* (Philadelphia, 2015). On Vermont, see Harvey Amani Whitfield, *The Problem of Slavery in Early Vermont, 1777–1810* (Montpelier, VT, 2014). On the economics of northern emancipation, see Robert William Fogel and Stanley L. Engerman, "Philanthropy at Bargain Prices: Notes on the Economics of Gradual Emancipation," *Journal of Legal Studies* 3 (1974): 377–401. For a corrective on the motivations behind northern emancipation, see Paul J. Polgar, "'To Raise Them to an Equal Participation': Early National Abolitionism, Gradual Emancipation, and the Promise of African American Citizenship," *Journal of the Early Republic* 31 (2011): 229–258.

18. *Pennsylvania Packet,* January 1, 1780.

19. *American Minerva* [New York], February 8, 1796.

20. Williams quoted in Polgar, "'To Raise Them,'" 230.

21. Berlin, *Many Thousands Gone*, 238.

22. *Pennsylvania Gazette*, February 2, 1780.

23. *New Jersey Journal*, September 20, 1780; "Negroes Memorial Octr 1788," in "Three Petitions by Connecticut Negroes for the Abolition of Slavery in Connecticut," ed. Vincent J. Rosivach, *Connecticut Review* 17 (1995): 79–92. A splendid meditation on the experience of gradual emancipation for blacks and whites—constructed largely from legal records—appears in Hendrik Hartog, *The Trouble with Minna: A Case of Slavery and Emancipation in the Antebellum North* (Chapel Hill, NC, 2018), esp. 38–86.

24. George William Van Cleve, *A Slaveholders' Union: Slavery, Politics, and the Constitution in the Early American Republic* (Chicago, 2010), 72. Van Cleve usefully distinguishes gradual emancipation from the exercise of eminent domain, which typically involves appropriating a specific piece of property, not an entire form, for public use. The slighting of gradual emancipation results in part from the fallacy of judging it against the standard of a later event, the general emancipation of 1865, and in part from the fallacy of judging it against what the most radical abolitionists at the time demanded.

25. Gavin Wright, *Slavery and American Economic Development* (Baton Rouge, LA, 2013), 41.

26. Edgar J. McManus, *Black Bondage in the North* (Syracuse, NY, 2001); Berlin, *Many Thousands Gone*, 47–63, 188–194, 228–255; White, *Somewhat More Independent*, 2–55.

27. Thomas Arnold quoted in Newman, *Transformation of American Abolitionism*, 25.

28. That American republicanism was built on racial slavery has become a familiar view, first enunciated forcefully in Edmund S. Morgan, *American Slavery, American Freedom: The Ordeal of Colonial Virginia* (New York, 1976). It was not a claim southern slaveholders made very often until after

1815. As in the North, southern proslavery claims rested primarily on the supposed inviolability of property in man. See Jan Lewis, "The Problem of Slavery in Southern Political Discourse," in *Devising Liberty: Preserving and Creating Freedom in the New American Republic,* ed. David Thomas Koenig (Stanford, CA, 1995), 265–300.

29. *Annals of Congress,* 1st Cong., 2nd sess., House, 1241; George Washington to Robert Morris, April 12, 1786, in *The Papers of George Washington, Confederation Series,* ed. W. W. Abbott (Charlottesville, VA, 1992–1997), IV:15. On these conservative grounds, some antislavery northern Federalists disdained the societies as well, including John Adams, who would have occasion to sneer at the "silly" efforts of the "self-constituted" PAS. See Chapter 4. On the attacks on the legitimacy of the Democratic-Republican Societies, see Sean Wilentz, *The Rise of American Democracy: Jefferson to Lincoln* (New York, 2005), 53–71.

30. William Pinkney, *Speech of William Pinkney, Esq. in the House of Delegates of Maryland, at Their Session in November, 1789* (Philadelphia, 1790), 9.

31. *New Jersey Gazette,* April 11, 1781.

32. *Pennsylvania Packet,* January 1, 1780.

33. Put slightly differently, one of slavery's defining evils was that it was an inherited and doubly perpetual condition, with the offspring of slaves (the radical abolitionist William Goodell would write in the 1850s) "held as Property, in perpetuity," the same as their parents: northern emancipation immediately ended slavery's double perpetuity. Freedom would come gradually, and conditions could be severe, but for these offspring, the condition of slavery was over. See Goodell, *The American Slave Code in Theory and Practice* (New York, 1853), 248.

34. *Pennsylvania Packet,* January 1, 1780.

35. Ibid.

36. The only previous comparable emancipation in the modern West was the French National Convention's abolition of slavery in all of France's

colonies in 1794, which Napoleon Bonaparte rescinded ten years later. On the 1817 New York law, which freed all slaves as of July 4, 1827, see Zilversmit, *First Emancipation*, 213–214, Gellman, *Emancipating*, 205–206.

37. *Gazette of the United States* [New York], February 20, 1790, quoted in Polgar, "'To Raise Them,'" 237; *New York Packet*, April 4, 1785, quoted in Gellman, *Emancipating New York*, 54.

38. *Pennsylvania Journal*, February 5, 1781. See also, among many other examples, *New-Jersey Gazette*, October 4, 1780.

39. Zilversmit, *First Emancipation*, 146.

40. *Boston Evening Post*, May 3, 1783.

41. Quotation in Zilversmit, *First Emancipation*, 116.

42. Ibid., 199.

43. *New-Jersey Gazette*, January 10, 1781.

44. Ibid., February 14, 1781. See also "Whig" in ibid., October 4, 1780, who objected to post-nati emancipation on the grounds that "all slaves are in reality as much the property of their masters as the gold and silver for which they were bought." There is no evidence that by agreeing to the extended indenture arrangements under the post-nati emancipation laws that the emancipationists conceded the legitimacy of property in man— quite the opposite, as the texts of some of those laws make clear.

45. *New-Jersey Gazette*, April 11, 1781.

46. *New-Jersey Gazette*, February 14, 1781.

47. *New-Jersey Gazette*, February 14, 1781; Brissot de Warville, *New Travels in the United States of America* (Dublin, 1792), 277–279; Duc de la Rochefoucauld Liancourt, *Travels through the United States of North America* (1799; London, 1800), III:704.

48. Smith, *An Inquiry into the Nature and Causes of the Wealth of Nations* (1776; London, 1904), I:123.

49. *New-Jersey Gazette*, November 8, 1780.

50. *American Minerva* [New York], February 6, 1796.

51. Crawford, *Observations on Negro-Slavery* (Philadelphia, 1784), 12–13. See also *Independent Gazetteer* [Philadelphia], August 10, 1782.

52. Samuel Miller, *A Discourse, Delivered April 12, 1797: At the Request of and before the New-York Society for Promoting the Manumission of Slaves* (New York, 1797), 15–16.

53. *New-Jersey Gazette*, March 21, 1781.

54. "An Act Authorizing the Emancipation of Negroes, Mullatoes, & Others, and for the Gradual Abolition of Slavery," ms., Office of the Secretary of State, Rhode Island, at http://sos.ri.gov/virtualarchives/items/show/71 (italics mine).

55. Randolph quoted in Davis, *Problem of Slavery in the Age of Revolution*, 170.

56. On the Virginia Abolition Society, see Gordon E. Finnie, "The Antislavery Movement in the Upper South before 1840," *Journal of Southern History* 35 (1969): 320, 322, 326, 333–334.

57. *Maryland Gazette*, May 15, 1783.

58. *Maryland Journal & Baltimore Advertiser*, May 30, 1788.

59. Eva Sheppard Wolf, *Race and Liberty in the New Nation: Emancipation in Virginia from the Revolution to Nat Turner's Rebellion* (Baton Rouge, LA, 2006), 1–38, quotations on 32, 34.

60. Fredrika Teute Schmidt and Barbara Ripel Wilhelm, "Early Proslavery Petitions in Virginia," *William and Mary Quarterly* 30 (1973): 133–146, quotation on 138.

61. Richard K. MacMaster, "Liberty or Property? The Methodists Petition for Emancipation in Virginia," *Methodist History* 10 (1971): 44–55, quotation on 48–49.

62. Quotation in ibid., 51. Washington later wrote favorably of the campaign to his friend the Marquis de Lafayette, with a note of despair that the emancipationist spirit had yet to "diffuse itself generally into the minds of the people of this country," George Washington to Lafayette, May 10, 1786, in *Papers of George Washington, Confederation Series*, ed. Abbott, IV:44.

63. Quotation in MacMaster, "Liberty or Property?," 48.

64. Quotation in Schmidt and Wilhelm, "Early Proslavery Petitions," 142.

65. Quotations in ibid., 139, 145.

66. Quotations in ibid., 142, 144.

67. Quotations in MacMaster, "Liberty or Property?," 53. MacMaster asserts that Madison was among the members who endorsed abolition. Certainly Madison was repulsed by the contempt shown by his colleagues to the emancipationists and their petitions, but I have been unable to confirm that he actually spoke in favor of emancipation.

68. Ibid., 54.

69. Washington to Lafayette, May 10, 1786, in *Papers of George Washington, Confederation Series,* ed. Abbott, IV:44. See also Washington to Robert Morris, April 12, 1786, ibid., 15.

70. McMaster, "Liberty or Property?," 53–54.

71. Constrained emancipation plans would continue to appear in Virginia after 1787, calling slavery indefensible but also insistent that blacks and whites could not live in harmony. The most auspicious of these prior to 1800, a scheme developed in 1796 by the jurist St. George Tucker, would have been extremely protracted, would have denied free blacks basic civil rights, and would have encouraged freed slaves to move elsewhere. As Manisha Sinha notes, it is "overly generous" to call Tucker's plan, or for that matter any of the others, emancipationist; instead, they helped define the middle ground, between the emancipationists and the prevailing proslavery forces. In addition to Sinha, *Slave's Cause,* 91, see Michael Kent Curtis, "St. George Tucker and the Legacy of Slavery," *William and Mary Law Review* 47 (2006): 1157–1212; and Paul Finkelman, "The Dragon St. George Could Not Slay: Tucker's Plan to End Slavery," *William and Mary Law Review* 47 (2006): 1213–1243.

72. Apart from Ingersoll and Franklin, Middle State delegates with antislavery records before 1787 included William Livingston and William

Paterson of New Jersey, Rufus King and Alexander Hamilton of New York (who at the very least was a member of the New-York Manumission Society), and, from Pennsylvania, Gouverneur Morris, George Clymer, and Thomas Mifflin (second cousin to the Quaker abolitionist leader Warner Mifflin).

73. The text of the petition appeared in the *Pennsylvania Gazette,* March 5, 1788, dated June 2, 1787.

74. Tench Coxe to James Madison, March 31, 1790, in Farrand, III:361.

75. New-York Manumission Society, Minutes, Volume VI, August 16–17, 1787, New-York Historical Society.

76. *Maryland Journal & Baltimore Advertiser,* March 28, 1786.

77. Farrand, II:443.

2

THE FEDERAL CONVENTION AND THE CURSE OF HEAVEN

1. Farrand, I:594, II:10.

2. It needs noting, however, that these reinforcements were not the special concessions to the slaveholding states that some neo-Garrisonian scholarship suggests they were. The framers did not, for example, include provisions on the suppression of domestic violence chiefly to compel northerners to help suppress slave insurrections. In fact, the convention debates almost entirely concerned domestic disturbances akin to Shays' Rebellion in 1786, which had been a catalyst for the movement to frame the Constitution. The relevant provisions in Articles I and IV protected both sections equally: so long as the nation included slaveholding as well as non-slaveholding states, northerners would be obliged to help put down any domestic violence in the South including slave insurrections, just as southerners would be obliged to join in putting down any Shays-like uprisings in the North. From time to time, as we shall see, northern delegates complained of being bound to put down slave rebellions, and

some antislavery Anti-Federalists raised the issue during the ratification, but the convention hardly approved it as a sectional proslavery
matter. Tellingly, there was only one sectional vote on either provision,
concerning a proposal by southern delegates to substitute "insurrections"
for "domestic violence" in Article IV; the proposal failed, six votes to five,
with New Jersey joining Virginia, North Carolina, South Carolina, and
Georgia in voting "aye." Ibid., II:467. See also Earl M. Maltz, "The Idea
of the Proslavery Constitution," *Journal of the Early Republic* 17 (1997): 40.

3. A few historians and constitutional experts have noted the Constitution's
exclusion of property in man and begun to suggest why it was important. Howard Albert Ohline remarked that "the most outspoken defenders of slavery from South Carolina were not able to obtain a national
sanction of the institution," in "Politics and Slavery: The Issue of Slavery
in National Politics," Ph.D. diss., University of Missouri, 1969, 65. A fuller
though still incomplete account appears in Don E. Fehrenbacher, *The
Slaveholding Republic: An Account of the United States Government's Relations to Slavery,* completed and ed. Ward M. McAfee (New York, 2001),
25–48. Donald L. Robinson's important study of slavery and early American politics astutely concludes that the framers "could not establish
straightforward constitutional guarantees against emancipation, as the
South Carolinians desired, because many Northerners, and perhaps
some Southerners, would not permit it." Yet Robinson also claimed that
the fugitive slave clause gave "a nationwide sanction to property in
slaves," the same argument advanced by slavery's defenders to back their
assertion that the Constitution established precisely that guarantee. See
Robinson, *Slavery in the Structure of American Politics, 1765–1820* (1971; New
York, 1979), 228, 244. Most recently—although he does not take up the
property issue per se—Mark A. Graber has evaluated how the Constitution protected slavery without formally acknowledging the institution,
and has explored the consequences for what he calls "the constitutional

politics of slavery." The arguments offered here differ sharply but also converge with his on several points. See Graber, *"Dred Scott" and the Problem of Constitutional Evil* (Cambridge, 2006), esp. 91–171. Two powerful articles, although not chiefly concerned with the Federal Convention, have established the centrality of contested views of property to the politics that led to the Civil War: Jan Lewis, "The Problem of Slavery in Southern Political Discourse," in *Devising Liberty: Preserving and Creating Freedom in the New American Republic*, ed. David Thomas Koenig (Stanford, CA, 1995), 265–300; and James L. Huston, "Property Rights in Slavery and the Coming of the Civil War," *Journal of Southern History* 65 (1999): 249–286. Broader considerations include Michael Kammen, "'The Rights and Property and the Property in Rights': The Problematic Nature of 'Property' in the Political Thought of the Founders and the Early Republic," in *Liberty, Property, and the Foundations of the American Constitution*, ed. Ellen Frankel Paul and Howard Dickman (Albany, NY, 1989), 1–22; and James W. Ely Jr., *The Guardian of Every Other Right: A Constitutional History of Property Rights* (New York, 1992).

4. Farrand, I:204.

5. Lewright B. Sikes, *The Public Life of Pierce Butler, South Carolina Statesman* (Lanham, MD, 1979); Pierce Butler, *The Letters of Pierce Butler, 1790–1794: Nation Building and Enterprise in the New American Republic*, ed. Terry W. Lipscomb (Columbia, SC, 2007), xv–xlvi.

6. Farrand, I:147.

7. John Hope Franklin, *From Slavery to Freedom: A History of American Negroes* (1947; New York, 1956), 143. Franklin's perceptive emphasis on the primacy of property for the framers, and its proslavery consequences, led him to conclude too hastily that the Constitution's protection of slavery amounted to giving "recognition to the institution of human slavery." To the extent that he implied that the framers recognized the legitimacy of slavery in national law, Franklin overstated his case.

8. Farrand, I:562. On this point, see especially Howard A. Ohline, "Republicanism and Slavery: Origins of the Three-Fifths Clause in the United States Constitution," *William and Mary Quarterly*, 3rd ser., 28 (1971): 563–584.

9. Farrand, I:196.

10. Ibid.

11. Ibid.

12. Ibid., I:201. Wilson's motion was seconded by Charles Pinckney of South Carolina, Charles Cotesworth Pinckney's fiercely proslavery younger cousin—a signal that Wilson and Pinckney had allied in a compromise to head off both Sherman's proposal and the one advanced by Rutledge and Butler.

13. *Journals of the Continental Congress, 1774–1789*, ed. Worthington Chauncey Ford et al. (Washington, DC, 1904–1937), XXVIII:239.

14. It had been the younger Pinckney, Wilson's seconder, who first circulated the idea of a three-fifths ratio for slave representation. See Ohline, "Republicanism and Slavery," 568–569.

15. Ibid. Gerry's observation echoed that of the South Carolinian Thomas Lynch Jr. in 1776 that it was absurd to treat slaves as persons. But in 1776, the debate was entirely over counting slaves for the purposes of taxation; in 1787, it was over counting them for purposes of representation and was later applied to taxation. If it meant gaining more political power, especially given the widely perceived unlikelihood that the federal government would enact direct taxes, proslavery southerners were now willing to put up with the absurdity.

16. Farrand, I:201. New Jersey and Delaware were the dissenting states, in line with their opposition, as smaller states, to any proposal that based representation on population. Not all states voted on every measure at the convention, as delegates would depart and return; Rhode Island did not even send a delegation.

17. Ibid., I:511, 542.

18. Ibid., I:559.

19. Farrand, I:561. At the close of the speech, Paterson stated in passing that the original wording of the three-fifths ratio by the Confederation Congress in 1783 was due to the members' "shame" over slavery, the line sometimes mistaken as a reference to the Federal Convention itself. In 1783, Paterson, while serving as New Jersey attorney-general, temporarily retired from politics on the death of his wife.

20. Farrand, I:566–567.

21. Ibid., I:567.

22. Ibid., I:570.

23. Ibid., I:580.

24. Ibid., I:580–587.

25. Ibid., I:588.

26. Ibid. Massachusetts, New Jersey, and Pennsylvania also voted against the clause; Connecticut, Virginia, North Carolina, and Georgia voted in favor. New Jersey, like Delaware, consistently opposed any plan based on proportional representation, which explains its votes more than the slavery issue. Paul Finkelman concludes from the tally that, despite the outcome, "it seemed that a majority in favor of [the clause] could be found." Paul Finkelman, "Slavery and the Constitutional Convention: Making a Covenant with Death," in *Beyond Confederation: Origins of the Constitution and American National Identity*, ed. Richard Beeman, Stephen Botein, and Edward C. Carter II (Chapel Hill, NC, 1987), 204–205 n. 43.

27. Farrand, I:594.

28. Ibid., I:593.

29. Ibid., I:595.

30. Ibid., I:596.

31. Ibid., I:597. Connecticut, Pennsylvania, Maryland, Virginia, North Carolina, and Georgia voted in favor of the clause; Massachusetts and South

Carolina were divided. New Jersey and Delaware, the two nay votes, may once again have been standing firm against any proportional allocation plan.

32. Ibid., I:603.

33. Ibid., I:604.

34. Ibid., I:605.

35. Ibid., I:605–606.

36. Cf. Finkelman, "Slavery," which argues, regarding the three-fifths clause, that "the slave states won a critical victory without making any important concessions" (196) and that the clause "was accepted without any quid pro quo from the South" (197), yet also observes that at least some southern delegates (Charles Cotesworth Pinckney specifically, but "presumably" others as well) "thought that the three-fifths rule for counting slaves was a great concession" (201). The slaveholding states certainly accepted the three-fifths rule and defended it against northerners who called for representation based on free inhabitants, but this does not mean the southerners did not think they had failed to make a concession. The three-fifths rule may indeed have been one of the things Pinckney had in mind when he later reflected on all that the slave state delegates had failed to win at the convention.

37. Farrand, I:604–605.

38. Jensen, XXIII:23. See also Farrand, I:561, 585, 586, 589, 595.

39. Lachlan McIntosh to John Wereat, December 17, 1787, in Kaminski, 165.

40. Farrand, I:567. As we will see later in this chapter, the prospect of an emerging southern and southwestern majority quickly proved a mirage.

41. Farrand, I:592, 601–602. Pinckney was referring to speeches by King and Morris during the debate that preceded the temporary rejection of the three-fifths clause, including Morris's remark that, by encouraging the Atlantic slave trade, the clause ran afoul of "human nature."

42. Farrand, II:30–32, 56–57, 58, quotations on 32 and 56. For a detailed account, see Paul Finkelman, "The Proslavery Origins of the Electoral College," *Cardozo Law Review* 23 (2002): 1145–1157.

43. Adding to the irony, the three opposing votes in this initial tally came from North Carolina, South Carolina, and Georgia. (Connecticut, Pennsylvania, Delaware, Maryland, and Virginia voted "aye"; Massachusetts was divided.) Although it solved the problem of nonvoting slaves, the electoral system still struck many southerners (and some northerners as well) as open to bribery and corruption, especially if those selected for the Electoral College were not, as Hugh Williamson put it, "the most respectable citizens . . . persons not occupied in the high offices of Govt." The convention wound up deliberating contentiously over every detail of the Electoral College until early September, when it finally approved a provision based on a special committee report. Farrand, II:58 (quotation), 493–494, 497–498, 528–529. The southern advantage widened further when the convention, after initially agreeing to place the power to nominate Supreme Court justices in the hands of the Senate, finally gave the nominating power to the executive, with the advice and consent of the Senate. Madison was again the prime mover, having argued that judicial nomination by the Senate would "throw the appointments entirely into the hands of ye Nthern states." Farrand, II:81.

44. Farrand, II:95.

45. On Rutledge, see James Haw, *John and Edward Rutledge of South Carolina* (Athens, GA, 1997), 12–216.

46. Robinson, *Slavery,* 218. In addition to Edmund Randolph of Virginia and James Wilson of Pennsylvania, the committee included Oliver Ellsworth of Connecticut and Nathaniel Gorham of Massachusetts. Overall, the selection appears to have been made with an eye to geographical balance, but it needs noting, first, that James Madison, who was bypassed for the committee, was a much firmer opponent of the Atlantic slave

trade than Randolph, and second, that Ellsworth and Gorham would go on to be especially supportive of the Lower South with regard to the Atlantic trade. The proceedings of the Committee of Detail have been too often neglected by historians of the Federal Convention. For a full discussion of the committee's work and the documentation related to it, see William Ewald, "The Committee of Detail," *Constitutional Commentary* 28 (2012): 197–285, on which I have drawn heavily.

47. Farrand, II:183.

48. Ewald, "Committee of Detail," 252–258.

49. Farrand, II:220.

50. Ibid., II:220–221.

51. Ibid., II:222–223.

52. On King, Robert Ernst, *Rufus King, American Federalist* (London, [1968]), 92–134, remains the best biography. Morris has received considerably more attention of late; see William Howard Adams, *Gouverneur Morris: An Independent Life* (New Haven, CT, 2003) and Mary-Jo Kline, *Gouverneur Morris and the New Nation, 1775–1788* (1971; New York, 1978), as well as Richard Brookhiser, *Gouverneur Morris, the Rake Who Wrote the Constitution* (New York, 2003); James J. Kirschke, *Gouverneur Morris: Author, Statesman, and Man of the World* (New York, 2005); and Melanie Randolph Miller, *An Incautious Man: The Life of Gouverneur Morris* (Wilmington, DE, 2008).

53. Ibid., II:223. Only New Jersey—opposed as ever to proportional representation—backed Morris's amendment; New Hampshire, Massachusetts, Connecticut, and Pennsylvania opposed it, along with all six of the slaveholding states from Delaware to Georgia.

54. Ibid., II:363–364. In the seven-to-four vote, Massachusetts and Connecticut provided the margin of victory. Every state south of Delaware voted in favor, although, notably, James Madison and George Washington—the president of the convention, who rarely intervened—dissented from the

Virginia majority. Like Gouverneur Morris and James Wilson, Madison argued in vain to the convention on behalf of export taxes, in part, in Madison's case, on the grounds that they would raise the price of export goods where the United States had no serious foreign rivals. Ibid., II:306. See also Erik M. Jensen, "The Export Clause," *Florida Tax Review* 6 (2003): 6–15.

55. Georgia would ban its Atlantic trade for good in 1798. South Carolina would ban its trade in 1792, only to reopen it in 1803.

56. *Maryland Journal*, December 15, 1789. On Martin, see Paul S. Clarkson and R. Samuel Jett, *Luther Martin of Maryland* (Baltimore, 1970).

57. Farrand, II:364.

58. Ibid.

59. Ibid.

60. Ibid., II:364–365.

61. Ibid., II:369–370.

62. Ibid., II:370.

63. Ibid. Mason's concluding antislavery remarks were almost certainly paraphrases of Thomas Jefferson's *Notes on the State of Virginia*.

64. Farrand, II:371.

65. Ibid., II:371–372.

66. Ibid., II:371.

67. Ibid, II:371–372.

68. Ibid. Pinckney's observation would also harden into accusations that the Virginians were entirely driven by greed, a charge endorsed by later historians. For a recent example, see Lawrence Goldstone, "Constitutionally, Slavery Is Indeed a National Institution," *New Republic*, September 17, 2015.

69. Farrand, II:373.

70. Ibid., II:372.

71. William Pierce, "Character Sketches of the Delegates to the Federal Convention," in Farrand, III:88–89. On Sherman, see Mark David Hall, *Roger*

Sherman and the Creation of the American Republic (New York, 2013), esp. 92–121.

72. Farrand, II:374.

73. Ibid.

74. Ibid., II:373.

75. Ibid.

76. Ibid., II:374.

77. Ibid. Connecticut, New Jersey, Maryland, Virginia, North Carolina, South Carolina, and Georgia voted "aye"; Massachusetts abstained.

78. Ibid. In the nine-to-two vote, New Hampshire, Massachusetts, Pennsylvania, Delaware, Maryland, Virginia, North Carolina, South Carolina, and Georgia approved, and only Connecticut and New Jersey opposed.

79. This committee is not to be confused with the earlier Committee of Eleven appointed in July to consider the issue of representation in the Senate.

80. On the "dirty compromise," see Finkelman, "Slavery," 218.

81. A friend of the prominent abolitionist David Cooper of western New Jersey, Livingston also had cordial relations with the New Jersey Abolition Society, which had been founded in 1786. During the year before his death in 1790, Livingston became a friend of and correspondent with the Pennsylvania Abolition Society and its president (Benjamin Franklin's successor), James Pemberton. See Richard S. Newman, *The Transformation of American Abolitionism: Fighting Slavery in the Early Republic* (Chapel Hill, NC, 2002), 22.

82. Farrand, II:400. The convention would eventually amend the maximum duty to ten dollars.

83. Pinckney in South Carolina General Assembly, January 17, 1788, in Jensen, XXVII:123–124; Luther Martin, "Genuine Information VII," *Maryland Gazette,* January 18, 1788, in Kaminski, 172–173; "Notes of a Conversation with George Mason," September 30, 1792, in Thomas Jefferson, *The*

Papers of Thomas Jefferson, Main Series, ed. Julian Boyd et al. (Princeton, NJ, 1943–), XXIV:428; Madison to Robert Walsh Jr., November 27, 1819, in James Madison, *The Papers of James Madison, Retirement Series,* ed. David B. Mattern et al. (Charlottesville, 2009–), I:548–549. On Mason, see also George Mason to Thomas Jefferson, May 26, 1788, in *Papers of Thomas Jefferson,* XIII:204–205.

84. Each of the delegates who provided the most direct information about the committee's work would have reason to make the deal look like a major concession by the North. Pinckney was trying to assure his South Carolina constituents that he and his colleagues had worked hard and completed an excellent deal; Martin and Mason were disgusted by the compromise and were inclined to describe it in the most sordid light; and Madison, by the time he wrote his recollection, was shading his account of the debates at the convention toward what was becoming the moderate proslavery position on the Constitution. On Madison's later views about what happened in 1787, see Chapter 5.

85. Farrand, II:373.

86. The convention allotted Virginia ten seats, South Carolina five seats, and Georgia three seats. Even with the admission of new western slave states—what would become Kentucky and Tennessee—the Lower South would have had to import a massive number of slaves to make up the disadvantage by 1800. And as it happened, any expectations that the slaveholders outside Virginia would enjoy a substantial enlargement of their representation in Congress were quickly dashed. Defining the North as all states north of Delaware, the southern states controlled 44.7 percent of the House in 1790; excluding Virginia, the South controlled 26.2 percent; take Maryland and Delaware out of the southern column as well, and the figure drops to 17.5 percent. The prospects for blocking abolition would not have been too much better by extending the delay past 1800. In the allocations based on the 1800 census, the southern states as a whole

controlled 46.1 percent of the House; the South excluding Virginia controlled 30.4 percent; and the South without Virginia, Delaware, and Maryland controlled 23.4 percent. In 1807, the bill abolishing the Atlantic slave trade passed the House by a margin of 63 to 49. Apportionment figures from Office of the Historian, U.S. House of Representatives, History, Art, and Archives website, at http://history.house.gov/Institution /Apportionment/Apportionment/.

87. Farrand, II:415. Mary Sarah Bilder argues persuasively that this sentence may have been one of many that Madison composed and added to his notes after the fact, casting doubt on whether he actually said it in the convention or put it in later to enhance his image. Indeed, Bilder suggests that he may have cribbed the "dishonorable to the National character" remark from a speech by Luther Martin. Bilder also points out other places where Madison revised his notes concerning discussions of slavery, but largely in order to clarify sentences that might be misunderstood. To be sure, as Madison composed all of his notes from late August (out of his on-the-spot jottings) after the convention concluded, there is reason to be cautious about all of this material, but some of it demands more caution than the rest. See Mary Sarah Bilder, *Madison's Hand: Revising the Constitutional Convention* (Cambridge, MA, 2015), 188–189, 194.

88. Farrand, II:415–416. New Hampshire, Massachusetts, and Connecticut joined Maryland, North Carolina, South Carolina, and Georgia voting in favor, opposed by New Jersey, Pennsylvania, Delaware, and Virginia.

89. Ibid., II:416.

90. Ibid.

91. There is another, much darker, albeit far-fetched construction of Madison's notes: that Langdon and King were saying that the objectionable wording, acknowledging men to be property, was the price for giving Congress the authority to abolish the slave trade. If that were the case, then the Lower South delegates on the committee drove a much harder

bargain than it appeared on the surface. By this reading, the committee was fully aware of the implications, and Sherman's complaint exposed a quiet effort to legitimize slavery in the Constitution without the convention realizing as much—an effort agreed to by, among others, William Livingston, Rufus King, Luther Martin, and James Madison. It is hard to believe that the wording Sherman seized upon was anything other than accidental—but there remains the slightest trace of a possibility that antislavery delegates as well as James Madison struck a deal over the slave trade that would have recognized property in slaves.

92. Farrand, II:416.

93. Ibid., II:417.

94. Ibid.

95. Ibid.

96. Madison to Robert Pleasants, October 30, 1791, in James Madison, *The Papers of James Madison, First Series*, ed. William T. Richardson et al. (Chicago and Charlottesville, 1962–1991), XIV:91.

97. On Madison and slavery, in addition to Noah Feldman, *The Three Lives of James Madison: Genius, Partisan, President* (New York, 2017), see Scott J. Kester, *The Haunted Philosophe: James Madison, Republicanism, and Slavery* (Lanham, MD, 2008), as well as Lance Banning, *The Sacred Fire of Liberty: James Madison and the Founding of the Federal Republic* (Ithaca, NY, 1995), esp. 76–110.

98. George Mason to Thomas Jefferson, May 26, 1788, in *Papers of Thomas Jefferson*, XIII:204–205.

99. Farrand, II:370.

100. On the background and meaning of Article IV, see David Skillen Bogen, *Privileges and Immunities: A Reference Guide to the United States Constitution* (Westport, CT, 2003), 11–16.

101. Ibid., 20.

102. Farrand, II:443. On slave property and the privileges and immunities clause, see also David R. Upham, "Exploring 'That Unexplored Clause of the Constitution': The Meaning of the 'Privileges and Immunities of Citizens' before the Fourteenth Amendment," Ph.D. diss., University of Dallas, 2002, 116–119; Paul Finkelman, *An Imperfect Union: Slavery, Federalism, and Comity* (Chapel Hill, NC, 1981), 34.

103. For differing views of the Northwest Ordinance, including its connections to the Constitution as well as to slavery, see Staughton Lynd, "The Compromise of 1787," *Political Science Quarterly* 81 (1966): 225–250; J. David Griffin, "Historians and the Sixth Article of the Ordinance of 1787," *Ohio History* 78 (1969): 252–260; Donald L. Robinson, *Slavery in the Structure of American Politics, 1765–1820* (New York, 1971), 378–383, 403; Paul Finkelman, "Slavery and the Northwest Ordinance: A Study in Ambiguity," *Journal of the Early Republic* 6 (1986): 343–370; Peter S. Onuf, *Statehood and Union: A History of the Northwest Ordinance* (Bloomington, IN, 1987), 109–132; David Brion Davis, "The Significance of Excluding Slavery from the Old Northwest in 1787," *Indiana Magazine of History* 84 (1988): 75–89; Fehrenbacher, *Slaveholding Republic,* 106–109; George William Van Cleve, *A Slaveholders' Union: Slavery, Politics, and the Constitution in the Early American Republic* (Chicago, 2010), 153–167.

104. On Cushing's decision and the larger issue of diverging slave law, see Emily Blanck, *Tyrannicide: Forging an American Law of Slavery in Revolutionary South Carolina and Massachusetts* (Athens, GA, 2014), esp. 115–170.

105. *Journals of the Continental Congress, 1774–1789,* XXVIII:164–165, 239.

106. Ibid., XXXII:343.

107. Farrand, II:443.

108. Ibid., II:453.

109. On these matters, see Fehrenbacher, *Slaveholding Republic,* 207–209.

110. Butler's papers at the Library of Congress include a draft fugitive slave provision, not in Butler's hand, which is basically the same as what Butler proposed except for the stipulation that "the legislatures of the several states shall make provision for the recovery of such person." This version dealt with James Wilson's objection by shifting responsibility from the state executive to the legislature, and left the exact procedures for the capture and rendition of fugitives in state hands. It remains unclear who wrote this version—apparently composed in a tavern—as well as why Butler did not later stipulate that the state legislatures would oversee the capture and return of fugitives. This draft, however, makes it all the more clear, first, that the clause was not intended to make the return of fugitive slaves a responsibility of the national government; and second, that it was not at all an effort to gain federal recognition of property rights in man. James H, Hutson, "Pierce Butler's Records of the Federal Constitutional Convention," *Quarterly Journal of the Library of Congress* 1 (1980): 68.

111. Farrand, II:454. For a perceptive analysis of the arguments over the fugitive slave clause, in and out of the convention, see Eric W. Plaag, "'Let the Constitution Perish': *Prigg v. Pennsylvania*, Joseph Story, and the Flawed Doctrine of Historical Necessity," *Slavery and Abolition* 25 (2004): 76–101.

112. In 1856, James Madison's former secretary Edward Coles wrote that Madison had informed him that the inclusion of the fugitive slave clause in both the Northwest Ordinance and the Constitution had been prearranged, securing southern support for the ordinance in exchange for "making the Constitution more acceptable to the slave holders." No other evidence of such a deal has, to my knowledge, come to light—but while it might explain the ease with which the ordinance passed in Congress and the fugitive slave clause was accepted by the convention, Coles's account does not gainsay the convention's insistence that the clause exclude

validation of property in man. See Coles, *History of the Ordinance of 1787* (Philadelphia, 1856), 28–29.

113. On American slaveholders' reactions to the *Somerset* principle, see Van Cleve, *Slaveholders' Union*, 31–40. More broadly on *Somerset's* impact, see William M. Wiecek, *The Sources of Antislavery Constitutionalism in the United States, 1760–1848* (Ithaca, NY, 1977), 40–61.

114. George William Van Cleve, "Founding a Slaveholders' Union: 1770–1797," in *Contesting Slavery: The Politics of Bondage and Freedom in the New American Nation*, ed. John Craig Hammond and Matthew Mason (Charlottesville, VA, 2011), 131.

115. Farrand, II:559.

116. Ibid., II:601–602.

117. In addition to the changes emphasized here, the Committee of Style removed the passage in Butler's proposal that referred to fugitives possibly gaining freedom "in consequence of any regulations subsisting in the State to which they escape." The committee may have thought the passage superfluous or even redundant: how might a fugitive slave claim freedom in a state with no regulations that might lead him or her to do so? Alternatively, the committee might have thought the words "any regulations" too vague and just dispensed with the entire passage.

118. Farrand, II:601.

119. Ibid., II:628, 662. As Mary Sarah Bilder notes, the commentary here, with Madison as omniscient interpreter, likely reflected "the distinct advantage of hindsight." Although there is no sense that he fabricated the Committee of Style's revision, Madison's gloss on why the committee made the revision is very much his own. That said, it is hard to see what other motivation would have led to these particular revisions—and, in any event, the change had the effect on the clause's meaning that Madison described. Bilder, *Madison's Hand*, 150. The symbols around the word "legal" mark Madison's interpolation to clarify an unclear reference in his original notes.

120. Paul Finkelman, *Slavery and the Founders: Race and Liberty in the Age of Jefferson* (2014; London, 2015), 34.

121. Fehrenbacher, *Slaveholding Republic*, 44.

3
SLAVERY, ANTISLAVERY, AND THE STRUGGLE
FOR RATIFICATION

1. *Columbian Herald* (Charleston, SC), July 26, 1787, in Kaminski, 161.

2. For a judicious discussion of the framers' motives, set against the broad question of political secrecy in the Atlantic world, see Katlyn Marie Carter, "Practicing Politics in the Revolutionary Atlantic World: Secrecy, Publicity and the Making of Modern Democracy," Ph.D. diss., Princeton University, 2017.

3. Matthew Mason, "Slavery and the Founding," *History Compass* 4 (2006): 943–955.

4. Important interpretations and commentaries on slavery and the ratification struggle include David Waldstreicher, *Slavery's Constitution: From Revolution to Ratification* (New York: 2009), 107–151; Kenneth Morgan, "Slavery and the Debate over the Ratification of the United States Constitution," *Slavery and Abolition* 22 (2001): 40–65; Robin L. Einhorn, "Patrick Henry's Case Against the Constitution: The Structural Problem with Slavery," *Journal of the Early Republic* 33 (2002): 549–573; John Craig Hammond, "'We Are to Be Reduced to the Level of Slaves': Planters, Taxes, Aristocrats, and Massachusetts Antifederalists, 1787–1788," *Historical Journal of Massachusetts* 31 (2003): 172–198; and Mark Boonshoft, "Doughfaces at the Founding: Federalists, Anti-Federalists, Slavery, and the Ratification of the Constitution in New York," *New York History* 93 (2012): 187–218. There is an enormous literature covering the entirety of the ratification struggle; I have relied most heavily on Pauline Maier, *Ratification: The People Debate the Constitution, 1787–1788* (New York, 2010);

and an excellent collection of essays, *Ratifying the Constitution,* ed. Michael Allen Gillespie and Michael Lienesch (Lawrence, KS, 1989).

5. Brown to Pemberton, October 17, 1787, in Kaminski, 70.

6. Rotch to Brown, November 8, 1787, in Kaminski, 74.

7. Hopkins to Levi Hart, January 29, 1788, in Kaminski, 95.

8. *Hampshire Gazette* (Northampton, MA), May 21, 1788, in Kaminski, 110.

9. See, for example, *Hampshire Gazette,* April 9 and April 16, 1788, in Kaminski, 100–108.

10. *Hampshire Gazette,* February 6, 1788, in Kaminski, 96.

11. *Hampshire Gazette,* June 4, 1788, in Kaminski, 111.

12. *Hampshire Gazette,* April 23, 1788, in Kaminski, 108.

13. Atherton, "Speech in the New Hampshire Ratifying Convention," ca. February 13, 1788, in Kaminski, 99.

14. *Providence Gazette,* October 6, 1787.

15. Lee to George Thacher, January 23, 1788, quoted in Howard Albert Ohline, "Politics and Slavery: The Issue of Slavery in National Politics, 1787–1815," Ph.D. diss., University of Missouri, 1969, 101.

16. *Massachusetts Centinel,* January 19, 1788, in Kaminski, 94.

17. Brown to Pemberton, October 17, 1787, in Kaminski, 70. See also William Rotch Sr., to Moses Brown, November 8, 1787, in Kaminski, 74, which recites the story of an escaped slave residing in Nantucket named Cato, who agreed to return to slavery after his master threatened to seize him under the fugitive slave clause.

18. "Speech by Benjamin Gale, 12 November [1787]," in Jensen, III:421, 424.

19. *Hampshire Gazette,* February 6, 1788, in Kaminski, 96.

20. *Hampshire Gazette,* April 9, 1788, in Kaminski, 69.

21. Massachusetts Convention, January 17, 1788, in Jensen, VI:12, 36–37.

22. *Hampshire Gazette,* April 25, 1788, in Kaminski, 108.

23. Massachusetts Convention, January 30, 1788, in Jensen, VI:1371.

24. *Massachusetts Centinel,* June 14, 1788, in Kaminski, 112.

25. Massachusetts Convention, February 4, 1788, in Jensen, VI:1422.

26. *United States Chronicle* (Providence, RI), July 17, 1788, in Kaminski, 114.

27. Massachusetts Convention, January 30, 1788, in Jensen, VI:1371.

28. Massachusetts Convention, January 18, 1788, in Jensen, VI:1245.

29. Simeon Baldwin, *An Oration Pronounced before the Citizens of New-Haven, July 4th, 1788* (New Haven, CT, 1788), 16.

30. Hopkins to Brown, October 22, 1787, in Kaminski, 73.

31. Belknap to Benjamin Rush, April 7, 1788, in Kaminski, 100.

32. Rush to John Coakley Lettsom, September 28, 1787, in Kaminski, 117; Rush to Elizabeth Graeme Ferguson, December 25, 1787, in Kaminski, 140.

33. Rush to Sharp, November 1, 1774, in John A. Woods, ed., "The Correspondence of Benjamin Rush and Granville Sharp, 1773–1809," *Journal of American Studies* 1 (1967): 13.

34. Pemberton to John Pemberton, September 20, 1787, in Kaminski, 116.

35. Prior to Brown, December 1, 1787, in Kaminski, 139.

36. *Freeman's Journal* (Philadelphia), November 28, 1787, in Kaminski, 134.

37. [Smith] Brutus III, *New York Journal,* November 15, 1787, in Kaminski, 128.

38. *Independent Gazetteer* (Philadelphia), May 6, 1788, in Kaminski, 153.

39. Prior to Brown, December 1, 1787, in Kaminski, 139.

40. *Freeman's Journal,* November 28, 1787, in Kaminski, 134; *New York Journal,* January 22, 1788, in Kaminski, 141. Neo-Garrisonian historians have singled out Hughes as a kind of exemplary (if rare) immediatist before the fact, but a closer look at his life as well as his arguments—he owned three slaves until at least 1790—has led one historian to describe him "not as New York's most committed antislavery voice during ratification, but one of the state's most fervent critics of the Constitution." Boonshoft, "Doughfaces at the Founding," 199.

41. *Independent Gazetteer,* November 3, 1787, in Kaminski, 122.

42. *Independent Gazetteer,* November 21, 1787, in Kaminski, 131.

43. *Independent Gazetteer,* November 6, 1787, in Kaminski, 125.

44. *Freeman's Journal*, February 20, 1788, in Kaminski, 146.

45. *Independent Gazetteer*, November 8, 1787, in Kaminski, 126.

46. *New York Journal*, November 15, 1787, in Kaminski, 127.

47. *New York Journal*, December 13, 1787, in Jensen, XIX:408–409. Clinton was writing as "A Countryman."

48. *Pittsburgh Gazette*, February 16, 1788, in Kaminski, 146.

49. Pemberton to Brown, November 16, 1787, in Kaminski, 129; Pemberton to John Pemberton, April 29, 1788, in Kaminski, 150.

50. *Independent Gazetteer*, October 29, 1788, in Kaminski, 119. The author, "Timothy Meanwell," did not mention Franklin by name, but his reference to "my friend . . . famed throughout the world as the champion of liberty" is unmistakable. The PAS itself would come to regard the Constitution favorably. See David Brion Davis, *The Problem of Slavery in the Age of Revolution, 1770–1823* (Ithaca, NY, 1974), 326. For another attack on Franklin, coupled this time with John Dickinson, see *New York Journal*, November 21, 1787, in Kaminski, 131.

51. *Pennsylvania Gazette*, October 24, 1787, in Kaminski, 119.

52. *Pennsylvania Gazette*, September 26, 1787, in Kaminski, 117.

53. *Independent Gazetteer*, October 30, 1787, in Kaminski, 121.

54. Pennsylvania Convention, November 28, 1788, in Jensen, II:417.

55. Rush to Belknap, February 28, 1788, in Kaminski, 147.

56. *An Additional Number of Letters from the Federal Farmer to the Republican Leading to a Fair Examination of the System of Government Proposed by the Late Convention* (New York, 1788), 179.

57. Waln to Richard Waln, October 3, 1787, in Kaminski, 118.

58. *Pennsylvania Gazette*, May 21, 1788, in Kaminski, 155.

59. *Independent Gazetteer*, October 30, 1787, in Kaminski, 121.

60. Ibid.

61. A Citizen of America [Noah Webster], *An Examination into the Leading Principles of the Federal Constitution* (Philadelphia, 1787), 40.

62. Rush to Belknap, February 28, 1788, in Kaminski, 147.

63. *Pennsylvania Herald,* December 26, 1787, in Kaminski, 135.

64. *American Museum,* November 7, 1787.

65. On Wilson, see Page Smith, *James Wilson, Founding Father, 1742–1798* (Chapel Hill, NC, 1956); this should be supplemented with Mark David Hall, *The Political and Legal Philosophy of James Wilson, 1742–1798* (Columbia, MO, 1997).

66. Pennsylvania Convention, December 3, 1787, in Jensen, II:463.

67. Ibid.

68. Tench Coxe, for his part, did not hesitate to speak very differently when trying to arouse support for the Constitution from southern slaveholders. Working closely with his friend Madison, Coxe composed an article (later a pamphlet) addressed to the Virginia ratification convention pointing out the Constitution's advantages to the slaveholding state, including the three-fifths clause. Even then, though, Coxe's maneuvering did not completely contradict his antislavery beliefs and commitments. His article also praised the Constitution for making individual states competent to undertake "the emancipation of the slaves already among us," a point unlikely to please Virginia slaveholders who believed their property rights precluded any sort of emancipation. See *Pennsylvania Gazette,* May 21, 1788, reprinted in *Virginia Independent Chronicle,* May 28, 1788.

69. See, for example, Thomas Jefferson's remark in 1770 that before "the enfranchisement of the slaves we have"—that is, emancipation—"it is necessary to exclude all further importations from Africa." Jefferson, *A Summary View of the Rights of British America* (Williamsburg, VA [1774]), 18.

70. Davis, *Problem of Slavery,* 41.

71. See also Matthew Mason, *Slavery and Politics in the Early American Republic* (Chapel Hill, NC, 2006), 12–16.

72. *Pennsylvania Gazette,* September 26, 1787, in Kaminski, 117.

73. *Pennsylvania Gazette,* March 19, 1788, in Kaminski, 149.

74. Burke quoted in Maier, *Ratification,* 250.

75. On ratification in South Carolina, see also Rachel N. Klein, *Unification of a Slave State: The Rise of the Planter Class in the South Carolina Backcountry, 1760–1808* (Chapel Hill, NC, 1991), 164–171.

76. *Poughkeepsie Country Journal*, March 11, 1788, in Jensen, XX:853.

77. South Carolina General Assembly, January 16, 1788, in Jensen, XXVII:108.

78. South Carolina General Assembly, January 17, 1788, in Jensen, XXVII: 123–124.

79. Ibid., XXVII:124.

80. The Georgia planter Lachlan McIntosh did write to a friend expressing concerns about the future of slavery under the Constitution and suggesting that Georgia try it out for several years before finally committing. Even McIntosh, though, seems to have assumed that the majority of Georgia citizens backed the framers' work; and, indeed, no overt Anti-Federal campaign appears to have arisen in the state. Lachlan McIntosh to John Weareat, December 17, 1787, in Kaminsky, 164–165.

81. Jonathan Elliott, *The Debates of the Several State Conventions, on the Adoption of the Federal Constitution* (Washington, DC, 1836), IV:102.

82. George Nicholas to David Stuart, April 9, 1788, in Jensen, IX:712. Between April 18 and May 22, the *State Gazette of Carolina* indeed reprinted, in whole or in part, seven installments from Martin's speech. These included, on May 8, excerpts from Martin's account of the slave trade compromise, which had also appeared in the Charleston *City Gazette* on April 14, 1788. See Jensen, XXVII:255.

83. Luther Martin, "Genuine Information VII," *Maryland Gazette*, January 18, 1788, in Kaminski, 172–174, quotation on 173; Luther Martin, "Genuine Information VIII," *Maryland Gazette*, January 22, 1788, in Kaminski, 174–175, quotation on 174.

84. For a brief antislavery attack on the Constitution aimed to arouse Quakers, and a reply, see *Virginia Independent Chronicle*, February 13 and March 12, 1788.

85. Thomas Jefferson, "Notes of a Conversation with George Mason," September 30, 1792, in *The Papers of Thomas Jefferson, Main Series,* ed. Julian Boyd et al. (Princeton, NJ, 1943–), XXIV:428.

86. Farrand, III:556 n. 2.

87. Virginia Convention, June 5, 1788, in Jensen, IX:964.

88. Virginia Convention, June 17, 1788, in Jensen, X:1338.

89. Federalist 42 and 54. On Madison's thinking on Federalist 54—"what is arguably the most unusual and distinctive of the Federalist Papers"—see also Malick W. Ghachem, "The Slave's Two Bodies: The Life of an American Legal Fiction," *William and Mary Quarterly,* 3rd ser., LX (2003): 809–842, quotation at 814.

90. Virginia Convention, June 17, 1788, in Jensen, X:1339.

91. Ibid., X:1341.

92. Virginia Convention, June 24, 1788, in Jensen, X:1476.

93. Virginia Convention, June 17, 1788, in Jensen, X:1341. A discerning analysis, which counters the oft-repeated charge that Henry's remarks were paranoid, appears in Einhorn, "Patrick Henry's Case."

94. Virginia Convention, June 17, 1788, in Jensen, X:1341.

95. Ibid., X:1343.

96. Virginia Convention, June 24, 1788, in Jensen, X:1483–1484.

97. Ibid., X:1503.

98. On the outcome in Virginia, see Maier, *Ratification,* 292–319.

99. On this point, see also Einhorn, "Patrick Henry's Case," esp. 570.

4

TO THE MISSOURI CRISIS

1. AC, 1 Cong., 2 sess., House, 1239. On the snubbing of the elderly Franklin, see Keith Arbour, "Benjamin Franklin as Weird Sister: William Cobbett and Philadelphia's Fear of Democracy," in *Federalists Reconsidered,* ed. Barbara J. Oberg and Doran Ben-Atar (Charlottesville, VA, 1998), 179–180.

2. *Federal Gazette* (Philadelphia), March 25, 1790.

3. AC, 1 Cong., 1 sess., House, 352.

4. For the entire debate, AC, 1 Cong., 1 sess., House, 349–356, quotations on 353, 354, 356. At one point, Madison justified assessing the duty on the grounds that the possessors of slaves considered them property, but he remained clear that the Constitution did not acknowledge slaves as property. Madison eventually agreed to seek a separate bill on slave imports later in the session, but that effort got nowhere. Congress did not take up the matter again until 1804, and would never approve a tax on slaves.

5. The PAS petition, presented a day after the Quaker petitions, appears in AC, 1 Cong., 2 sess., House, 1239–1240. More sweeping than the Quaker petitions, the PAS petition was also far more ambitious than the one the group had planned to send to the Federal Convention, which asked the delegates only to consider suppressing the Atlantic slave trade. See the 1787 petition, dated June 2, in *Pennsylvania Gazette,* March 5, 1788. On the sophistication of the Quaker and abolitionist campaign, see William C. diGiacomantonio, "For the Gratification of a Volunteering Society: Antislavery and Pressure Group Politics in the First Federal Congress," *Journal of the Early Republic* 15 (1995): 169–197. Other important studies of the petition controversy include Howard Albert Ohline, "Politics and Slavery: The Issue of Slavery in National Politics, 1787–1816," Ph.D. diss., University of Missouri, 1969, 126–169; Howard A. Ohline, "Slavery, Economics, and Congressional Politics, 1790," *Journal of Southern History* 46 (1980): 335–359; Donald Robinson, *Slavery in the Structure of American Politics* (New York, 1971), 302–312; and Richard S. Newman, "Prelude to the Gag Rule: Southern Reaction to Antislavery Petitions in the First Federal Congress," *Journal of the Early Republic* 16 (1996): 571–600.

6. AC, 1 Cong., 2 sess., House, 1241, 1242, 1243–1244. Smith was particularly sensitive on the subject, as during his campaign for Congress in 1788 he had promised specifically to stand firm on slavery, and even to persuade

northerners of why slavery needed protection. See George C. Rogers Jr., *Evolution of a Federalist: William Loughton Smith of Charleston, 1758–1812* (Columbia, SC, 1962), esp. 162–166. In talking about "our country," Smith meant South Carolina and perhaps the entire slaveholding South, not the United States at large.

7. AC, 1 Cong., 2 sess., House, 1246–1247. Gerry began his speech talking about congressional authority to regulate the slave trade, then shifted to his hypothetical emancipation plan, leaving it somewhat ambiguous whether the "business" he was referring to was the slave trade or slavery itself. His remarks did reveal, though, how easily talk of one could shift into talk of the other.

8. AC, 1 Cong., 2 sess., House, 1246; Farrand, II:324.

9. AC, 1 Cong., 2 sess., House, 1246; *Gazette of the United States*, February 17, 1790. These accounts leave it unclear whether Madison was talking about Congress halting the introduction of slaves to states created out of territories or to territories before they became states. On Madison's dismay at the Lower South's "virulent language" and intemperate reaction to "the most distant approach of danger," see James Madison to Benjamin Rush, March 20, 1790, in *The Papers of James Madison, Congressional Series*, ed. J. C. A. Stagg (Charlottesville, VA, 1962–1991), XIII:109.

10. John Langdon of New Hampshire, lately an antislavery (although compromising) delegate at the Federal Convention, had assured his abolitionist friends that a large Senate majority was friendly to the petitions, but the effort was squelched with the help of influential northerners led by Vice President John Adams, who saw no reason to support what Adams called "the silly petition of Franklin and his Quakers." Adams to Thomas Crafts, May 25, 1790, Adams Papers, Massachusetts Historical Society. On the struggle in the Senate, see Ohline, "Politics and Slavery," 134–137.

11. Smith to Edward Rutledge, February 13, 1790, in George C. Rogers Jr., "Letters of William Loughton Smith to Edward Rutledge," *South Carolina Historical Magazine* 69 (1968): 108.

12. AC, 1 Cong., 2 sess., House, 1247. In the *Annals*, the tally of nay votes is misreported as fourteen, when only eleven names are listed. Only one northerner, one Marylander, and two Virginians voted with the solid Lower South minority. Some accounts have called it a victory for securing citizens' rights to petition their representatives, but that issue was submerged in the debate over the constitutionality of the petitions.

13. On the abolitionists' work with the committee members, see John Pemberton to James Pemberton, March 2 (quotation) and March 14, 1790, Pennsylvania Society for Promoting the Abolition of Slavery Papers, Historical Society of Pennsylvania [hereafter PAS Papers]; Ohline, "Slavery, Economics and Congressional Politics," 345–346; and Gary B. Nash, *Warner Mifflin: Unflinching Quaker Abolitionist* (Philadelphia, 2017), 166–172. The committee consisted of Abiel Foster (NH), Elbridge Gerry (MA), Thomas Hartly (PA), Benjamin Huntington (CT), John Laurence (NY), Josiah Parker (VA), and Thomas Sinnickson (NJ). Parker, although a slaveholder, was the same Virginia congressman who had spoken out against the slave trade in Congress in 1789.

14. John Pemberton to James Pemberton, March 2, 1790, PAS Papers.

15. AC, 1 Cong., 2 sess., House, 1465–1466. William Loughton Smith interpreted the clause accordingly, as a move toward general emancipation. Ibid., 1504–1505. It would not have been the boldest idea bruited by the committee. According to John Pemberton, the members only narrowly rejected the radical abolitionist claim that the Constitution's preamble, declaring the government's goals to "promote the General Welfare, and secure the Blessings of Liberty," gave Congress the power to emancipate the slaves immediately. John Pemberton to James Pemberton, March 14, 1790, PAS Papers.

16. AC, 1 Cong., 2 sess., House, 1465–1466; W. E. B. Du Bois, *The Suppression of the African Slave-Trade to the United States of America 1638–1870* (1896; New York, 1904), 78.

17. AC, 1 Cong., 2 sess., House, 1508, 1520. John Pemberton, keeping close tabs on the proceedings, was especially worried about New Englanders "who here to fore professed highly respecting freedom" but who had now "slipped away"; March 16, 1790, PAS Papers. Howard Ohline argues persuasively that the vacillation of some northerners on the petitions stemmed from their desire to win southerners' support for Hamilton's *Report on the Public Credit*. See Ohline, "Slavery, Economics, and Congressional Politics," esp. 349–350, 354–359.

18. Ohline, "Slavery, Economics, and Congressional Politics," 350–353, offers a clear narrative.

19. See the full report on the debate in *Pennsylvania Packet*, March 30, 1790. Madison's conflict with Smith prompted John Pemberton to laud Madison as the abolitionists' chief ally in the House, notwithstanding Madison's removal from the report of any suggestion that Congress could emancipate the slaves. John Pemberton to James Pemberton, March 20, 1790, PAS Papers.

20. AC, 1 Cong., 2 sess., House, 1523.

21. William Wiecek originated the term in *The Sources of Antislavery Constitutionalism in the United States, 1760–1848* (Ithaca, NY, 1977), 16.

22. George Washington to David Stuart, March 28, 1790, in *The Papers of George Washington, Presidential Series*, ed. W. W. Abbott (Charlottesville, VA, 1987–), V:288. Washington agreed to meet with Warner Mifflin on March 16, when he told the abolitionist that he "was not inclined to express any sentiments on the merits of the question" until and unless it came to him as a piece of official business. George Washington, *The Diaries of George Washington*, ed. Donald Jackson and Dorothy Twohig (Charlottesville, VA, 1976–1979), VI:47.

23. AC, 2 Cong., 2 sess., House, 728, 730–731.

24. On the persistence of antislavery politics, see esp. Matthew Mason, *Slavery and Politics in the Early American Republic* (Chapel Hill, 2006), 9–41, as well as Wiecek, *Sources,* 84–105, and Manisha Sinha, *The Slave's Cause: A History of Abolition* (New Haven, CT, 2016), 105–113.

25. Congress would toughen the 1794 law six years later by substantially raising the fines for persons convicted of illegal participation in the trade. Three years after that, it would enact new fines for bringing newly imported slaves into states that banned the international slave trade.

26. On the origins, framing, and passage of the Fugitive Slave Act, see above all Paul Finkelman, "The Kidnapping of John Davis and the Adoption of the Fugitive Slave Law of 1793," *Journal of Southern History* 56 (1990): 397–422.

27. PAS quotations in ibid., 420.

28. AC, 2 Cong., 2 sess., House, Appendix, 1415.

29. The territory was created out of lands ceded by North Carolina in April 1790, in payment for obligations owed to the federal government.

30. On Mississippi Territory, see Robert V. Haynes, *The Mississippi Territory and the Southwest Frontier, 1795–1817* (Lexington, KY, 2010), esp. 7–26. On the politics of the territory's organization, see Ohline, "Politics and Slavery," 298–303; Donald L. Robinson, *Slavery in the Structure of American Politics, 1765–1820* (1971; New York, 1979), 386–400; and, above all, John Craig Hammond, *Slavery, Freedom, and Expansion in the Early American West* (Charlottesville, VA, 2007), esp. 19–29.

31. There is now a strong and growing historical literature on the Haitian revolution's impact inside the United States. See, for example, Ashli White, *Encountering Revolution: Haiti and the Making of the Early Republic* (Baltimore, 2010), quotation on 1–2; and, most recently, James Alexander Dun, *Dangerous Neighbors: Making the Haitian Revolution in Early America* (Phliadelphia, 2016), which delineate the variety of American responses.

32. AC, 5 Cong., 2 sess., House, 1306.

33. Ibid., 1310. Thacher (his name is also spelled Thatcher) has received far too little attention from historians. Howard Ohline offers some intriguing material, especially on Thacher's involvement with Warner Mifflin, based on research in various collections of Thacher's papers; see, e.g., Ohline, "Politics and Slavery," 152–154.

34. AC, 5 Cong., 2 sess., House, 1306–1308.

35. The states north of Delaware held a 57-to-48-seat majority in the House; see Office of the Historian, U.S. House of Representatives, History, Art, and Archives website, http://history.house.gov/Institution/Apportionment /Apportionment.

36. AC, 5 Cong., 2 sess., House, 1308.

37. Ibid., 1306–1307, 1309–1310.

38. Ibid., 1309–1311.

39. On this point, see Hammond, *Slavery*, 23, 25–27. I am persuaded by Hammond's argument that the southern-northern Federalist alliance prevailed by gearing their arguments "less to opening a new frontier to slavery than to accommodating the Natchez planters in order to secure America's borders in an unruly but critical region, a matter of urgent concern" (27).

40. AC, 5 Cong., 2 sess., House, 1306.

41. See, for example, the sources quoted in Jed Handlesman Shugerman, "The Louisiana Purchase and South Carolina's Reopening of the Slave Trade in 1803," *Journal of the Early Republic* 22 (2002): 273.

42. Pickering, a Federalist delegate to the Pennsylvania ratification convention, said nothing at all about slavery, let alone the three-fifths clause, in a warm and lengthy defense of the Constitution that he composed late in 1787. See Pickering to Charles Tillinghast, December 6 and December 24, 1787, in Jensen, XIV:192–206. Nor did New England Federalists coalesce against slavery until the Louisiana Purchase in 1803, when po-

litical concerns led them to attack the three-fifths clause as the corner-stone of Jeffersonian power. See Matthew Mason, *Slavery and Politics in the Early American Republic* (Chapel Hill, NC, 2006), esp. 36–40.

43. *Aurora* [Philadelphia], November 23, 1803, quoted in John Craig Hammond, "'They Are Very Much Interested in Obtaining an Unlimited Slavery': Rethinking the Expansion of Slavery in the Louisiana Purchase Territories, 1803–1805," *Journal of the Early Republic* 23 (2003): 361 n. 21.

44. Ibid.

45. On the Hillhouse amendments struggle (in addition to the detailed account of the politics surrounding Louisiana Territory in Ohline, "Politics and Slavery," 353–398), see Hammond, *Slavery*, 37–40; Hammond, "'They Are Very Much Interested'"; and Padraig Riley, *Slavery and the Democratic Conscience: Political Life in Jeffersonian America* (Philadelphia, 2016), 102–107. *Annals of Congress* reported roll call votes but little of the Senate debates over Louisiana, so historians must rely instead on the notes and memoranda compiled by Senator William Plumer of New Hampshire, published as *William Plumer's Memorandum of Proceedings in the United States Senate, 1803–1807*, ed. Everett Somerville Brown (New York, 1923), 111–122. An odd alliance of senators, including James Jackson of Georgia and Israel Smith of Vermont, opposed the closing of international slave imports to Louisiana, in part out of concerns that it would undermine what might be a luxuriously rich economy, in part out of concerns of estranging resident slaveholders in Louisiana. Of the senators from states south of Virginia who voted on the amendment, two, Jesse Franklin and David Stone, both of North Carolina, voted with the majority—just as two Lower South senators, Abraham Baldwin and James Jackson, both of Georgia, voted against. The roll call tally appears in AC, 8 Cong., 1 sess., Senate, 240–241.

46. On this point, see Hammond, *Slavery*, 39.

47. *Plumer's Memorandum*, 124.

48. Ibid. As there was no debate over the amendment, it is unclear whether any concerns about property rights were primarily on the senators' minds. The roll call tally appears in AC, 8 Cong., 1 sess., Senate, 242.

49. See *Plumer's Memorandum*, 126.

50. Ibid., 114. There are numerous fine biographies of Adams, but none that surpasses Samuel Flagg Bemis's two-volume classic, *John Quincy Adams and the Foundation of American Foreign Policy* (New York, 1949) and *John Quincy Adams and the Union* (New York, 1956).

51. *Plumer's Memorandum*, 125. The roll call tally appears in AC, 8 Cong., 1 sess., Senate, 242.

52. *Plumer's Memorandum*, 116.

53. Ibid., 129.

54. AC, 8 Cong., 1 sess., Senate, 242. Opponents offered various other reasons for opposing the amendment as well, ranging from New York senator John Smith's claim that any effort to prevent slaves from being admitted to Louisiana from existing states was bound to fail to a more general attack by Jackson of Georgia on all of the Hillhouse amendments as incendiary, not least in raising alarms among resident Louisiana creoles. The debate on the bona fide amendment appears in *Plumer's Memorandum*, 127–130.

55. *Plumer's Memorandum*, 142–143.

56. Ibid., 129. Breckinridge squared his concern for slaveholders "of wealth" with his oft-stated antislavery professions by advancing a version of the already familiar "diffusion" argument (also favored by President Jefferson) that to disperse slavery would weaken it. The thrust of the administration's plan was to accelerate this diffusion, particularly by halting the importation of slaves from abroad.

57. Ibid., 130.

58. Ibid.

59. AC, 8 Cong., 1 sess., Senate, 244. The proposal to strike failed by a vote of 15 to 13. Only two southerners, from Kentucky and North Carolina, voted against striking the provision; three northerners, from New Jersey, New York, and Ohio, voted in favor of striking it. Notably, John Breckinridge, evidently more torn about the matter than it appeared, did not vote.

60. Ibid. Breckinridge, along with most of the Upper South senators, wound up voting for the amendment. The opposition consisted of an alliance of six southerners, including both of the Georgians and both Virginians, and five northerners, including John Quincy Adams and Timothy Pickering.

61. AC, 8 Cong., 1 sess., Senate, 255.

62. AC, 8 Cong., 1 sess., House, 1186. As the *Annals* neither recorded whether there was any debate over Sloan's bill nor the roll call tally, it is impossible to know much about the proposal. Like George Thacher, Sloan is a fascinating figure, but unlike Thacher, he has received an extended and informative biographical study: Bruce Bendler, "James Sloan: Renegade or True Republican?," *New Jersey History* 125 (2010): 1–19. Two years later, Sloan would lead an effort in the House to remove the capital back to Philadelphia, free from slavery—a symbolic attack on slavery that very nearly won House approval to be committed to a Committee of the Whole. Riley, *Slavery and the Democratic Conscience*, 129–131.

63. The U.S. district attorney in what became Orleans Territory, the wealthy planter James Brown, disturbed by the restriction as approved in 1804, was assured by legal counsel that additional legislation enacted a year later—which assimilated Orleans Territory to the terms of the Northwest Ordinance but with the exemption of slavery removed—repealed the Hillhouse provision. Brown to Albert Gallatin, December 11, 1805, in *The Territorial Papers of the United States*, ed. Clarence Edward Carter (Washington, DC, 1934–1969), IX:548. On the backlash among Louisiana

Territory slaveholders to the restrictions and Congress's abandonment of the bona fide regulation, see Hammond, "'They Are Very Much Interested,'" esp. 370–380.

64. AC, 8 Cong., 2 sess., House, 995–996; *Journal of the House of Representatives*, 8 Cong., 2 sess., 93–95.

65. AC, 9 Cong., 1 sess., 364–365.

66. On the slave trade abolition debates, see Matthew E. Mason, "Slavery Overshadowed: Congress Debates Prohibiting the Atlantic Slave Trade to the United States, 1806–1807," *Journal of the Early Republic* 20 (2000): 59–81; as well as Riley, *Slavery and the Democratic Conscience*, 119–125.

67. AC, 9 Cong., 2 sess., House, 221.

68. Quotation in Josiah Quincy, *Figures of the Past* (Boston, 1926), 178.

69. On Randolph, William Cabell Bruce's classic two-volume *John Randolph of Roanoke* (New York, 1922) should be supplemented with David Johnson, *John Randolph of Roanoke* (Baton Rouge, LA, 2012); and Robert Dawidoff, *The Education of John Randolph* (New York, 1979).

70. AC, 9 Cong., 2 sess., House, 626–627.

71. Quotations in Mason, "Slavery Overshadowed," 71.

72. Williams, *An Oration on the Abolition of the Slave Trade; Delivered in the African Church, in the City of New-York, January 1, 1808* (New York, 1808), 19.

73. On slavery and partisan fights between Jeffersonians and revived Federalists during the War of 1812, see Mason, *Slavery and Politics*, 42–74.

74. Figures from Office of the Historian, U.S. House of Representatives, History, Art, and Archives website, http://history.house.gov/Institution/Apportionment/Apportionment.

75. Based on the 1810 census, the House was apportioned for 103 representatives from states north of Delaware and 78 representatives from Delaware southward, creating a solid northern majority of twenty-five votes in contrast to the northern majority of just eleven votes after 1800 and nine votes in 1790. Approaching the debates over Arkansas and Missouri,

antislavery northerners were well aware of their widening advantage, which would grow even further to a thirty-three vote House majority after 1820. Figures in ibid.

76. In 1818, building on the growing ferment, a special meeting of the American Convention for Promoting the Abolition of Slavery (which had fallen into a lull in recent years) appointed a committee to prepare a mass memorial to Congress "requesting the adoption of such provisions, as will exclude slavery from the limits of such territorial governments as may hereafter be established within our country, and prevent any such future territories from being erected into a state, unless slavery shall be prohibited by the constitution thereof." *Minutes of the Fifteenth Session of the American Convention for Promoting the Abolition of Slavery and Improving the Condition of the African Race* (Philadelphia, 1818), 42. More memorials and petitions would follow, from many quarters. On the Livermore amendment, see AC, 15 Cong., 1 sess., 1675. More generally on slavery and politics and continuing antislavery activity during the misnamed Era of Good Feelings, see Mason, *Slavery and Politics*, 75–86, 130–176; Sinha, *Slave's Cause*, 160–191.

77. AC, 15 Cong., 2 sess., House, 306–311, quotation on 309.

78. In the large literature on the Arkansas and Missouri crisis, two works are essential: Glover Moore, *The Missouri Controversy, 1819–1821* (Lexington, KY, 1953); and Robert Pierce Forbes, *The Missouri Compromise and Its Aftermath: Slavery and the Meaning of America* (Chapel Hill, NC, 2009).

79. AC, 15 Cong., 2 sess., House, 1066, 1170–1217.

80. Ibid., 1222.

81. John Quincy Adams, *Diaries 1779–1821*, ed. David Waldstreicher (New York, 2016), 533.

82. AC, 15 Cong., 2 sess., House, 1223–1224, 1225–1226.

83. Ibid., 1226–1235, quotations on 1226.

84. Ibid., 1224–1225.

85. Ibid., 1228, 1232. Pro-extensionists would also cite the 1803 treaty with respect to slavery in Missouri. See, e.g., John Hardin of Kentucky's speech, AC, 16 Cong, 1 sess., House, 1069–1091.

86. AC, 15 Cong., 2 sess., House, 1229–1230.

87. Some opponents of restriction claimed that Article IV, Section 3 of the Constitution authorized Congress to make "needful rules and regulations" only with respect to the actual land and other property belonging to the United States. This reading turned on the meaning of the word "territory." See, for example, Alexander Smyth's later remarks in AC, 16 Cong., 1 sess., House, 1003, or, for that matter, McLane's own later remarks, ibid., 1160.

88. AC, 15 Cong., 2 sess., House, 1226, 1229.

89. Quotation in Don E. Fehrenbacher, *The Slaveholding Republic: An Account of the United States Government's Relations to Slavery,* completed and ed. Ward M. McAfee (New York, 2001), 218.

90. Ibid.

91. AC, 15 Cong., 2 sess., House, 1276.

92. *Minutes of the Sixteenth Session of the American Convention to Promote the Abolition of Slavery and Improve the Condition of the African Race* (Philadelphia, 1819), 26.

93. AC, 16 Cong., 1 sess., House, 994.

94. Ibid., 736. See also the emphatic statement by Samuel Smith of Maryland, ibid., 941.

95. Ibid., 1076.

96. Ibid., 994, 1005–1006. See also, for example, remarks by Robert Reid of Georgia, ibid., 1027, and Alney McLean of Kentucky, ibid., 1153–1154.

97. Ibid., 1388, 1391.

98. Ibid., 351. See also, for example, remarks by Philip Barbour of Virginia, AC, 15 Cong., 2 sess., House, 1188; Alexander Smyth, 16 Cong., 1 sess., House, 1009; and Louis McLane, 16 Cong., 1 sess., House, 1160.

99. AC, 16 Cong, 1 sess., House, 1310–1329.

100. Quotations from the remarks of Alexander Smyth, ibid., 1013–1014, 1220–1221; Charles Pinckney, ibid., 1323; and Philip Barbour, ibid., 1222. See also ibid., 1341, 1372.

101. AC, 15 Cong., 2 sess., House, 1192.

102. AC, 16 Cong., 1 sess., House, 1091–1113, quotations on 1104.

103. Ibid., 1350.

104. The outstanding work on the history of antislavery constitutionalism remains Wiecek, *Sources*.

105. AC, 16 Cong., 1 sess., House, 1394–1403, quotations on 1395, 1396, 1399.

106. AC, 15 Cong., 2 sess., House, 1280–1282.

107. Macon quoted in Moore, *Missouri Controversy,* 109.

108. AC, 16 Cong., 1 sess., Senate, 428. Ten senators, eight southerners plus the two from Indiana, voted against the Thomas amendment alone; six of them, all southerners, ended up voting for the bill itself with the amendment included. Fifteen northerners and one senator from Kentucky who supported the amendment wound up voting against the bill; only four northerners backed the compromise as a whole. In sum, all but one of Macon's southern allies, William Smith of South Carolina, finally went along with the amendment if it meant winning Missouri, while for a sizable number of northerners, the 36° 30′ restriction was not enough to offset the admission of Missouri with slavery.

109. The tallies for the final votes appear in AC, 16 Cong., 1 sess., House, 1586–1588.

110. The results for the Thomas amendment were especially telling. The amendment passed the House by a vote of 134 to 42. Representatives from slaveholding states broke 39 for and 37 opposed, in contrast to 95 for and 5 against from the free states. Clearly, southerners were more willing to give way over the 36° 30′ restriction, but this reflected the primacy of the Missouri issue in most people's minds. That nearly half of the slave state

representatives in the House, as well as half of the senators from the Deep South and both senators from Virginia, opposed the amendment was a sign of considerable southern resistance.

111. *Daily Advertiser* (New York), March 7, 1820.

112. Randolph's famous remark first appeared in the *Statesman* (Pittsburgh, PA), April 26, 1820, cited in Moore, *Missouri Controversy*, 104.

113. *Charleston City Gazette*, March 10, 1820.

114. Donald E. Fehrenbacher, *The South and Three Sectional Crises* (Baton Rouge, LA, 1980), 19.

115. *Richmond Enquirer*, March 7, 1820; *Herald* (Norfolk and Portsmouth, VA), March 10, 1820; William Brown quoted in Moore, *Missouri Controversy*, 230.

116. R. King to J. A. King and Charles, March 5, 1820, in *The Life and Correspondence of Rufus King*, ed. Charles R. King (New York, 1894–1900), VI:291; quotation in Leonard L. Richards, *The Slave Power: The Free North and Southern Domination 1780–1860* (Baton Rouge, LA, 2000), 84.

117. Plumer quoted in Sean Wilentz, *The Rise of American Democracy: Jefferson to Lincoln* (New York, 2005), 231. See also Mason, *Slavery and Politics*, 178–179.

118. *Minutes of the Seventeenth Session of the American Convention for Promoting the Abolition of Slavery, and Improving the Condition of the African Race* (Philadelphia, 1821), 10.

5

ANTISLAVERY, THE CONSTITUTION,
AND THE COMING OF THE CIVIL WAR

1. John Quincy Adams, *Diaries 1779–1821*, ed. David Waldstreicher (New York, 2016), 532, 545.

2. Whitemarsh Seabrook, *A Concise View of the Critical Situation and Future Prospects of the Slave-Holding States in Relation to Their Coloured Population* (Charleston, 1825), 5.

3. William Henry Smith, *Charles Hammond and His Relations to Henry Clay and John Quincy Adams* (Chicago, 1885), 41.

4. Quotation in Donald J. Ratcliffe, "The Decline of Antislavery Politics, 1815–1840," in *Contesting Slavery: The Politics of Bondage and Freedom in the New American Nation,* ed. John Craig Hammond and Matthew Mason (Charlottesville, 2011), 280.

5. Van Buren to Thomas Ritchie, January 13, 1827, Martin Van Buren Papers, Library of Congress.

6. Ibid. There is an abundant and contentious literature on slavery and the Jacksonian party system. For a concise and judicious account, see Ratcliffe, "Decline," esp. 276–281.

7. William C. Nell, quoted in C. Peter Ripley, ed., *The Black Abolitionist Papers* (Chapel Hill, NC, 1985–1992), III:6.

8. *The Constitution of the American Anti-Slavery Society with the Declaration of the National Anti-Slavery Convention at Philadelphia, December 1833* (New York, 1838), 4.

9. On slavery and antislavery in Washington, see Paul Finkelman, "Slavery in the Shadow of Liberty: The Problem of Slavery in Congress and the Nation's Capital," in *In the Shadow of Freedom: The Politics of Slavery in the Nation's Capital,* ed. Paul Finkelman and Donald R. Kennon (Columbus, OH, 2011), 3–16; Stanley Harrold, *Subversives: Antislavery Community in Washington, D.C.* (Baton Rouge, LA, 2003).

10. On the Lundy petition campaign and Lundy's alliance with Miner, see Don E. Fehrenbacher, *The Slaveholding Republic: An Account of the United States Government's Relations to Slavery,* completed and ed. Ward M. McAfee (New York, 2001), 68–71. For a detailed accounting of Lundy's journey from Baltimore to Bennington to find Garrison, see William Clinton Armstrong, *The Lundy Family and Their Descendants of Whatsoever Surname* (New Brunswick, NJ, 1902), 366–368.

11. Lundy quotation in Fehrenbacher. *Slaveholding Republic,* 71.

12. *Liberator* (Boston), January 1, 1831.

13. RD, 24 Cong., 1 sess., Senate, 672.

14. Susan Zaekse, "'A Nest of Rattlesnakes Let Loose among Them': Congressional Debates over Women's Antislavery Petitions, 1835–1845," in Finkelman and Kennon, *In the Shadow of Freedom,* 100. On the ominous political climate surrounding the campaign, see Fehrenbacher, *Slaveholding Republic,* 73–74.

15. On the gag rule controversy, see above all William Lee Miller, *Arguing about Slavery: John Quincy Adams and the Great Battle in the United States Congress* (New York, 1995).

16. RD, 24 Cong., 1 sess., House, 2449.

17. Ibid., 3757. That Pinckney was the son of Charles Pinckney, the former framer and redoubtable proslavery advocate, made his seeming apostasy all the more galling to Hammond and the hard-liners, who retaliated by denying him renomination to his congressional seat in 1836.

18. A middle position also emerged in time, arguing that as efforts to abolish slavery in Washington and in the territories were intended to begin the destruction of slavery in the existing states, they were therefore unconstitutional. See the remarks of Charles Atherton, CG, 25 Cong., 3 sess., House, 22–23.

19. RD, 24 Cong., 1 sess., House, 2449.

20. Ibid., 2225.

21. Ibid., 2071.

22. *Charleston Courier,* January 14, 1836, quoted in Fehrenbacher, *Slaveholding Republic,* 80.

23. RD, 24 Cong., 1 sess., House, 2024–2034, quotation on 2028.

24. Ibid., 2029, 2225.

25. On Adams and the gag rule, in addition to Miller, *Arguing about Slavery,* see Leonard L. Richards, *The Life and Times of Congressman John Quincy Adams* (New York, 1988).

26. Slade is another figure who deserves more attention, but see Andrew S. Barker, "Chauncey Langdon Knapp and Political Abolitionism in Vermont, 1833–1841," *New England Quarterly* 73 (2000): 434–462; Corey Brooks, "Stoking the 'Abolition Fire in the Capitol': Liberty Party Lobbying and Antislavery in Congress," *Journal of the Early Republic* 33 (2013): 523–547; and Corey Brooks, *Liberty Power: Antislavery Third Parties and the Transformation of American Politics* (Chicago, 2016).

27. "To the Congress of the United States," petition, ca. 1835, Moore Family Collection, Old Sturbridge Village, Sturbridge, MA.

28. RD, 24 Cong., 1 sess., House, 2047.

29. Ibid., 2049. Francis W. Pickens of South Carolina along with the Virginian Bouldin were among the southerners who also insisted that there was no difference between immediate and gradual emancipation with respect to property rights. Ibid., 2225, 2248.

30. Ibid., 2052.

31. On Weld, see Robert H. Abzug, *Passionate Liberator: Theodore Dwight Weld and the Dilemma of Reform* (New York, 1980) and, with special emphasis on the 1830s, Owen M. Muelder, *Theodore Dwight Weld and the American Anti-Slavery Society* (Jefferson, NC, 2011). An older work is valuable as well: Benjamin Platt Thomas, *Theodore Dwight Weld, Crusader for Freedom* (New Brunswick, NJ, 1950). Other abolitionists were also exploring Congress's powers over slavery, some coming to more sweeping conclusions than Weld about the Constitution's antislavery meanings. See Stanley Burton Bernstein, "Abolitionist Readings of the Constitution," Ph.D. diss., Harvard University, 1969; and Helen J. Knowles, "The Constitution and Slavery: A Special Relationship," *Slavery and Abolition* 28 (2007): 309–328.

32. Theodore Dwight Weld, *The Power of Congress over the District of Columbia* (New York, 1838), 12–13 n.

33. Ibid., 39.

34. RD, 24 Cong., 1 sess., Senate, 97.

35. RD, 24 Cong., 2 sess., Senate, 711.

36. CG, 25 Cong., 2 sess., Senate, 55; *The Works of John C. Calhoun,* ed. Richard K. Crallé (New York, 1854–1860), III:185.

37. CG, 26 Cong., 1 sess., Senate, 188, 191.

38. On Morris, see Jonathan H. Earle, *Jacksonian Antislavery and the Politics of Free Soil, 1824–1854* (Chapel Hill, NC, 2004), 37–44. A detailed account of Morris's fight against Calhoun's resolutions appears in B. F. Morris, *The Life of Thomas Morris* (Cincinnati, OH, 1856), 95–106.

39. The 1819 exchange between Madison and Robert Walsh Jr., a prominent antislavery Philadelphia lawyer and man of letters, appears in Walsh to Madison, November 11, 1819, and Madison to Walsh, November 27, 1819, in *The Papers of James Madison, Retirement Series,* ed. David B. Mattern et al. (Charlottesville, 2009–), I:548–549. Had Madison admitted to Walsh his own role in excluding slavery, he might have had to deal squarely with his relevant passage in his notes on the debates. There he cited himself stating that the Constitution could not admit "the idea that there could be property in men"—a far more definitive statement than his remark to Walsh about "some states" desiring to avoid "acknowledging expressly a property in human beings." On slavery in the territories, Madison told Walsh that, given the "ductile character" of Congress's authority, it was at least plausible that Congress could interdict slavery—but he inferred that Congress might never have read the Constitution that way, "since in none of the Territorial Governments created by them is such an interdict found." In any event, he noted, any authority Congress possessed over the territories did not extend to incoming states. Regarding the Northwest Ordinance's slavery provision, Madison said it remained to be decided whether states formed from the Northwest Territory could introduce slavery but that in any case the ordinance "proceeded from the old Congress, . . . acting under a charter which contains no shadow of the authority exercised." (Having registered no objection to the ordi-

nance at the time, he now ignored how the new Congress had reaffirmed it in 1789.) Madison also said that the ordinance may have been approved not so much to prevent slavery's expansion as to discourage further importations from overseas "by narrowing the space open to them." Overall, while trying to stay consistent, Madison found himself subtly sidling away from his earlier emancipationist sympathies and closer to the mildest of the proslavery positions, with regard to the Constitution as well as Missouri. As times changed, so did James Madison. All of that said, though, Madison did not edit out from his manuscript notes on the Federal Convention his remarks on excluding property in man, leaving to posterity what would become a key passage for later antislavery advocates. For another view of the Madison-Walsh exchange, see Drew McCoy, *The Last of the Fathers: James Madison and the Republican Legacy* (Cambridge, MA, 1989), 105–113.

40. On the publication of Madison's notes and its importance, see Michael Kammen, *A Machine That Would Go of Itself: The Constitution in American Culture* (New York, 1986), esp. 87–91.

41. On the Liberty Party, the masterly account in Richard H. Sewell, *Ballots for Freedom: Antislavery Politics in the United States, 1837–1860* (New York, 1976), esp. 43–130, may now be complemented with Reinhard O. Johnson, *The Liberty Party: Antislavery Third Party Politics in the United States* (Baton Rouge, LA, 2009); and Brooks, *Liberty Power.*

42. Quotation in Frederick J. Blue, *Salmon P. Chase: A Life in Politics* (Kent, OH, 1988), 43–44.

43. On Chase, along with Blue, *Chase,* and John Niven, *Salmon P. Chase: A Biography* (New York, 1995), see Eric Foner, *Free Soil, Free Labor, Free Men: The Ideology of the Republican Party before the Civil War* (New York, 1970), 73–102, and Matthew Axtell, "American Steamboat Gothic: Disruptive Commerce and Slavery's Liquidation, 1832–1865," Ph.D. diss., Princeton University, 2016. On Chase's blend of idealism and intense personal

ambition, see Steven P. Maizlish, "Salmon P. Chase: The Roots of Ambition and the Origins of Reform," *Journal of the Early Republic* 18 (1998): 47–70.

44. Quotation in Foner, *Free Soil*, 76.

45. "Proceedings and Resolutions of the Ohio Liberty Convention," *Philanthropist*, December 29, 1841.

46. Chase to Joshua Giddings, May, 19, 1842, quoted in Foner, *Free Soil*, 85.

47. William Goodell, *Views of American Constitutional Law, in Its Bearing on American Slavery* (1844; New York, 1845), 62.

48. Frederick Douglass, "What to the Slave Is the Fourth of July? An Address Delivered in Rochester, New York, on July 5, 1852," in *The Frederick Douglass Papers*, ser. I, ed. John Blassingame (New Haven, CT, 1982), II:385–386.

49. Manisha Sinha, *The Slave's Cause: A History of Abolition* (New Haven, CT, 2016), 474–477.

50. Quotation in Fehrenbacher, *Slaveholders' Republic*, 218.

51. *Prigg v. Pennsylvania*, 41 U.S. 16 Pet. 539 (1842). On Story's opinion, the proslavery myth, and the mistaken claim of historical necessity, see Fehrenbacher, *Slaveholding Republic*, 219–222, and Eric W. Plaag, "'Let the Constitution Perish': *Prigg v. Pennsylvania*, Joseph Story, and the Flawed Doctrine of Historical Necessity," *Slavery and Abolition* 25 (2004): 76–101.

52. *Liberator*, November 25, 1842.

53. Phillips, *The Constitution a Proslavery Compact* (1845; New York, 1856), ix.

54. On the Garrisonians' use of Madison's notes, and specifically the way Phillips used them, see William M. Wiecek, *The Sources of Antislavery Constitutionalism in the United States, 1760–1848* (Ithaca, NY, 1977), 245.

55. Phillips, *Constitution*, 186.

56. Ibid., 147.

57. Ibid.

58. Ibid., 159.

59. For reviews of these events from different but complementary angles, see Sean Wilentz, *The Rise of American Democracy: Jefferson to Lincoln* (New York, 2005), 547–594, and Sinha, *Slave's Cause*, 461–478.

60. On Wilmot and the proviso struggle, see above all Earle, *Jacksonian Antislavery*, 123–144.

61. CG, 29 Cong., 1 sess., House, 1218. The first roll call vote on the proviso went unrecorded, but this tally on the bill it amended gives a clear idea of the sectional breakdown.

62. CG, 31 Cong., 1 sess., House, 29.

63. CG, 29 Cong., 2 sess., House, 115.

64. Douglass remained a Garrisonian to this point, but the Wilmot struggle helped set him on a path where he would endorse the schismatic Free Soil Party, successor to the Liberty Party, in 1848. See David W. Blight, *Frederick Douglass's Civil War: Keeping Faith in Jubilee* (Baton Rouge, LA, 1989), 29.

65. CG, 29 Cong., 2 sess., House, Appendix, 138.

66. CG, 30 Cong., 1 sess., Senate, 619.

67. CG, 30 Cong., 1 sess., House, Appendix, 968.

68. CG, 29 Cong., 2 sess., Senate, Appendix, 356–359.

69. CG, 30 Cong., 1 sess., Senate, Appendix, 868–873, quotation on 868. In this speech, on the status of Oregon Territory, Calhoun cited the three-fifths clause and not the fugitive slave clause as the key enshrinement of property in man. He also rehearsed his common-property doctrine. Note, though, his seemingly offhand remark about the Constitution's "express guarantee" of property in man.

70. AC, 15 Cong., 2 sess., House, 1227.

71. *Great Speech of the Hon. George M. Dallas upon the Leading Topics of the Day* (Philadelphia, 1847), 36.

72. Oliver Dyer, *Phonographic Report of the Proceedings of the National Free Soil Convention* (Buffalo, 1848), 19–20.

73. See Wilentz, *Rise*, 610–636.

74. Ibid., 637–645.

75. The full text can be found in *Statutes at Large,* 31 Cong., 1 sess., chap. 60, Law Library of Congress website at https://www.loc.gov/law/help /statutes-at-large/31st-congress/session-1/c31s1ch60.pdf. The measure's formal title simply repeats that of the 1793 law: "An Act to amend, and supplementary to, the Act entitled 'An Act respecting Fugitives from Justice, and Persons escaping from the Service of their Masters,' approved February twelfth, one thousand seven hundred and ninety-three."

76. CG, 31 Cong., 1 sess., Senate, Appendix, 1622.

77. CG, 31 Cong., 1 sess., 1807.

78. Quotation in Wilentz, *Rise,* 653.

79. *Georgia Journal and Messenger* (Macon), October 16, October 30, and November 13, 1850, quoted in James L. Huston, "Property Rights in Slavery and the Coming of the Civil War," *Journal of Southern History* 65 (1999): 279.

80. Preston King to Francis Blair, February 26, 1852, Blair-Lee Papers, Princeton University. My thanks to Bryan LaPointe for alerting me to this letter.

81. *Appeal of the Independent Democrats in Congress to the People of the United States* (Washington, D.C., 1854), 2.

82. Abraham Lincoln, *Collected Works of Abraham Lincoln,* ed. Roy C. Basler (New Brunswick, NJ, 1953), II:514, VII:281.

83. Ibid., I:247–283, quotations on 255, 266, 274.

84. Ibid., I:274.

85. *Dred Scott v. John F. A. Sandford,* 60 U.S. (19 Howard), 393, 451 (1857). The essential work remains Don E. Fehrenbacher, *The Dred Scott Case: Its Significance in American Law and Politics* (New York, 1978).

86. Office of the Historian, U.S. House of Representatives, History, Art, and Archives website at http://history.house.gov/Institution/Apportionment /Apportionment.

87. AC, 16 Cong., 1 sess., House, 1003.

88. AC, 15 Cong., 2 sess., House, 1229; CG, 30 Cong., 1 sess., Senate, Appendix, 868. On the legal doctrines contained in the various opinions, see Fehrenbacher, *Dred Scott*, 365–414.

89. *New York Herald*, March 8, 1857.

90. Douglas, *Remarks of the Hon. Stephen A. Douglas on Kansas, Utah, and the Dred Scott Decision* (Chicago, 1857), 6; *Chicago Press and Tribune*, September 13, 1858.

91. Lincoln, *Collected Works*, III:257.

92. *Chicago Press and Tribune*, September 6, 1858.

93. CG, 36 Cong., 1 sess., Senate, 494.

94. Douglas, "The Dividing Line between Federal and Local Authority. Popular Sovereignty in the Territories," *Harper's New Monthly Magazine* 19 (1859): 519–537, quotation on 531.

95. Ibid., 532.

96. Quoted in Fehrenbacher, *Dred Scott*, 523.

97. Lincoln, *Collected Works*, III:405.

98. Ibid., III:522–550, quotation on 528. Lincoln either overlooked or had no way of knowing about several important occasions on which either the House or the Senate had seriously considered and even approved interference with slavery in the territories, including James Sloan's proposal, approved by the House, to block completely the importation of slaves into Louisiana Territory.

99. Ibid., III:535.

100. Ibid., III:543.

101. Ibid., III:543–544.

102. Ibid., III:545. For this paragraph, the annotated version of the Cooper Institute speech, prepared as a campaign pamphlet by Charles C. Nott and Cephas Brainerd with Lincoln's assistance, cites James Madison's notes on the Federal Convention debate over the Atlantic slave trade on August 25, 1787. The citation includes the transcripts of Roger Sherman's objections about property in slaves and Madison's remark about how the

Constitution should not admit property in men. The annotations also liberally cite Madison's notes on other matters.

103. Harold Holzer, *Lincoln at Cooper Union: The Speech That Made Abraham Lincoln President* (New York, 2004).

104. Frederick Douglass, "The American Constitution and the Slave: An Address Delivered in Glasgow, Scotland, on 26 March 1860," in *The Frederick Douglass Papers*, series I, ed. John Blassingame (New Haven, CT, 1985), III:340–366, quotation on 346. There are variant texts of this speech, including three that appeared in the Glasgow press. The second quotation here comes from the version published in Philip S. Foner, *The Life and Writings of Frederick Douglass* (New York, 1950), II:480.

105. *North American* (Philadelphia), September 13, 1860.

106. James A. Hamilton, *Reminiscences of James A. Hamilton, or, Men and Events at Home and Abroad, during Three Quarters of a Century* (New York, 1869), 448.

107. Ibid., 450; *New York Times*, July 4, 1860; Hamilton to Luther Bradish, July 4, 1860, and Bradish to Hamilton, July 14, 1860, Luther Bradish Papers, New-York Historical Society. The essay also appears in Hamilton, *Reminiscences*, 624–631. My thanks to Michael T. Ryan for alerting me to the Hamilton-Bradish correspondence.

108. Hamilton also attributed to Madison a line that, though Madison never used it, turned up in several places in the mid-nineteenth century: "We intend this Constitution to be the great charter of human liberty to the unborn millions who may enjoy its protection, and who should never see that such an institution as slavery was ever known in our midst." The earliest reference I have found is in Henry M. Dexter, *Our National Condition, and Its Remedy; A Sermon, Preached in the Pine Street Church Boston* (Boston, 1856), 16.

109. *New York Times*, July 4, 1860.

110. Ibid.

111. Hamilton, *Reminiscences*, 446–448.

112. Ibid., 448.

113. *Substance of a Speech of Hon. John C. Breckinridge, Delivered in the Hall of the House of Representatives, at Frankfort, Kentucky, December 21, 1859* (Washington, DC, 1860), 5.

114. *New York Times*, September 6, 1860.

115. *Declaration of the Immediate Causes Which Induce and Justify the Secession of South Carolina from the Federal Union* (Charleston, SC, 1860), 8.

116. Ibid., 8–9.

117. Aedanus Burke in AC, 1 Cong., 2 sess., House, 1241.

118. Constitution of the Confederate States of America, Ms., Hargrett Rare Book and Manuscript Library, University of Georgia, transcription at www.libs.uga.edu/hargrett/selections/confed/trans.html.

119. Robert H. Smith, *An Address to the Citizens of Alabama, on the Constitution and Laws of the Confederate States of America* (Mobile, AL, 1861), 19.

EPILOGUE

1. On the legal and political background, see James Oakes, *The Scorpion's Sting: Antislavery and the Coming of the Civil War* (New York, 2014), 104–265.

2. Butler to Cameron, July 30, 1861, and Cameron to Butler, August 8, 1861, *Private and Official Correspondence of Gen. Benjamin F. Butler during the Period of the Civil War* (Norwood, MA, 1917), I:187, 202.

3. On the process of emancipation, see James Oakes, *Freedom National: The Destruction of Slavery in the United States, 1861–1865* (New York, 2013), 49–488.

4. The Confederate Congress approved Davis's policy with a modification, stipulating that white officers would be handled by the Confederate government itself. Fearing retaliation by the Union on Confederate prisoners of war, the Confederacy never put the policy into effect. That

decision, though, did not prevent several Confederate generals and soldiers from murdering captured black soldiers and sometimes their white officers.

5. Lee to Grant, October 3, 1864, Grant to Lee, October 3, 1864, and Lee to Grant, October 19, 1864, in *The Papers of Ulysses S. Grant,* ed. John Y. Simon et al. (Carbondale, IL, 1967–2012), XII:263, 325. Several months later, when Confederate leaders and the public were debating the enlistment of blacks to fight for the Confederacy, the Confederate government silently changed its policy and began exchanging Union soldiers who had been slaves.

6. Charles Sumner, *Freedom National, Slavery Sectional: Speech of Hon. Charles Sumner, of Massachusetts, on His Motion to Repeal the Fugitive Slave Bill* (Boston, 1852), 17.

7. Charles Sumner, *No Property in Man: Speech of Hon. Charles Sumner on the Proposed Amendment of the Constitution Abolishing Slavery throughout the United States* (New York, 1864), 5, 18.

8. Ibid., 14.

INDEX

Due process clause, 19, 166, 196, 220

Duties: on exports, 58, 72, 88, 91; on imports, 83, 84–85, 95–97, 154; on slaves, 154–155; on slave trade, 78–79

Dwight, Theodore, 203

Early, Peter, 182

Electoral College, 70–71, 187, 243

Ellsworth, Oliver, 74, 81, 83, 85, 87

Emancipation: J. Q. Adams on, 264; antislavery assumptions about, 134; Constitution and, 134–135; expansion of slavery as hastening (diffusion argument), 191, 318n56; gradual emancipation laws, 31–37, 39–41, 46, 186; as invading property rights, 39–40; Methodist campaign for, in Virginia, 49–53; in northern states, 5, 14, 25, 26–27, 31–32; politics of, 263–264; post-nati, 33, 39, 43, 215; practical, 264; racism in counterattack on, 41; southern fears of, 149–150. *See also* Manumission

Emancipation Proclamation, 264–265

Emerson, John, 242

Era of Good Feelings, 187

Expansion of slavery: in Arkansas Territory, 190–193; as hastening emancipation (diffusion argument), 191, 318n56; Kansas-Nebraska Act and, 239–241; Louisiana Purchase

and, 174–175; in Missouri, 201–205; political abolitionists and, 17–18; in territories, 234–235; toleration of, 169–173; Wilmot Proviso and, 231–233

Exports, national duties on, 58, 72, 88, 91

Federal consensus, 162, 163

Federal Convention: abolitionist societies and, 53–55; on amendment power, 110; antislavery delegates to, 7–8, 14–15; Committee of Detail, 71, 72, 73–76, 78; Committee of Slave Trade, 87–101; Committee of Style and Arrangement, 110–112; as creating paradox, 22–23, 113–114; Madison notes on, 7, 17, 116, 194, 222–223, 229, 329n39; pro-slavery politics in, 2–3, 56–57; records of proceedings of, 6–7; representation debates of, 60–70; secrecy of, 115–116, 272n5; slavery debates of, 112–114; slave trade debates of, 79–87. *See also* Constitution, U.S.

The Federalist, 115, 145

Federalist Party, 177, 187

Federalists: antislavery, 128–136, 147–148; overview of, 116; in ratification debates, 121–122; in Upper and Lower South, 136–137. *See also* Madison, James

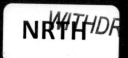